the Awakened BEING

LIVING IN LIBERATION, ABUNDANCE & BLISS RIGHT NOW

SunDari

MARCI LOCK

ISBN: 978-19-5-036717-7

Published by

LIFESTYLE
ENTREPRENEURS
P R E S S

If you are interested in publishing through Lifestyle Entrepreneurs Press,
write to: Publishing@LifestyleEntrepreneursPress.com

Publications or foreign rights acquisition of our catalog books.
Learn More: www.LifestyleEntrepreneursPress.com

Printed in the USA

Dedication

This creation is dedicated to all those committed to stepping out of their comfort zones, changing their stories, and living their best lives that in turn change the world we all live in. Thank you for having the desire, intention, and bravery to investigate and get curious about what else is available to you so that you too can be an influence for the greater good of the planet. We all are worthy of experiencing the life we desire and each one of us can be a gift to create a greater change.

I wouldn't be where I'm at in life without my greatest teachers and mentors, my epic ultimate growth partners—my boys, Skyler (aka Super Sky Guy) and Gavin (aka Gavin the Great). I cherish them beyond human words can express for the gift they've been to grow, learn, expand and reflect with through life's fabulous journey. I also wouldn't be experiencing the life I am and here in service for others to receive the same without the many experts, mentors, teachers, and leaders who were willing to go first in their own journeys so that I could learn from their wisdom and specific gifts to evolve. It is also with great honor and appreciation I acknowledge and witness every single person and experience I've had throughout my current holy human journey for all they have allowed me to learn and expand into.

A special thanks to Kami Jensen, a divine Sister of Light who has been a very special and sacred contract of support by my side in SunDari / Marci Lock Enterprises for many years in delivering these messages and truths through all the ways we share and serve for the greater good of humanity. Thanks to my entire team, who are so dedicated to our contribution to the expansion of consciousness, and to their own journeys, which lead them to be here and to be my divine family support for this mission and purpose. Thank you to my dear Best Life Tribe Community, fans, followers, and supporters who have all participated on this path, willing to be alchemists of their own life and transform their deepest wounds to greatest strengths; they have chosen to become the change. The same goes for the high-level leaders I've been so blessed to mentor; they too are making an even greater impact for humanity.

Lastly, thank you to all my divine allies and besties of light, twin ray reflectors, sacred soul family, and beloveds in all forms who have been such gifts of inspiration and support through all of my experiences and expansion. I appreciate you immensely for all you are. To each of you here reading, thank you again for joining me for this journey. I love and appreciate you.

Contents

Introduction 1
What Can You Expect from This Book?. 3

Chapter 1: My Story of Normal 9

Chapter 2: I Changed My "Normal," and You Can Too 16
How'd I Do It? 21
Commit to Something Different 22
Give Yourself Permission. 24
What is True Freedom? 25
What is Normal for your "True Self"? 26
Your "True Self" Normal Is Acting as an Effortless Creator 27
Seek Accountability 28
Discovery Opportunity #1: Assess the Results You've
Created 29

Chapter 3: Everything Is Energy 31
Fear and Faith-Based Energy 33
The Importance of Living in the Moment 37
Radical Responsibility 38

Chapter 4: Your Mental Programming Is Creating
Your World 40
Operating System #1: Your Thoughts and Beliefs 40
Your Perceptions are the Result of Your Beliefs 44

Operating System #2: Your Perceptions 44

You Traded It All for Love 48

The Act of Noticing 51

Chapter 5: What Are You Really Saying? 52

Operating System #3: Your Language 52

Chapter 6: The Emotional Feeling Body 71

Operating System #4: Your Emotions 71

Matching the Physical Symptom with the Emotional Issue 72

My Body Taught Me How to Overcome Breast Cancer ... 75

Your Body Is Getting Younger Every Day 80

Have You Cut Yourself Off from Your Emotions? 83

You Get to Look Back to Move Forward 87

Sky Guy's Story 89

This Gift Isn't Just for You 94

Discovery Opportunity #2: Feel Your Feelings. 96

Your Shifting Essentials 98

The Foundational Pre-Steps to Effectively Utilize
the 5 Steps 98

Chapter 7: Pre-Step 1: You Can Always Start with a Breath 99

Working with and through Your Emotions 99

Integrate Movement. 101

Chapter 8: Pre-Step 2: Give Yourself Permission to Get Curious 103

The Power of Quality Questions to Guide Your Life 103

The Gift Is in the Shit 108

Pain Without Drama or Suffering 111

Chapter 9: Pre-Step 3: Acceptance of All Things Is the Key 113

Comparison Is the Thief of All Joy 118

ALL Things Have a Right to Exist. 119

The Sacred Contract and Purpose of You 126

The New Model Is the Embodiment of Being 133

5 Steps to Freedom: Quick Reference Guide. 140

**Chapter 10: When, How & What to Expect with
the 5 Steps to Freedom** 143

Chapter 11: Step #1: What Am I Feeling Right Now? 150

Creating Awareness in Your Body 150

The Hack to Open Up to Your Emotions 152

Discovery Opportunity #3: Explore the Unconscious 161

Chapter 12: Step #2: Asking Why? 163

Know Why You're Feeling It 163

What Is a Trigger & Why Is It Important? 164

The Conscious Response to your Unconscious Reaction .170

Get Off the Merry-Go-Round 173

The CONTAINER of Unconditional Love, Support
& Acceptance 194

The Power of Becoming Conscious 196

Discovery Opportunity #4: Get to the Root
of Your Core Beliefs 199

**Chapter 13: Step #3: What Do I Really Want?
(In the Future and in This Moment)** 201

Calling Yourself on Your Bullshit. 202

"You Never Get What You Don't Ask For". 215

Trust & Assume Only the Very Best to Be What's
Really True 217

Be Specific and Go Deeper if You're Struggling. 219

If You're Not Defining What You Want, You're Also
Making a Choice 220

Your Results Are Your Truths 221

Discovery Opportunity #5: Discover What
You Really Want and What's in the Way 222

Chapter 14: Step #4: Align to New Beliefs and Perceptions 224

Choose Freedom.................................... 224
Check in on Your New Belief........................ 230
Your Inner Child Knows the Way.................... 236
Break Down Will Always Lead to a Break Through 240
My Association to It Is SHIT 242
You Can Completely DESIGN a Brand-New Story 248

Chapter 15: Step #5: What Is the Action I Get to Take to Give Me What I Want?.................252

Create Your Solution 253
Bring It to This Moment 254
Alignment Comes from Inside....................... 261
Be Proactive About Your Action..................... 264
I'm Just Practicing 265
Discovery Opportunity #6: Act Accordingly & Create
the Support to Achieve 269

Chapter 16: The Power of Checking In 272

Tying It All Together: The 60-Second Shift to Awesome and
Check-In Tool 273
Consciously Choose to Feel Even MORE 280
Specific Check-Ins................................. 285
Check in with Your Inner Child:..................... 285
Discovery Opportunity #7: Create Joy................. 290

Conclusion..291

Parting Thoughts as You Continue Your Journey into MORE...................................... 302

Introduction

Thank you. I acknowledge and witness you, my friend. You've taken a huge step in choosing this book as a support in discovering how else you can have an even greater life experience. No matter how bad, good, or even great of a life you might be currently experiencing, it shows you're seeking even greater and you're ready to receive what can absolutely transform your life into even more peace, love, joy, abundance, and bliss every day as your norm. Before we get started, though, I want to be very vulnerable, upfront, and authentic with you, as being completely transparent with nothing to hide and nothing to prove is what gives me, and I believe all of us, pure freedom. I'd love you to take a moment to hear more clarity in what you can expect. This way, you can honor your precious time, effort, and sacred energy to be super-ass effective in moving forward and producing the results you want to be experiencing.

There are a few things I want to share with you, and it will then be up to you to decide what feels good for you to do with this information. My intention is to share with you everything I am guided to, and I will always honor whatever response you choose that will then create the experience you want.

This transmission isn't meant to be another traditional self-help book or bible deemed full of truth that only gives you a surface view that keeps you experiencing the same cycles and results. I call that surface-level self-empowerment. I believe results speak for themselves because results don't lie. The result of our society is that 19 out of 20 people are failing at getting what they want and less than 1% of people achieve the vision they desire. What we are doing and the ways we've been taught and programmed to operate simply aren't working unless we are choosing to stay in struggle and suffering.

This isn't to discredit all the beautiful teachings and teachers we've had that have gotten us to where we are; we can only be grateful and appreciative of all of that. Yet, we have a lot more joy, abundance, and freedom to expand into and now receive. What we can see based on our results is there has obviously been something missing in our alignment. Instead of being aligned to what we want, we've been aligned to what we currently have and are experiencing. We aren't living fully in our most amazing, magical, blissful, abundant, pleasurable, passion-filled, and purposeful lives by doing what we've been doing.

Instead, in these pages, I believe you will find something very different that could liberate you to your full experience and expression of pure freedom now. It is a path to take you step by step to an even greater and greater experience, so it can only continue to take you to the next level, and the next level, and the next because these tools applied give you an ever-expansive growth into more of what you want when you continue to apply them. That is, if you are open to looking outside the box, parameters, conformed ideas, and programs that you have been taught and the operating systems you've been using.

That simply means, my loves, that we are going to play a new game of curiosity. If you choose to simply remain open to all ideas and possibilities available to you now and even allow yourself to experiment with them, I can promise you that this will continue to open up the capacity for you to receive only more of what you want in your life. *Only you can give yourself permission to live the life you love.* This means that it is up to you to discover the truths that fit and serve you best to receive the result you desire.

My commitment to you through this book is to simply share with you how I discovered and implemented living a life I absolutely love in ALL areas. I will share with you the gifts and tools I learned that can allow you to receive your greatest joys and freedom as the results in your life. By consciously choosing my own journey, I discovered how to go from broken to bliss. Now, I'm honored to share the journey and support and teach countless others to do the same.

If you are seeking more peace, love, awesomeness, abundance, magic, miracles, blissings, and blessings to live your best life in every area, my friend, you are here for a reason. I'm excited to share these tools with you to expand your life into your greatest creation and adventure.

What Can You Expect from This Book?

This book will most likely challenge some of your truths, programs, perceptions, and parameters. It might feel uncomfortable. It could also make you question everything, and that might very well piss you off. I want you to hear the perfection in this. All of these triggers and emotional experiences are powerful because they mean you're now seeing what has been hidden and kept you from growing into the greatest life experience you've been seeking, have always been worthy of, and simply didn't know how to see clearly to accept and integrate into your life and way of being.

I also invite you here to not believe everything you hear or read in this book and begin to practice questioning all of the information for yourself. Only you can know what's right for you, and most of us have been going through the motions of life, believing subjective truths without consciously questioning them. We've lived our whole lives fighting for our beliefs that originated in early childhood to be true and have created the very reality we live in based on them. The truths I share here are simply my subjective truths that gave me and the many others I've been blessed to share with the results we were seeking to be living and experiencing. The opportunity I'm suggesting here is to drop the fight and simply get curious about what isn't serving you anymore and what now can allow you to have more of what you really do want.

With that said, I want to reassure you that this process doesn't have to be serious, scary, or hard—in fact, it's the opposite. It has only been our silly human stories and ways of operating that have been keeping us locked in the programs and parameters that make it hard. Moving through these steps can be as easy or hard as you choose to make it depending on how much you give yourself permission to lean in, embrace what you find, and continually dance and play with the discovery of the journey to your ultimate freedom.

Some of my messages will resonate so deeply within you that you will feel them unlocking a remembrance in your being. And some might not resonate at all. All responses are perfect because all things are perfect feedback and true for each individual based on their perception, which again is a subjective truth. With this awareness, I honor your response, knowing it actually has nothing to do with me at all but everything to do with what's going on inside of you. I won't take it personally nor do I have any attachment or expectation around any of your responses and I will only continue to see you as a divine being worthy of every emotion and experience you are choosing.

Right now, the only inner-standing I want you to witness and support yourself with is a commitment to practice being open to receive what shows up right in front of you in each moment. That means all thoughts, perceptions, emotions, and any experiences you have are perfect the way they are. Otherwise, we aren't going to change anything or get out of the cycles that are already creating your own self-fulfilling prophecies and suffering. It is through this gift of seeing what shows up and being willing to get curious about why there would be a particular thought, emotion, perception, projection, or trigger that allows us to get clear and create something different. This journey can only allow you to access and create an even greater life experience. *No one can save you but yourself.* If you are going to continue on this journey, get clear with yourself now, give yourself permission, and commit to yourself that you will support yourself to get to the results you want by allowing and being open to and authentic with all your responses. They are all perfect.

That said, if you find an idea doesn't resonate or you don't quite understand it, my suggestion is to simply remain open and curious to allow whatever is hidden beneath the surface to come up. If you think I'm nuts on a specific point and you want to shut down, then yes, of course, you can skip it. All responses are a choice. What I'd love for you to remember through this journey is: *how you choose to respond will always determine what you get next.*

Please simply give yourself permission instead to get curious because the things we want to run past and not really look at or have resistance to are the very things that hold the greatest gems to our healing and liberation. We've created behavioral patterns to stay in our comfort zones. It is these unconscious commitments that have formed our perceptions and the behaviors that are blocking us from receiving our greatest gifts.

The pattern to shrug it off, create a distraction, or say, "I don't know," and want to skim past it to only go through the motions and continue to ignore it might show up for you here. I want to reassure you, loves, the value of leaning in here because this is where the gold is—just beyond what you see and know now. All of these reactions will also reveal and reflect exactly how you show up in your life as well. Your shit will continue to happen until you choose to respond consciously versus react unconsciously and lean in to allow a shift to happen. This means a shift gets to take place in how you choose to respond, operate, and be for a different result to now be created in your life. I'm here to share with you my lifelong journey in discovering, testing, and implementing those tools that allowed me also to create those shifts, and you can use these tools, clear direction, and guidance to move right through it to create a different result.

The only request I have for you to get all you can out of this process is to simply do your best to breathe into it, lean into it, allow it to reveal what's there, and remain open to the discovery of all things. This doesn't mean you have to attach to any of it or decide now if it's true for you. You are just here to play a game of curiosity and practice this new life skill, which will, by itself, create incredible changes in your life by allowing you to become curious in all things and open to receiving even greater. You can now give yourself the freedom to explore new territory. If you aren't willing to look, you will never know of the gifts waiting for you just beyond it to receive. Whatever you aren't willing to fully "be" with will continue to create resistance and not let you "be." Remember that you are here not by default but by design because your inner guidance system is asking you for even more of all you are and can receive in your life. I'm so excited for your journey to see what infinite possibilities are awaiting you.

I can promise you that on this path of seeing more, life can only get greater for you. I urge you, for your greater good and the greater good of all those that you interact with and are an influence to, to come to the end of this journey that is in this book to give yourself your grandest life experience. You choosing it for yourself can only exemplify for those you love and others that they too can do the same.

Throughout this experience, you will discover nuggets of truths and ways of being that will bring you to a completely different life experience if you choose. By the end of this book, you will have seen and been taught exactly how to live in and operate out of the next version of the remembrance of your true nature, highest self, and divinity, incorporating the clear wisdom and inner-standing to create and experience your best life. You will, of course, always continue to evolve, as life is never stagnant. I am not claiming that reading this book will be the end of your journey for you, and instead what is available is that as you will continue to incorporate these same tools, revealing more and more for you as you remember how worthy you truly are and have always been of everything you desire to experience. What I share here is how my life has continued to become more magical, miraculous, and amazing in every area.

Most importantly, this all really does get to be fun and easy. You might think that seems way too good to be true. Again, that's OK. Let's notice and get curious to what really is going on inside of you if you feel any resistance to that as a possibility for you. It's all just interesting feedback. I did tell you this could challenge your comfort zone, and I am so happy for you if it does. It has already begun, as you are noticing your beliefs and parameters being confronted by a simple statement. These are the micro catches we are after that will make the macro changes in your life.

So, are you now open to making everything fun and easy in your life, even if in your past experience it hasn't been? Can you now allow yourself to get curious about how it can be? Are you willing to play a game now with it and how your entire life experience could become that way? You can start choosing this right now. How? Start by choosing to smile and realize this is a new moment that can be experienced in any way you want. Now, you can get excited because your wholeness, divinity, and pure badassery that is you is already here, always has been, and is inevitable. Today is worth celebrating, and so are you because you are alive, breathing, and always have infinite possibilities in front of you of ways to see, feel, act on, and experience whatever it is you want.

Let's begin the adventure of living your best life!

As we start this journey together, I have several free gifts I'd love to share with you for support. *"The Ultimate Life of Having It All"* is a free guided meditation and activation to support you in creating and aligning with the life you desire. It's something you can utilize again and again to support your journey of growth and expansion. To also allow you to expand your capacity to create and receive Joy in your life, you'll have access to this training, *"Living In 100% Joy Now."* To receive these and several other support gifts, simply visit the book resources page at Book.marcilock.com/resources. I am truly excited for you to IN-JOY all there is for you to discover within through these and through our journey here to live in Liberation, Abundance, and Bliss now as you integrate living a life you absolutely love filled with your greatest joys.

For support in creating solutions and freedom, we dive deep into several aspects of life in my show, *The Awakened Being: Conversations to Create Change,* where each episode is designed to shift your reality and awaken your full liberation. We'd love you to check out what shows are available and see if any specifically can support you in whatever you are alchemizing to a greater life experience. As you tune in, subscribe if you feel called to continue to participate. You can listen directly to the show at Marcilock.com/show or find it on all other major platforms as well.

And, of course, to support you with implementing the tools in this book, you can get all the resources we share here, the pdf guides for the 5 Steps to Freedom, Discovery Opportunities, and all the gifts at Book.marcilock.com/resources. You will find many additional resources as well to support you in wherever you are at in your journey to living your very best life. I'm so grateful you are here. I'm honored to walk with you and be a part of your journey.

1

My Story of Normal

By six years old, the scent of Lysol was ingrained in my tiny fingers and hands from scrubbing church pews alongside my parents, who worked as custodians, cleaning churches. I was woken up sharply at 6:00 a.m. with bright lights suddenly flipped on and piercing my tiny eyes, prompting me to help my parents on our farm and then off to their job with them as custodians. Of course, my parents intentions weren't for me to be child labor. It was simply that there wasn't any money for someone to watch me as my older brothers and sister went off to school. So, I got to join my parents in the daily activities of their job and help out.

Growing our own food was not a hobby; we did so that we could survive and had food to eat. I'd work in the garden and do chores on the farm before making myself a glass of powdered milk and pick a piece of fruit for breakfast before starting on another job. From a young age, it was all I knew: work, struggle, sacrifice, survive. It was my normal. Accordingly, I took on that same belief system as I grew, never feeling I'd ever be worthy of anything else.

Besides being dirt poor, I was scared. Actually, more like terrified of life. I was constantly fed and internalized the stories of scary people in the world doing scary things. I was afraid of disappointing God, of sickness, of disease, of being attacked, of being heard, of being seen, of being rejected. I basically lived in fear of being anything at all other than what I was told was expected of me and of life itself out of what I was told was safe. What I attracted and experienced because of what I believed the world to be and my level of worthiness was a very scary world and extremely difficult reality.

As a teenager, I worked my ass off as I ran between multiple outside paying jobs on top of any needs expected to be fulfilled at home. I was timid and awkward, always thinking about how I was supposed to act for others to approve instead of how my actions would make me feel. It was all about pleasing others, my parents, God, and the church. I never had a voice or expressed my opinion. I did anything and everything to be who "they" wanted me to be and please whatever person or persons I was with, always terrified of being rejected.

I watched my father's fight with his health from the time I was born. At age 15, I watched him die. In his own childhood, he was programmed to believe that his role on earth was to toil, work, suffer, and endure the tests under the belief that when he died, he'd earn his kingdom in heaven for eternity. And he did exactly that. He worked his entire life to endure, serve, struggle, and survive, and then he died. From a young age, death was something I became acquainted with as I experienced many people in our family and close circles dying, mostly from sicknesses and unseen freak accidents. At 15, just six days after my father passed away, I lost my best friend in a car accident. As I was taught, life was just one intensely painful "test" of suffering, sacrifice to make, and one scary experience after another to endure and it continued to show up that way.

My dear mother struggled, too. She shared the same beliefs— to always serve, do good for others, and put herself last, yet she strived to appear perfect and keep it all together. At a young age, I specifically was influenced by her struggle to love and accept herself, and it was the most seen through her dissatisfaction with her weight.

At four years old, I remember my mother coming out of her room in tears saying that she worked so hard to lose five pounds just to gain it right back again. At the time, I didn't understand and I only saw her as someone I deeply loved and who was perfect just the way she was. I didn't really know what the "weight" was she was referring to, so I didn't understand why she was upset. What I did see is that it had to do with her body, and she wasn't happy with it. I have a clear memory of my exact response to my mother that day. I looked up at her through complete love and innocence and said, "Maybe God gave it back to you because you needed it."

Then, on another day as a young girl, I remember my mother saying she was going to go for a walk and asked if I'd like to come. Excited and overjoyed to join her, I ran outside. As my mother arrived next to me, I reached up my hand to hold hers. She then said to me that she couldn't hold my hand because she needed to move her arms briskly at her sides to burn more calories.

Now, my mother is one of the sweetest, most caring and compassionate people I've ever known and in no way was she intending to hurt me. It wasn't like anything even traumatic really happened. Yet, what happened in that moment was I made a decision that would influence my entire life experience. The decision I made was that how the body "looked" was so incredibly important and that it looking a certain way was what determined I was "good enough." I learned that for her, if the body wasn't "good enough," that it meant she wasn't happy or felt good enough. To me, this translated as: To be accepted and good enough, I had to be beautiful, and to be beautiful was to be thin. And I discovered that to be thin is a fight and battle, which wasn't much different from what I was being taught about everything else in life. I took on the story that the body is a struggle—you can't trust it, and you don't have control of it. From that moment, I took on my own fight with my body. I began to feel like a victim and like I had no control over it. I carried that knowledge and programming with me onward into my future life experiences.

As a teenager, I suffered from anorexia, bulimia, ulcers, migraines, and physical sickness and symptoms that were constantly a part of my life. I struggled to sleep because I never felt safe. When I had a stalker at age 11, I completely stopped sleeping altogether—a problem that only caused more sickness and internal stress on my nervous system. When I was 19, I had a heart attack.

Although my biggest health scare was yet to come, these health issues in my youth were already based on complicated, deep-rooted programs. I assumed I'd have a life where I would scrape by financially, settle in relationships, and not believe my body was capable of anything other than letting me down. All I knew was one loss after another.

After my dad died, I went to night school and became certified as a nurse assistant that I could earn more money and figured out a way to buy a car even before I was 16 so that I could get around to all my jobs. There were several times while I was driving that I'd feel so incredibly tempted and wondered, *What if I just veered across the road and killed myself?* The only thing that stopped me at the time was thinking that I might hurt someone else or just end up handicapped and as a vegetable for the rest of my life instead of dying. I couldn't bear to think of my mom in more pain after already experiencing the passing of my father. Plus, there was work left to be done, and I felt the responsibility to take care of my mother, earn enough to pay our rent and the bills, and make it work to keep surviving.

At age 17, I began studying self-empowerment, yet nothing went deeper than shifting your thoughts and perceptions. Although I strived to do that, I didn't believe I was really worthy or deserving of anything different or feel that any of that could be true for me and I didn't know how to really apply it other than self-affirmations and forcing myself to focus on other thoughts.

Just wanting to be safe and loved, and only knowing the programs I'd learned, I chose what was comfortable and what I thought would give me that safety. I was taught my entire life that God just wanted me to be a mom, raise a family, and serve others. So, at age 21, I did what I thought I was supposed to do and got married for safety and approval.

I remember saying to myself over and over in my thoughts, *If I am the perfect mom and wife and always look perfect, then my husband will always love me and appreciate me and never cheat on me.* This was the exact thought consistently playing in my head, the perceptions I looked for, and the beliefs that I felt to be true. If I could just do everything right—or at least pretend to—I would be accepted, validated, and safe. I believed that's how I'd always keep this man (and everyone else) happy and loving me. Even after being diagnosed with breast cancer at the age of 24, I was always striving to fit the picture by being the perfect wife and mother. I had no idea at the time that the breast cancer was just one of the many external results I'd created as a byproduct from all the pain and emotional turmoil inside.

I thought this strategy was the way to control my own safety, and it's all I knew and had ever known.

I was creating my own safety according to what I believed was really safe. It felt comfortable to stay in and expect struggle, sacrifice, hardship, and survival. Again, life showed up exactly as I believed it would (and in accordance with the very reality that I was afraid of).

When my boys were less than one and four years old, I found out my husband was cheating on me when he texted me and told me he'd left a note for me to read. I was devastated to read he had cheated several times with his assistant manager of the fast food restaurant he managed. Later, I discovered he was forced to tell me because her boyfriend was about to.

I was crushed and, of course, all my limiting beliefs were re-affirmed as I continued to create the very circumstances that reflected the inner environment I was living in—that I was never enough and there was only one struggle after another to overcome to survive.

Being raised Mormon meant being raised in what I experienced as a strict religious environment based on beliefs of what is good, bad, wrong, and right. In the eyes of the church, divorce was one of the worst things you could ever do. I remember going to my bishop to share what was going on with my husband, and I told him my plan I'd come up with: to start work as a waitress right away in hopes I could earn enough for now to pay the bills and feed and support my boys. His advice to me was to take back my husband because if I didn't, I would be folding napkins as a waitress for $2 an hour for the rest of my life. He didn't seem interested in how I felt as a person; it was more about what I was expected to do to: serve, sacrifice, and act in the way that he deemed God wanted me to.

For probably the first time in my life, I realized that none of that view felt good or sat with me as true. I began, at a deeper level, to question who I was really listening to and the kind of results they really had in their lives. I had a realization that continuing to do what everyone else expected of me or said I "should" be doing was literally killing me. It made so much sense as to why I'd had so many sicknesses and struggles with my body and health my entire life—I was in constant emotional turmoil that created sep-aration with myself as source, constant dysfunction inside, which was the byproduct of sickness and disease (out of ease with life).

The truth I wasn't able to see as the cause until that time was that I didn't love myself. I'd never given myself the permission to find out who I was because my entire life was built on pretending to be what I thought I should be. I was simply trying to control the environment to keep my little girl inside who was scared of rejection, judgment, comparison, and not being good enough to feel safe by staying unheard, unseen, and hiding in the shadows. Since that is exactly what was inside of me, that is exactly what kept reflecting externally for me to face.

In the end, I got a divorce—against the advice of everyone from my church and childhood—and took a ridiculously low-paying waitressing job of just $2 an hour to scrape by making enough for basic food and rent to support the three of us. I paid a friend to sleep on my couch at night so I could take care of my kids by day and waitress at night to earn enough to get by. Life was extremely hard, and I was only focused on one day at a time to survive, but it felt normal—I'd always been miserable, after all, and I knew how to work hard and survive. I couldn't imagine it any different.

Yet, I had taken a baby step and an inch onto a new path and moving beyond the misery of living as others thought I had to. This was a new behavior and step into creating something different by giving myself permission to begin living a life I was choosing to now do and be something different.

2

I Changed My "Normal," and You Can Too

It was just six years after feeling completely broken as a tired, overwhelmed single mother and $2-an-hour waitress that I was mentoring personal clients at a million-dollar-plus level. I had built a multi-million-dollar enterprise, was living in my dream home in paradise with my epic growth partners and my beloved, and was traveling the world, doing exactly what I love: sharing what gave me this freedom.

How did I go from struggling and broken to living the fantastical life I do today in bliss? It's simple: I said no to what had held me back for so long—an operating system where every decision, every perception, and every thought I had was rooted in scarcity, fear, or feelings of inadequacy and unworthiness. How? I started by taking full radical responsibility that everything I was thinking, speaking, and feeling about the world was creating my reality.

By going internal and focusing on my inner-standing to come into full alignment, I allowed myself to receive a completely different experience. A life of infinite possibilities of awesomeness was the result of choosing to live consciously.

On my path, the main tool that allowed me to overhaul my life and I'll be sharing with you here was "the 5 Steps to Freedom," which walks you through overcoming any conflict, unconscious programs, or resistance in the way of getting what you want. I became committed to creating freedom and expansion in each moment instead of subconsciously projecting the negativity of my past onto my present and continuing to live in contraction.

In short, I had been living in a story that said I had to struggle and fight my body for every pound and every bit of health while being afraid of the world and the people it held. I believed in a story that said the sacrifices I was making both financially and personally were simply "it" for me because that's all I deserved.

And you know what? It all changed for me when I finally realized I was the one creating that shit story. One day, when someone mentioned the flowers and horses we had just passed, I realized I never saw them. What I did see were the weeds growing on the side of the road. I completely missed the pasture of flowers behind them, the horses running in the fields, the mountains, trees, and the beauty that was everywhere and in everything because I had only been focused on the weeds. It was one of the first realizations I had in seeing why I had what I had and how I was the only one creating my own suffering. I was the one living in the behaviors, parameters, ideas, and programming that kept that story alive and true. So, I chose to change it—and you can change yours, too.

Today, I truly live my ideal dream as my reality and still use these tools that gave me freedom to continue to only expand into even greater and greater. Living in Peace is my top priority, bliss and joy are my norm, and I choose to live in complete freedom in all aspects of my life. Of course, that means freedom of time to do what I want, when I want, and with whomever I want, being the source of my own experience and reality. Freedom of money to live the lifestyle I desire, provide for my boys in the way I want, and utilize the tool of money for funding the projects we create and philanthropic endeavors we are passionate about, utilizing it as a resource for the greater good. Freedom to only allow and engage in the most aligned, conscious, awakened relationships with beautiful beings that magnify love and light. The thing that led to all of those external results of freedom was aligning to the freedom of who I truly was, lying hidden and dormant inside.

Physically, I continue to thrive in my ideal body of health, where I actually look and feel younger every day, which I'll share more on later. From this knowing I direct my energy, and I am fully worthy of whatever I want as my experience. I give my cells and my body directions to stay in optimal health and alignment. My body supports all aspects of my creations, sexuality, power, gifts, and abilities to serve and expand continually and easily as my norm.

I love and adore what I do, which is in alignment with my highest self, and get paid extremely well, aligned to my true self-worth. On the journey of discovering and allowing all of me to come through, I found and get to share my unique gifts, genius, passion, and purpose. From my personal coaching and master-minds, to leading a tribe of freedom seekers through my online programs, on stages, podcasts, and TV worldwide, I've made more money than I ever thought possible doing only what I love while discovering more of who I am and offering that light.

I have been extremely selective with who I've chosen to work with as my personal clients, as I learned to value myself and hold my energy as sacred. This has allowed me to work close-ly with some of the most influential leaders and the most rec-ognized corporations out there, who choose to create and be the change for the planet. The value I give and have aligned to has allowed me to also personally coach at a price point of over a million-dollar-plus level, and I have become recognized as "The Million Dollar Mentor." I share this simply for you to see the drastic change in my own self value as well as the ability to be seen, heard, express, and give my gifts to the world. I am truly blessed to get to work with the most amazing light leaders and beings from all over the world, who I adore and cherish going the journey with.

Even though I have and continue to work with individuals at a very high financial level of investment as well, my calling continued to expand, as I was passionate about how many more people could be served. The vision I've received and known we have as an opportunity in our path of evolution as humanity is to choose a New Earth experience where we operate as awakened beings, in our full divinity and in peace and harmony with each other and all of life. To create a New Earth, we get to align to the highest frequency and consciousness as New Humans to operate from our Divine Natural State of Bliss, Joy, Peace, and Love. I had a deep desire that everyone who truly was seeking to find peace, freedom, and the remembrance of their true divinity could be supported in that discovery. We do this through our many online programs, activations, meditations, sharing through my podcast *The Awakened Being: Conversations to Create Change*, and supporting our online community along with experiential transformations through our retreats worldwide.

I thoroughly enjoy hosting my Ascension Adventures Breakthrough Retreats, VIP and Group VIP experiences, and events all around the globe because I truly love experiential transformation. One of the spaces I love and thrive in the most is where I believe our greatest playground for our freedom is. That is accessed by being willing to dive into all the places that feel scary, messy, or most shy away from. I love all aspects of the messy human and the multidimensional mystic that we are, and this is where I will hold and love people through to the remembrance of their wholeness. This is where massive transformation and complete recalibration to our true internal alignment takes place, and it is available for you too.

Love is the inclusion of all things, not the exclusion of anything. I've been blessed to witness the awakenings and remembrances as the outcomes of countless souls who chose to create their freedom by leaning in to release all of the unseen internal blocks, awaken dormant DNA, and discover many of our multidimensionality, capabilities, and gifts within as you align all parts of you to the remembrance of the divine being you've always been. These processes have empowered myself as well as many of the greatest influencers to share their gifts more fully and freely, and the same gifts are awaiting inside you. The opportunity is available for you to discover how easily you are meant to create and how worthy you've always been to choose and receive an amazing and magical life in all ways as your divine birthright. You can begin to do this now, no matter where you are at or what you've experienced.

Although my boys' father and I are no longer married, he and I are truly the dearest friends and partners in this parenting journey. You'll notice I refer to him as my "former" rather than my "ex." Every single relationship and all these beautiful beings who have been a part of my life's journey of experiences are those I called in and asked for, so I only see them through the eyes of pure love, honor, and appreciation for the gifts we gave each other and contracts we held to assist each other in our growth and ascension. This is freedom. There is no blame, shame, or trying to prove yourself right. I was not the victim—I was the creator of my experiences, and they simply showed up in what I was asking to receive. From business to my personal life, all my relationships are magnifying, beautiful, honoring, and free. There is no room for settling, tolerating or sacrificing in my chosen current experience; there is only continually receiving greater and greater.

As I received the direction and began channeling the writing of this book, I was living in my dream home in San Diego we called "The Magical Manifestation Mansion," overlooking the beach with my two growth partners and best friends—i.e., my sons and my divine-sacred-union beloved in my life. I had visualized and manifested this dream home and land, which came with everything I desired for the service I was being called to give. I was able to utilize it for events to support the community, for retreats, and as a space where my million-dollar-plus clients could come and stay for deep-dive-VIP transformational experiences with me. My boys and I had created our normal as lives we absolutely loved. Choosing to live authentic and free to be fully expressed and transparent in everything we're experiencing. We travelled the world for my retreats and our own personal adventures and chose our lives to be operating from a level of absolute freedom to be able to go wherever we feel called, whenever we feel called.

At the time of completing this book, I was called to the next greatest adventure of discovery, freedom, and service on my journey and began travelling the world as a Global Citizen to serve wherever, whenever, and in whatever way I felt called. By the time you read this, all I know is that I'll be continuing to experience an even grander capacity of light, love, abundance, and joy in life as I continue to come into even more remembrance. Life can only continue to get greater and greater.

This is what is available and so much more as an Awakened Being. This is the new way of the New Human, fully awakened to their divinity and creating the New Earth where we remember we are the source of our experience and we can let go of any old constructs that created our own suffering.

How'd I Do It?

I know what it's like to feel broken. I know what it means to feel invisible. To feel used, thrown away, and objectified. To be broken in your life, mindset, and bank account. To put others before yourself. There were several times in my life I thought about killing myself.

Today, everything has changed, and my reality and way interacting and being with life is completely different. I've gone from broken to bliss. I changed my life, and all I continue to see and experience is more happiness, growth, expansion, and joy. I have the freedom to be my full self, unapologetically as me, and the ability to encourage others to do the same, and that has given me internal peace. I can't put a value on this gift.

I got here by dropping my old story of normal, caring about what others think, and looking for permission outside of myself. If you aren't moving towards what you want and what is right for you, even if it is taking the next inch, then, my friend, the reality is that you're stuck in some bullshit story, excuse, or validation that you can't have it. That is what normal has trained you to do—instead of seeing all the infinite possibilities and being fully worthy and capable of receiving them, you've been trained to stay stuck in the shit, looking for all the reasons why you can't have what you want.

I did it too. I strived to live in normal. Having been there and done that, normal wasn't what it is all cracked up to be. Actually, it was what it's cracked up to be—shitty and hard. We'll be diving into each operating system to understand clearly what creates conflict, disconnect, and limitation and get clear on how you can shift each one of these operating systems to align to how you've been designed to create and be. Let's discover what your NEW normal can be.

Commit to Something Different

My life gets better every day, and all of this comes to me easily because I've chosen to grow, learn, expand, and continue to receive bliss, joy, ease, and grace instead of struggle, hardship, and sacrifice. Not only can you have all of this, but you are built to have all of this. In this book, I will teach you the five steps tool you can use to transform your own existence—to go from unconsciously reacting to consciously creating. You'll discover how to go inside and shift your operating systems to cut through your own unconscious programs and reprogram them to allow only more peace, love, and joy into all aspects of your life.

Bottom line: what you can't ignore is your results. See, we can use stories and make excuses all over the place, but your results can never lie. They will always prove the truth and show you exactly what you have been and are currently committed to. Think about your own life right now. Are you just going through the motions and settling for what you believe you deserve? Even if your life is what you would say is good, why stop there? Wherever you are and whatever you are experiencing, can you now allow yourself to be on a continual path of accepting greater and greater? Now is the time to commit to the greatest asset you will ever have, which is you. You and your life experience are the greatest assets, which create everything else. What is more important than the life you choose to create that influences everything else? If you want something different, it is available for you to create and receive as the divine powerful creator you already are designed to be. Now is the time to say yes to your own happiness. Nobody else can do it for you. Only you can give it to yourself.

What do you want to be experiencing? What would an epic existence look like for you? Would you love to wake up each day in complete joy and alignment, excited and prepared to grow and excel in business, in your relationships, and in your physical and spiritual wellbeing?

I know you could be in a place in your life where everything I'm saying sounds crazy. I was there too, and if it wasn't for those people willing to speak up that began to open up my world to what else was available, then I definitely wouldn't be here. I'm also here simply in support to walk with you and share if you are open to it and willing because I too have lived in that place. Something happened for me to shift my reality, and I want to offer the same for you. I'm definitely not anyone's guru preaching at or to you. You are and always be your own guru and only you can know what is best for you. I'm here as a friend and fellow light being, knowing that your happiness adds to all our happiness. Together we grow and rise in love and an even greater experience for all. I am here with outstretched arms to embrace you in love with a desire that by sharing my own journey, you too can see infinite possibilities for yours. These are the shifts that worked for me and those who I've shared them with—to align to a very direct path to more love, pleasure, abundance, joy, passion, and play.

Most people stop themselves from change because they have a distorted picture and idea of what change is. Life is always consistently changing, and change is the most natural thing. We are always evolving and changing, and wouldn't we be completely bored if we weren't? So, why do we strive so tightly to hold onto and control things to be the same? This only leaves us stuck in the comfort zones that aren't really comfortable. Change is our most natural, beautiful process for new opportunity, new freedoms, new joys, and greater experiences. It is easy when you take it a breath and a moment at a time. Breathe into it, my loves, become at ease with the dance and flow of life that naturally is always bringing us change and our evolution for what is our greatest joys, guiding us to more than we ever could have been able to see through our current lens of consciousness.

Give Yourself Permission

Get curious and see what is possible for you. What I can and will do is walk with you and share the tools that gave me my own freedom and that can empower you to do the same for yourself. From there, the number of individuals who are affected by you and, as a result, will then give themselves permission, is infinite, just as you will discover you are infinite possibilities.

So, do this for yourself. Nothing is as important as how you are experiencing your life. I'll continue to remind you that you, my friend, are your greatest asset. It isn't anything that you own; it is you. You are the only one who can change your life experience and the only one who can give yourself permission to create it. You are the most sacred experience of your life. Can anything be as sacred and important as how you are experiencing you? Can anything be as important of an investment as your life experience? If you see this new opportunity for you as a commitment to yourself to continually move forward just a breath and a moment at a time, you will always only be changing and evolving into receiving a greater and greater life than you currently have. Isn't that way easier than settling, struggling, surviving, and staying in your uncomfortable comfort zone of suffering?

What is True Freedom?

The tool you will be mastering in this book is called the 5 Steps to Freedom, but what is freedom? The odds are that even the loftiest definition allowed by your subconscious mind isn't quite there because you've got years of experiences, attachments, limiting beliefs, and fears that created these parameters that are blocking your allowance to ultimate freedom.

True freedom means giving yourself permission to always be fully you, unapologetically. Liberation means letting all of you be accepted, known and letting both your light and dark times and experiences serve you. Just as love is accepting all things, freedom is expressing and accepting all emotions and utilizing them all in a way that leaves out the bullshit and the judgment.

When you're operating in ultimate freedom, you feel light and buoyant—confident to be heard, to be seen, and to feel everything and use everything that happens to you, for you on your own terms as the source of your own experience. This allows you to receive because there are no rules; there is only freedom of infinite possibilities, and this is available to you as your new and true normal.

What is Normal for your "True Self"?

Forget the "either/or" game that has become a normal idea of existing for so many. We are all infinite, limitless, capable, and worthy. Will you take a moment and feel into a specific moment in your life with me? What happened when you were born? You might be using your mind to try and think of a memory, such as crying or seeing your mother. We are tuning into what happened even before that...

I'll remind you that the very first thing that ever happened to you, my friend, was that you were born perfectly. Take a moment to feel that and please take that in. This knowing is a part of what will begin to shift everything. What happened next my love? You simply began to take on *stories*. From these stories, you began to feel and take on the **hurt** from them. You then took on **ideas** from these stories and hurt. **Time** continued to build on these and anchor them into who you believed yourself to be. Stories, hurt, ideas, and time built into your specific "**SHIT**." This separation of who you have always been, still are, and always will be is what created your own suffering. It's not who you are; it's just what you learned. It can now be a choice to dissolve these illusions creating a false reality because you can now unlearn, deprogram, and de-story what isn't working and shift to experience a very different new normal aligned to the perfect being you actually are.

You are uniquely designed in this life to experience whatever it is you want to be experiencing, to create the result you want, and to come into full alignment in a way that changes your reality.

Your normal can be a place of unconditional love, freedom, bliss, abundance, joy, and pleasure. You can exist without limits, fear, lack, or scarcity. You are designed to thrive in love and awesomeness as a sovereign master creator of whatever it is you want to be experiencing, and you are designed to do it effortlessly.

Your "True Self" Normal Is Acting as an Effortless Creator

You are here to discover the expression of your full divinity. That means you have the opportunity to uniquely design this life experience. You have the power and ability to create the result that you want. Operating out of who you truly are and how you are designed, your natural normal is a place without limits or scarcity. Your normal is where you're thriving in infinite love, joy, bliss, abundance, and all awesomeness you choose as the creator of your reality and source of your every experience rather than a spectator of life or a bitch to circumstances.

It is effortless, just as you are effortless. This is extremely important for you to realize. I want you to simply notice something. Stop moving or doing for a moment and focus on yourself right now just being. What's happening right now? Are you able to witness it? Well, it's really simple. Just being, you are breathing, aren't you? And you are doing it effortlessly, aren't you? I know; it's not rocket science I'm breaking down here, and that is what makes this so doable, simple, easy, and available for everyone. It's very simple because it is the way we are designed. You're breathing, and you're not even trying. It is happening naturally.

What else is happening?

Just sitting or standing here "being" you, can you notice that your mind is having thoughts that come and go? Your eyes are seeing and perceiving the world around you. Your body is experiencing feelings and sensations. None of this is taking effort because all of these thoughts, perceptions, and feelings are what you've been training yourself in and doing your entire life. The point is that you are effortlessly creating right now.

If you look outside today, the sun rose again. It didn't struggle. Birds are still flying with ease. The grass, trees, fruit, vegetation, and all of life is continuing to grow. Both you and nature are always creating effortlessly. Do you realize, though, what you were and are actually creating? Can you see that exactly what you have right now is what you've been creating effortlessly because it's been what all your operating systems have been focused on and doing to get that as your result? Do you know exactly how you have done that? All it takes now is to simply lean in and get curious as to why your results are what they are, as they will never lie and can be a clear reflection for you on what you have been committed to getting. It takes just as much effort to create your own suffering as it does your liberation because it is all a direction of energy, which you effortlessly are and have been already applying to all of life. Maybe you haven't known or fully understood it, and as you continue here, it will become crystal clear. Now, choosing a conscious direction shift, it can now be just as easy to get what you actually want instead.

Seek Accountability

You can also make this process easier by knowing that you are not alone. In fact, I recommend you invite someone to do this with you, read with you, and take on this new change. Accountability is only taking positive responsibility toward getting to the result you want in your life.

Who else is seeking greater and could be a support to you and you a support to them? Step together in creating greater in your lives and know that you have a place of support. I highly recommend you get as much support around you and engage with that support as much as possible. This is your life experience we are talking about. Whether you choose to take that recommendation and create more support or not, know that I'm here with you and there are countless individuals and a community who are freedom seekers, living as the New Humans and are also on their path and journey to their remembrance and liberation.

You can also join me and this entire community of those choosing their best life in the Best Life Tribe. This is where we offer step-by-step support, trainings, tools, live Q&As with me for breakdown to breakthrough, and a supportive environment to guide you through resistance, which would normally be where we stop ourselves, and assist on the pathway to living an absolutely amazing life.

You can get access into the Tribe and Facebook Community Support in the resources guide at book.marcilock.com/resources.

Also, know that everyone else in your world, your children, family, friends, and those you don't even know will be affected by who you now choose to be. Thank you for giving yourself the healing you seek, creating peace within yourself, and therefore creating peace for our entire planet.

Discovery Opportunity #1:
Assess the Results You've Created

There are several discovery opportunities throughout this book, which will give you the practice of going within to witness what's happening and allow you to reflect on the material in the chapter. This might be completely new for you and it might not. Give yourself a chance to tune into deeper insight, facilitate healing, and create clarity as to what has been operating internally to now manifest something different externally. Take a few minutes to reflect and contemplate on these questions and allow any feelings to arise. We'll be going into more depth as you continue on exactly how to utilize all of it and get clear with yourself.

Stop and really evaluate what the results are that you currently have in your life; this will give you insight into what gets to shift if you want to create something different. The more detailed and thoughtful your responses, the more helpful these assignments will be, so take your time and respond from the heart.

1. What is the "normal" feeling and experience I am living in most of the time?

2. What are my beliefs about how life works and what is attainable for me?

3. What are my current results in these areas: Relationships with others? Body and health? Finances? Relationship to myself?

4. How much have I been able to receive joy and live my passions so far in my life? How free do I feel and give myself permission to be? How much do I allow myself to receive sex, pleasure, and play?

5. Looking at your authentic answers from the questions above, what is it that you see you have been believing you deserve? Are there things you have been tolerating in your life, and if so, what have you been tolerating?

6. What would you like to now create and experience as your new normal and current reality?

3

Everything Is Energy

In every moment, you're creating energy. The energy you emit is why you have the things you have and behave the way you behave. You can always quickly and easily get the solid answer of exactly what is happening and why by looking directly at the "energy.

Again, please breathe and practice staying open if you think that is airy fairy and makes no sense at all because it is the piece you may have been missing that can set you free. I'm not here to blow smoke up your ass or to make anything more complicated in your world. We are here to get super clear and allow everything to become extremely simple in manifesting and receiving the life you absolutely love. Soon you will easily be able to know exactly how to see everything happening in any situation like a superpower you never knew you had that makes life so amazingly easy. It is through feeling and witnessing the energy present that allows you to shift what was unseen to create a different result.

So, how do you detect this energy?

It's simple; you just look at or tune into how it feels. How you feel as you do each and every thing in your life is a reflection of your energy. How you feel when you interact with a friend as you are laughing is very different from how you feel when you are interacting with someone who you dislike. How you feel doing something you love is different than how you feel when you are doing something you feel forced to do or dislike doing.

Have you really looked at and noticed how everything you choose to say, choose to think, or choose to do actually feels? Have you noticed what you feel when you enter a room? Why is it that you might enter a room of people and feel drawn to a certain crowd, person, or direction? Have you ever put an outfit on, and it just didn't feel right, so you changed it? Have you ever walked into a gathering, place, or restaurant and then decided to leave because it just didn't feel right or good? Have you said yes to doing something, and it actually felt heavy and didn't feel good? How different is it when you've said yes to doing something you genuinely wanted to do, were excited about, and that felt in alignment? Have you ever hugged someone, and it felt extremely awkward like you were hugging a big, stiff rock with legs? How about when you've hugged someone and found yourself sinking into their embrace, drawn into their warmth and safe feeling as you were held? These are different ways of experiencing energy. Same hug—two vastly different experiences because of the energy of the two beings in the mix and your feelings and energy towards them. This is what we are talking about when we simply witness energy in all its different forms and ways of existing in life. That's not so airy fairy and woo woo now is it? What it is, is the gold that is present in everything, it is the foundation of life happening, and it is what will give us whatever experience we want when we acknowledge and work with what life itself is made up of. Whether it is to bring the formless into form, or to shift and change what we have in form to become a completely different experience, it is all made up of energy.

Everything has an energy that you can feel. In everything you do, you are sending out a powerful signal to everyone and everything else that says exactly what you want to experience and what you believe you are worthy of. We're all radiating and living in a vibration that reflects our energy toward whatever we are experiencing. So, what is the energy you emit when it comes to relationships? In other words, what is your relationship to relationship? Do you feel fear? Are you afraid of connection because it has only brought pain, heartache, and rejection in the past? Is it an energy of sacrifice, settle, and difficulty? Or is what you give out a feeling of joy, happiness, support, and love? When it comes to money, is there an energy of scarcity, lack, worry, struggle, and unworthiness to receive it? How about the energy you have towards your own body? Is it a fight and struggle of never being enough that you are constantly in? Is your body something you shame, judge, and feel negative about? Is your body something you love, appreciate, and adore? Everything you are doing carries an energy and is a direct reflection of what you are receiving in your health and body, wealth and freedom, pleasure and play, in all of your relationships with others and with yourself. All of your beliefs, perceptions, behaviors, programming, and patterns therefore exude the energy you are living in, feeling, and vibrating out to be received, and by emitting this energy, you are unconsciously creating the same results. Recognizing the energy you are putting out there is the first step to becoming a *conscious creator*.

Fear and Faith-Based Energy

There are two core type of energies that you are choosing to operate from: fear energy or faith/love energy. You could also label these in many other ways, such as you are either in an energy of contraction or expansion, exclusion or inclusion, separation or unity, shrinking or growing, enslaving or empowering. Are you getting the concept and feeling of the difference? I describe fear-based energy is an energy of lack, scarcity, separation, anxiety, worry, not enough-ness, or unworthiness. This type of energy comes from a feeling of force, fight, strive, struggle, and trying to get something because you believe you have to, should, or need it to be whole, worthy, or have what you want. The truth is that this energy is manmade and created from our programming of stories, ideas, attachments, and expectations that are all coming from lack, and it isn't how you were designed to operate; it was learned. When you start anything with the energy of fear, you are planting a seed that grows until you get exactly what you were afraid of because that is what it was built on.

Faith-based energy I feel and describe as love energy. It is in love energy that everything is created because creation comes from getting curious, being in wonderment, discovery, and getting excited about the possibilities you can find. That is how we create. We can also see this as the "inclusion" and the "unity" or the "expansion" into all things. When you come from this energy, you are open to all the possibilities and can keep moving forward in the curiosity of what will show up, how it could be possible, and what other ways it could be available, work, or be created. What happens is then you receive exactly that. New possibilities as each step appears to get you closer to receiving more of what you want. Can you see the difference? Are you on the energy channel of creating a happy, abundant life or operating from the fear, scarcity, and survival energy channel?

It is love—not fear—that is our natural energy. Love is the acceptance of all things. When we allow ourselves to look at all of the challenges we've had out of the eyes of love, hear the stories and reflections through the ears of love, and choose to even feel it through love, we can see how it is and actually always has been love and how it supported us to be who we are today. It was the scared little boy or girl inside you who developed the belief system they aren't good enough, and so they are always afraid of not being good enough. When we see it out of those eyes, it doesn't make sense to shame, blame, or judge the little boy or girl for feeling that way. That only causes it to feel and be more and more true.

It is when we see what's really happening energetically, it makes sense why we attracted it, perceived it that way, felt that way, and had the experience we had. We called in this very experience out of love for ourselves to grow and align to receiving greater and move beyond the limited programming and remember the truth of who we are. When we simply apply curiosity and look for the feedback that is provided through energy and the curiosity available in our wonderment and excitement, we find how we can awaken to an even greater capacity and ability to receive.

Now if the energy you give something then gives you the same thing back, we can see how when we choose to apply love energy to everything we've ever experienced and are experiencing now, we can only receive even more of what we want instead of staying in the same cycle. To do this means that we choose to apply love to every relationship, every experience, and every moment. Just be open to experimenting with this because if it happened or is happening, then what good does it do for us to fight what is currently here or already happened? We would only keep creating a fight and suffering. If we can get curious to see if we can witness it through love, knowing if energy never lies and you can only manifest what you are vibrating, then obviously our energy we were vibrating attracted this very experience. You'll have a lot more support coming up if that feels difficult to take in, as I know we can view many experiences in life as happening to us and not for or by us, especially as we look at having experiences we did as children. Again, breathe and just witness what comes up as we become more aware of what is underneath.

Tune in for just a moment and get curious with me. How does it feel if you choose to think that you were put here to suffer, bad things happen, and that life is suffering? I was raised that way and so I know exactly how that can feel. Do those thoughts feel good in your body? Is that something your Highest Self believes as true? Again, I want you to continue to get curious to decide what feels good for you. Right now I want you to just play with an experiment about how other views can feel. What if for now, you believed that everything that ever happened to you was for your benefit because every single experience gives you more growth, compassion, understanding, and more wisdom?

What I want you to witness in your experience of viewing and feeling these two different ways is that these are the two energy channels we've been looking at. You can either choose to go down the fear energy channel that is creating contraction, constriction, and enslavement of your divinity or you can choose to get curious about all the ways this has always been the energy of love leading you to the expansion of all you are truly here to be. Now there are many levels of energy and vibration. I share it this way because for me it becomes super easy and simple to clarify what the energy in anything and everything is doing when I evaluate it as one or the other: fear- or faith-based energy. Meaning, is this idea, belief, thing, view, situation, or whatever I am looking at serving me or enslaving me? Is it expanding me into all I am or creating my own suffering? Is it inclusion and unity or exclusion and separation? Is it taking me UP or bringing me DOWN? One path is choosing to operate and see it as a victim, and the other is taking responsibility and directing the energy, choosing to operate as a Sovereign Creator. Which one do you want to be experiencing?

The power of choice is always ours, and we have the power to choose what energy channel we are creating and vibrating. When we can practice now getting curious to see it all out of love, then what becomes available is we will begin to see and discover what we never saw before that can give us our freedom. We can choose to apply love energy to fully feel, fully heal, and move through it and receive even greater because we are and always have been worthy of having it all and experiencing our heaven on earth now. To create is to apply love energy. To create is to grow, to change your story. But here's the thing—we've been raised and trained to ignore our feelings, especially if they're based in fear or pain, and to mask who we are.

One of the greatest lessons I have learned along my journey is that fear and pain are important parts of our process. They tell us what's not working and are simply there as feedback. Pain is for us to PAY ATTENTION INSIDE NOW to what beliefs, paradigms, attachments, and ideas we chose to create that fear. Fear can be there to allow you to pay attention, keep you safe and aware. You can use it to serve you when you simply notice it and shift into curiosity around it. It doesn't have to be in the driver's seat. It doesn't have to cause drama or suffering either. You can use fear-based energy without living in it.

The Importance of Living in the Moment

Instead of living in love energy—your natural energy—maybe you've found yourself falling into patterns of self-sabotage that continue to give you exactly what you're expecting. It's a cycle you're unconsciously choosing to be in: past, future, past, future, past, future. This cycle of projection has you looking at your past experiences and then projecting those stories and beliefs onto your future. That is how you continually create it. If you're like many people I've coached over the years, you're unaware that you aren't living in the present, which is this very moment, the only time that is actually happening. Living in this moment gives us the ability to create consciously and respond consciously to create what we do want. When you are operating out of unconscious thoughts that you are projecting from your past and thinking about your future with those same worries, beliefs, and unconscious programming, then you're only creating more of it for you to receive. This isn't living in the moment in curiosity, wonderment, and excitement. With time, practice, and the tools in this book, you will learn to live in the present moment and create your reality consciously. Now you have the gift of knowing you are the creator, and everything you speak, focus on, and feel will shift into your world.

Radical Responsibility

To become a conscious creator is to take radical responsibility for everything. When you choose to take radical responsibility, you will get really clear with the results you are creating and what you are doing that is creating them. That means instead of ever looking outside of myself and blaming anyone or anything, I take responsibility that this is the result and experience in my world and I ask myself how I attracted and created it and get curious about what it is here to teach me. We stop fighting and we start allowing and receiving. It might sound easier to point the finger at an excuse or reason why things aren't showing up the way you want them to, and that will only keep you digging yourself into an even deeper hole that you are standing in. We get to take responsibility of every thought, word, feeling, action, and experience to begin to shift it. It isn't outside of us; it is all available right here within us and has created our external world. You are the medicine you have been seeking.

I would recommend you begin to practice taking full responsibility of everything you see, think, and feel as a beautiful new gift you are opening for yourself. You are awakening to all you are and the power and capabilities you have that will change everything. Not just in the area of your life that you think you want to fix. You aren't and have never been broken; you are just remembering who you really are and learning how to realign to operate from that place. You are already worthy of experiencing all you desire in every area of your life. So, begin to put that special focus on what your thoughts, words, and actions have been and how you've been reacting or responding to life. Witnessing and curiosity allows us to see how that same pattern, program, or paradigm is showing up in all of our world as all areas of your life are being affected to match that comfort zone and identity you chose. We'll create even more clarity in the next few chapters to practice and apply. As an enlightened creator, you are now conscious to and taking full radical responsibility for all the ways you emit energy. You choose to align it with what you desire and who you choose to be. Now it's time to see clearly how each operating system is creating what we put out and receive so that we can align all we do and all we will be with the highest vibration of our divinity.

4

Your Mental Programming Is Creating Your World

Operating System #1:
Your Thoughts and Beliefs

Albert Einstein once said, "No problem can be solved from the same state and level of consciousness that created it." What does that mean? You can't find the solution to a problem while looking at it through the same paradigm that created the problem in the first place. We can't manifest a different life experience by continuing to do things out of the same root beliefs, frequency, and energy. You can say affirmations and mantras all day long, yet if at your core you believe you aren't worthy, good enough, or deserving and that is the ENERGY and frequency you are attuned to and giving out, that is saying something completely different. Your words don't match your inner feelings, so affirmations alone won't create the result because you are still aligned to the energy you are giving out at your core.

Your Inner Child

Are you wondering why you are living on the energy channel that you are? Why would you pick living on the fear channel versus the high-vibe awesome life of bliss and joy channel if you are a powerful creator who can simply choose?

This is why: it wasn't you in the "now" who picked it; it was you "then," in that moment in time when you didn't have the ability to understand any better. Your inner five-year-old is in the driver's seat and is currently running your life.

To be more specific and clear, before age seven, you learned your programs, patterns, and beliefs and forged your identity. You picked up the programming of your parents and/or adults around you, who domesticated you to their ideas, beliefs, and constructs of how life operated and what things meant.

See, here's the thing: the subconscious mind has no logistical understanding, and at this age this is what you are operating from. At pre-seven, you didn't have an understanding as to why you experienced the events taking place in your life because you were operating only out of the subconscious mind. There was no logic to make sense of anything; you didn't have a voice of reason to guide you. You didn't have an understanding of why things looked, sounded, or appeared the way they did and how your perception could be untrue. You simply had the ability to see, hear, and then internalize how that made you feel. You learned something and made a decision based on it without logic or understanding, and so everything you felt, heard, and saw before that age is now controlling how you create your reality.

When you were born, you were simply discovering and creating yourself. You were curious about what you liked and how you could move. Moment by moment, you were discovering your world. You are here and your purpose is to discover and express all you are, and this world of infinite possibility is your playground to dance in and create.

For a young child, everything they see is for play and discovery. Consider this scenario: As a child, you notice one of your daddy's things, and to you it looks like a big toy. You begin to get curious about what it is, what it does, and what magnificent things could be possible with it. Suddenly, Daddy comes in and sees you playing with his things. He reacts by raising his voice, getting mad, and spanking you. Before this moment, you simply were happy creating and playing, and then suddenly you are being hurt. You are still not sure why. You know your daddy takes care of you, but now you can't trust that he won't hurt you. You could have had a reaction to hit back. Maybe you experienced him getting even angrier and so you learned to not do anything at all.

Before this moment, you felt free and happy. After this moment, taking on what you heard, saw, and felt, you have now learned whatever you chose to take on from the experience. You began to forget the perfect innocence of who you are and how you are designed to operate. Now you've taken on the emotional pain and have taken the emotional memory into your body. You could've taken on the belief that you can't trust others, trust life, or trust you are safe to exist let alone discover and get curious about life because your emotional body told you that.

Here's another example: Say a five-year-old little boy is playing with his toys, and Mom comes into the room and begins to yell. He sees her upset, frustrated, and angry and hears the words she is using, such as "bad," "wrong," maybe even "stupid" or "lazy." He feels sad, hurt, and maybe even afraid. Afraid to make her upset again, afraid to be himself, to just simply play and be free. He makes a decision in that moment about how he has to be and what he has to do to be safe.

A five year old who gets scolded does not think his mother raised her voice because she is stressed or tired nor does he have the ability to have a logical understanding of it. Instead, the subconscious mind could only clarify what it saw, heard, felt, and therefore learned from it.

What he learns is that if he doesn't behave a certain way, he is a bad child. This decision and belief as well as the programming he takes on from this modeling will now shape his patterns, behaviors, and entire identity he builds around how and who he has to be.

One of my clients, a highly successful doctor with a large practice, told me she was feeling "off" and upset but couldn't understand why. I took her through the same process I'll share with you on how to identify what she was feeling in her body, which led her to pinpoint a heaviness in her chest. Continuing to discover why the heaviness was there, which reflected sadness, we were able to get back to one of her core belief systems and stuck emotional energy in her body that was causing the pain.

The core belief we found was that she didn't trust herself. A doctor who didn't trust herself? The role and the emotion didn't seem to match up, but it all made sense when we looked back into her pre-seven-year-old mind, experiences, and belief systems.

When she was two, she was out in public with her father. As happens to many toddlers during the process of this age and potty training, she did not make it to the restroom in time and peed on the floor. In response, her father yelled at her, and she felt ashamed of her body and what it had done. From that moment, my client developed a belief system that she could not trust herself—not even her own body—to perform. We saw how this had shaped her experiences, perceptions, and reality through all of life. Doing the internal cleansing and reprogramming she experiences life now in full trust and would tell you that this old belief doesn't even hold any energy or truth for her anymore.

She is not alone in holding onto core beliefs formed during early years that subconsciously limit adult perceptions. Many of us, in fact, will find we're carrying around one or more and sometimes even all of the five main core beliefs I see show up:

1. *I'm not good enough.*
2. *I'm not worthy.*
3. *I'm not loved or lovable.*
4. *I'm not deserving.*
5. *I can't trust life, I can't trust others, or I can't trust myself.*

Without logical understanding, you've likely been learning these limiting belief systems and behavioral patterns since birth. In fact, they've formed your identity, which built your reality, and you're not sure how to change it. The truth is that you might not have even been aware of it running because it is all you've ever known.

Now you can get curious as to why you have the beliefs that you do. For example, think about your beliefs when it comes to money, your body, or relationships. If you discover that you believe relationships are hard, a struggle, a sacrifice, a responsibility, or anything that doesn't create peace, bliss, joy, magic, miracles, or more awesomeness in your life, then you can see exactly why you are experiencing that. Identifying the beliefs you've taken on that have formed your world is key to allowing you to create new ones.

Your Perceptions are the Result of Your Beliefs

Operating System #2:
Your Perceptions

Ultimately, having the right beliefs and perceptions moves you toward what you want—whatever that may be. They also can move you toward what you don't want—more scarcity, struggle, settling, and surviving, which we know now is not your true design or nature.

I've found it extremely important to understand and help my clients to understand that everyone creates their own world. It's also important to know this: **You will always do whatever it takes to prove yourself right.** In other words, whatever you believe, you're always looking for and working to prove that belief right.

Now, moving into your world of perceptions as one of your main operating systems, you can begin to see why you see things the way that you do. Proving your beliefs right can happen unconsciously in a few ways. Say, for example, you go into a room with anywhere from just a few to even a few hundred people. Suddenly, you notice someone looking at you, and immediately, your mind begins to churn with a chatter based on your belief system. *They're judging me*, you might think. *Do I have something on my face? Are they looking at my shirt? Is there something on it? Why are they looking at me? Do they think I'm ugly?*

In that moment, you're creating a perception that is based on your inner core beliefs. If you have a common core belief that you are not enough, you can see why you could have these perceptions and can notice you aren't comfortable with being seen. This can reflect so many things, as how can you allow yourself to be adored, cherished, and loved if you aren't comfortable being seen and adored? Many times not feeling like we are enough as we are can result in training from a young age to wear a mask, being afraid to fully be you, or holding back from being seen or heard because it could lead to the feeling of rejection, which is just what the little girl or boy inside is afraid of. If you have this core belief, then this is why the chatter in your head sounds like this. That perception becomes the story you write for yourself as you go through this life.

Let's look at the reality. There are infinite possibilities and perceptions that can exist, and all of them are true because what you find as true for you is what you are always looking for.

Maybe the person looking at you from across the room was actually admiring you as a sharp dresser. Maybe they thought you were beautiful. Maybe—and this happens all too often—they were just feeling uncomfortable in their own body in their own little corner of the room. Whatever you are perceiving is always all about what's going on inside of you.

How Shitty Beliefs and Perceptions Produce Shitty Results and Relationships

Most of us want epic, amazing, phenomenal love; that is a common desire for most people. Yet again, the world you are experiencing without will always be a perfect reflection of the world within.

I referred to the question before, "What is your relationship to relationship?" This can be intimate relationships, committed relationships, a marriage, a partnership, co-worker, friend—any relationship. Whenever you are having an issue with a relationship, it is your relationship to that relationship and the relationship to the aspects inside you it is reflecting that is causing the issue. Consider this: you can never fully know anyone outside of you. You can't know what's going on in their head, heart, and body or what their intentions are. You *can* have thoughts, ideas, feelings, and beliefs about the relationship that are creating an energy, experience, and even the behaviors you then operate from within that relationship.

With my clients, what we often find is a distrust or limitation attached to the concept of love itself. How can you accept and create amazing love if you don't trust love, think it's hard, or are afraid of connection, intimacy, or being fully loved, seen, heard, supported, and vulnerable? That distrust, although buried deep down into your cellular and emotional memory, has usually played into the downfall of their relationships. So, what do they do? They find ways to push away partners—even partners who could be amazing—because they're on a subconscious mission to prove themselves right.

They put their guards up in one way or another; create a fight or disconnect when things are going well; become clingy, anxious, irrational and distrusting; build an assumption, idea, thought, or worry in their mind; project their past experiences onto the relationship; and create a clear way to prove themselves and their beliefs right in the relationship. Although their mouths and maybe even hearts are saying they're open to finding an ultimate love, their actions don't match up. Why? Those actions—getting jealous, showing resentment, putting their guards up—are still rooted in those limiting core beliefs that say they're not worthy of love; that say they're unlovable; that say they can't trust themselves, others, or love; and that say they will get hurt.

Can you now see that we can't allow unconditional, amazing love when deep down we don't even love ourselves as whole and complete? We can only allow the amount of love into our life that we have for ourselves.

Prioritizing Yourself

Most of us have been taught its safer to show up for others, take care of others, and try to make others happy—putting ourselves last, but let's break down what's really happening when we give, give, give and put ourselves last.

Let's continue with the example of love relationships. When we neglect ourselves and put others first, we are actually giving a very low-vibrational level of love. It comes from a place of "have to," "should," and "need" and becomes a resentment-energy-based love. *I have to do this for them so they will like me, love me, approve of me. I should do this, so they are happy.* Whenever we are putting ourselves last, we are empty, and there is nothing to give. Giving to others for these reasons doesn't come from love; it comes from fear. So, what kind of love are you receiving in return? A very low-vibrational level and amount of love that reflects the same amount you are willing to give to yourself by putting yourself last and being afraid to be fully you, take care of yourself, or even ask for what you want.

Struggling with negative patterns in relationships is just one example of how core beliefs and perceptions can be reflecting the unconscious commitments you made that are only sabotaging what you really want. This concept applies to and effects every-thing—who you believe yourself to be in the world and even the amount of abundance, love, and joy you believe you are deserving and worthy of having.

You can now see what is available when you allow yourself to lean in and evaluate your beliefs and perceptions operating. It can become clear as to why you took on a belief from an experience you had, how you are perceiving situations and circumstances in your life to prove that belief right, and how you are behaving to ensure this outcome, even if you've been doing it unconsciously.

You Traded It All for Love

"IF you do this, I will give you my love and acceptance."
"IF you don't do this, I will withhold my love."
"IF I do that, they will love and approve of me."
"IF I am that, I will love and approve of myself."

What I've just described is how we've been domesticated from our desire to experience love. Every form of domestication boils down to "If you do this, I will give you my love, acceptance, and approval. If you do not do this, I will withhold my love." Every form of attachment or expectation begins with "If this happens, I'll be happy, and then I'll get or feel love" or "If this doesn't happen, I will suffer." Maybe no one has ever come right out and said it in these clear terms for you yet, but this is exactly how we've been trained to give and receive love. What has been embedded in our system is that love is conditional; it includes the word "IF" to receive it.

We could view this through two main paradigms of love and the many little ways to operate within the two: unconditional love and conditional love. What is the difference? Conditional love includes the word "IF" and it comes with attachments, expectation, and a list of to-do's in order to receive the love, acceptance, and approval you are seeking. Conditional love only gives you a limited perception that giving and receiving love can only look a certain way. When someone or something doesn't fit into this image, we then use these conditional behaviors and patterns to conform them into the same box we've all been stuck in because it's what we've known.

We became domesticated through conditional love. Do you remember getting a reward for doing what your parents asked? If you didn't, do you remember getting a punishment, receiving guilt, or even being shamed for not doing exactly what they wanted? Were you ever told what good boys and girls do and act like? These are all forms of domestication and conditional love. As you grew up, you most likely didn't even realize that we were implementing the same programming and continuing to operate from self-domesticating patterns and ways of living. As a grown up, you can do and be and experience whatever you want and create life according to your terms. Do you? Are you? What are you doing and how are you living your life? Is it because of what your family wants and approves of, the religion or community you were raised in taught, or what you decided was the way it was supposed to look like and be? Are you engrained subconsciously in the same patterns of domestication that you are unconsciously applying to yourself?

Domestication is a system of control we bought into, and conditional love is the main tool. The moment you are trying to control others is the moment you put conditions on their love and acceptance of them, just as whatever you are trying to control is really the very thing controlling you. Did you get that?

Whatever you are trying to control is really controlling you....

That was a huge game changer in my reality as I released all desire to ever control anyone or anything. Remember, everything is a reflection and mirror of what gets to be healed and loved. You can only give to another what you have, and so when you find yourself applying conditions to people and circumstances, you can see the perfect reflection of everything you've created as conditions you are also imposing on yourself. No wonder we only love ourselves if things look or show up a certain way. You have certain results, and you've been blaming, shaming, guilting, and punishing yourself with self-domesticating patterns attempting to control your own actions, conditions, and world. What if instead we now chose to operate from a place of unconditional love that honored everyone and everything in their perfect process and experiences of life? We have a choice to love and interact conditionally or unconditionally. If the mirror we are looking at is clean, we see ourselves as a beautiful, perfect, whole, complete, divine, and worthy being of our own perfect expression of who we are, which is a perfect reflection of the divine. We can then see others as the same perfect expressions of their divinity.

Ultimately, our journey is to give ourselves the love we are seeking as we come to the remembrance that we are and have always been whole. When we begin to live life through this lens, we give ourselves and others the healing and freedom that have always been available beyond the conditions and illusions. Now that you've more clearly looked at the operating system of your perceptions and why you see what you see, it is most likely getting more and more clear and you can see how each system is connected. With this clarity, we can move beyond chaos and now make the micro shifts to come into alignment with the true essence you really are. When we remember that everything is a reflection, it makes it really easy to get curious and to find what is actually true for you.

The Act of Noticing

These micro shifts start by simply the act of noticing. Notice the conditions you've put on yourself and others and allow yourself to catch them. The 5 Steps tool will assist you with this to see through the illusion and re-align yourself to the Divine worthy being you truly are. The reason we want to really practice becoming aware and noticing is because most of what you are doing is memorized and unconscious. Research has shown by the time you are 35 years old, 95% of your thoughts and actions are memorized. Think about it: do you drive the same way to certain locations, do the same things when you get out of bed, have the same streams of thoughts or standard talk in your head? If we look even closer, you'll see the same patterns that you've applied when you've responded to pain or pleasure.

You've created a lifetime of neuropathways that define how you respond, and it is how you are living and operating unconsciously. There is nothing to judge, blame or fix here, just to notice and apply that unconditional love as we take it one inch, one moment, and one step at a time. I constantly told myself, "Inch by inch life is a cinch, yard by yard it's hard" as I was focused on one inch at a time to be able to move forward in my life. The amazing news is that each day as you lean into the feedback, you'll uproot these unseen programs and you can begin practicing new ones as you micro align and create the reality in alignment to your divine natural birthright. With each bit of context and understanding you are receiving now, you are remembering the truth of who you are, how you are innately designed, and that you are and always have been worthy of living a life you love.

5

What Are You Really Saying?

Operating System #3:
Your Language

In speaking with someone, it usually only takes a few words or sentences for me to pick up on their entire internal belief systems operating, their perceptions creating their world, and to have a clear view of what is running their world. It also becomes super clear what specific blocks are keeping them from living the life they truly want.

Why is it so clear? Because I can hear what they are really saying; their words reveal everything. What they are saying is why they can't have what they want, and here's the kicker: they don't even know they are doing it.

As you become awakened to this, you will begin to hear everything with this understanding too. You'll be able to pick up on others' most intimate beliefs and experiences simply through their language. What comes with this superpower is that you'll also never be able to view what comes out of your own mouth the same way. You may suddenly want to get really clear with what you choose to say, listen to, and allow in your field of energy as well. Yes, it is that powerful and something you will not be able to ignore when you truly understand and align to the power of your sacred energy exactly how it is creating your world and affecting your reality.

Each word you say aloud or to yourself does several things for your internal system. It is most commonly and instantly linked to a visual and a vibration. That's easy enough, right? It is not the word you are saying that matters as much as it is the message it is giving you internally, the vibration you feel in your body from it, as well as the frequency it then carries to the Universe.

Your words and the language you use will either limit and enslave you into that very experience or magnify and empower you into infinite possibilities. We've been trained in a really low-vibrational language system, and now it's time to get clear and align to the language of your highest divine self that knows its power to create and the sacred energy and focus of its words.

To truly understand this, take notice of what we tend to talk about and what we practice with our words and communication. We are taught from a very young age to focus on what we don't want to happen, what we don't want to do, what we want to avoid, what we don't like, what's wrong, or what's not working. Why? Because again, we've been taught to be big ass complainers through a very limiting language system of conditioning, parameters, restraints, and control. It doesn't work with the laws of the Universe or even how we were designed. Actually, I'll rephrase that. It is working perfectly with the laws of the Universe; when you focus on what you don't want, that is exactly what you continue to receive.

Think about this for a minute: you tell your kids, "Don't jump on the furniture." You complain to your husband he "doesn't take out the trash." You tell yourself, "Don't eat the chocolate." What's truly happening in the mind when those phrases are said?

The first thing to notice is that whatever we say, we tend to see. That is how our mind works and, as I mentioned above, we receive both a vision and a vibration from our language. Whatever it is that we focus on, we find. Our language system puts the image in your mind to focus on the very thing you are saying you want to avoid; your kids see themselves jumping on the furniture, your husband sees the trash full and you unhappy with him, and you see chocolate.

Notice what else is really happening when we say those things. First, is there any clear communication regarding what you actually want? No, you are only focused on what you *don't want*. Instead of "Don't jump on the furniture," what if you requested, "Please sit down on the furniture and jump on the trampoline or up and down on the floor!" Wouldn't giving clear direction to what we do want actually make more sense?

As trained complainers, you've most likely been practicing complaining your entire life. It's how you now know to relate to others, yourself, and the world. We've been taught from the time we were little to focus on complaining about life and what we don't want to happen or are afraid of happening. We are stuck in a world of "don't," "can't," "should," "shouldn't," "have to" and "need." Instead of moving towards creating and receiving the very thing you think you need to get to the result you want, you actually are sabotaging it.

It's not just a head game, and in fact, there is so much more happening here with your words than just the visual being created. What is also happening inside is that you are saying something so concrete that is locking in at your very core. With this system, over and over again, we are only reaffirming the limitations you are so desperately seeking to find freedom from. What you are actually communicating to your core self is "I'm bad"; "I'm wrong for doing this"; "I'm not good enough"; I'm not worthy." You are vibrating "shame" within. That is the lowest vibration that exists and will always block manifestation and anything you want to receive.

That may sound harsh, yet "don't do that," "you should do this," "you have to do that," or "you need this" all say "I'm not good enough as I am." They reaffirm that there is something you need to do to be good enough and to therefore be worthy. Inside it always feels like there's something wrong. This is just striving to continue to operate from the perceptions I mentioned earlier that we unconsciously live out of saying that we aren't perfect and we "need" to continue to strive to be so that someday we'll be good enough, accepted, worthy, and loved...aka "Perfect." All of that is bullshit; we are perfectly experiencing every moment just as we are. We can never make a mistake or be wrong because what we are being is simply life happening.

You might not be willing to receive that yet, as your mind still is operating from conditioning and stories that say otherwise. So, let's continue to evaluate simply what is, and you can decide what's working for you and what you might want to try on and practice for a different experience.

A Conversation with Yourself

How do you feel when you say you have to do something? How do you feel when you say you should or shouldn't do something? For just a moment, tune into how those words feel in your body. Do any of those feel good, empowering, or like you are in control? Or are they screaming lack, unworthiness, not enough, settle, sacrifice, force, and powerlessness with their energy?

"I should" Is coming from a place of fear, lack, scarcity, and shame. It comes from a perception that you should do something so you can be accepted or loved by something outside yourself versus it being something you want to do and are choosing to do because it feels good and is right for you. "I should do this for so and so" comes from fear they won't approve of you or accept you unless you do the thing you think you should do. "I should do that" behavior comes from a thought or idea that you aren't enough if you don't. It isn't coming from a clean love energy that creates what you want; it is coming from a resentment, blame, or shame energy. For example, "If I don't work out, I'll be fat, overweight, unattractive, etc." Choosing to do something because this is the underlying belief behind it is only re-affirming the limiting core belief you are not enough, and it's re-affirming you aren't enough now. On top of this, every time you are taking the action towards what you want, it is being done out of this shame energy that only emits that as the vibration. What is normally the next outcome? You sabotage because everything you are doing is just re-affirming and creating that self-fulfilling prophecy that you aren't enough now, and you "need" this thing, and "should" do this so you are enough.

Apply this same exact understanding to "should" in business, in relationships, in your health, and in every single way of operating, and you'll see now what has really been going on. For a moment, think about something you've said you "had to" do or "should" do. Are you willing to try something else instead? Replace the words "have to" or "should" with "get to" or "choose" and just see how that feels. When I first understood this, I realized every time I was saying I had to do something or should, I was giving my power away. I was showing up as a victim, as if I had no choice or control. I committed to catching my words and shifting back to operating as a powerful creator in choice.

I would say things like, "I have to clean my house" or "I have to go get my kids from school." I was speaking about these things as if someone was forcing me to do them. I didn't *have to* clean my house. What was true is that I wanted a clean house, and so I chose to clean it. Then I got to evolve to the next level of receiving and realize if I truly didn't want to do something, what else was possible? I got to pay cleaners to come and support by cleaning my house. I didn't *have to* go get my kids from school; no one was holding a gun to my head. Of course, I wanted to go pick up my babes from school because I love them and keeping them safe and supported was my agreement with them. Do you see how unconscious this language is and how by using it you are giving up your power, when, in fact, you really do always have a choice? Being a conscious creator means we come into alignment with all we speak, think, act on, and create.

How do you feel when you need something? When you need something outside of yourself to be whole and complete? What you're saying to your internal self and your core is "I am not worthy and whole. I need something to be enough and whole." In other words, "I need to look like this to feel good about myself"; "I need this amount of money in my bank account to be enough"; I need a relationship or this person to like me for me to like myself"; "I need this THING to have THAT as my RESULT."

"I don't," "I can't," "I have to," "I should," "I need"...all of these come from a place of you being out of sovereignty and out of choice, and these are the main phrases that have made up our everyday conversations and are exactly why we have the results and reality we currently do.

Instead of saying "I need something," I began to replace it with conscious language: "For me to create...I am choosing this, or I GET to..." I began speaking from the truth that I am a powerful creator.

This very important operating system that is our learned language continues to engrain and imprint the principle of "have-do-be" as the way we operate: "When I have that, I will finally do the thing I want to do, then I'll be happy and successful"; "When I have the body, have the money, have the time, then I'll (fill in the blank of how you'd participate in your life) go out to the parties, I'll date, and I'll be seen, I'll get on stage for my business or video, I'll go to the pool with my kids, I'll go on vacation, spend time with my family, travel, enjoy, play, do that thing I want to do. I'll be happy and fulfilled! Free!"

Everything we are speaking in this manner is outside of us and waiting for some magical future someday date to show up and give us access to happy. The crazy part is we are always making it outside of our reach, in the future, which now you can see is why it is never here.

Have you noticed that something always continues to show up to keep it outside of your reach? That is because you aren't claiming it! It isn't yours now, and you aren't being it now. You can't change what you won't claim and vibrate now.

If you want something, you get to start with the first step and first inch to receiving it. As I began to understand the world of manifestation and our effortless ability to create and receive, I began calling myself on my bullshit by checking in on it. If I say I want something and instead of getting curious and looking at options to take the next step towards it, I find instead a survival archetype stepping in to bring in a story, excuse, validation, or anything taking me out of radical responsibility, then I get to pay closer attention to why that came up and bring myself back in alignment as the creator to be moving towards it now.

Let's say that you want to participate in a program to be able to learn how to do something you want, yet you don't have the money that is required for it. What do we tend to say or tell ourselves? *I'll do it when I have the money.* Now, in surface self-empowerment, this can be seen as a good thing. *I'm going to go create the money so I can do that program or get that thing.* However, what happens at your core, or what is the vibration and imprinting, when you say this? The message is: *I'm not giving myself permission. I'm not worthy now. I'm lacking something to have that. If I had the money, then I'd do it or give myself permission.* Can you see the inner feeling of lack or unworthiness because you are attributing your actions to something outside of yourself?

When I have the money, then I'll give it to myself. This only re-affirms the exact someday paradigm we've been talking about. You are in a story that you can't have it now because of a specific experience outside of you that is in control.

Have you ever saved up for something, and then before you got to use the money for the thing you saved up for, something else showed up that required the money?

Let's say you again are saving to participate in this program or experience. You begin saving up and suddenly, your car has an issue and requires a repair. The creation of "someday" and it being in the future for you has to manifest because that is the energy you've vibrated into the quantum energetic field and are clearly speaking out to the Universe/Multiverse as well as held and vibrating within your body by not giving yourself permission. It manifested from outside of you in the exact form it was spoken, felt, and believed.

Do you see it?

Now, you might have decided to save for something and had a different experience. Please, know that it all comes down to being in an energy that matches the vibration of it to receive. If the energy is coming from a place of *I want it, and so what do I get to do to create and give it to myself?* then it is the energy of saying, *Yes, I get to have that. What's next, and what do I do to receive it?* If the energy is coming from a place of lack versus this place of em-powerment, you are unconsciously creating sabotage because you never deemed yourself worthy of it in the first place. This is very different then, *OK, what can I do? How can I participate?* You may have saved up the money and gotten exactly what you wanted, and there are a few key steps in aligning the declaration with the action. It is a NOW vs. SOMEDAY mindset and action along with the alignment of the energy of it. The 5 Steps to Freedom tool will assist you in always getting clear to move from the unconscious program to the conscious action to receive.

Speaking in Appreciation

Your words reflect your internal world and everything that you believe, think, feel, and therefore are being. So, what will you now choose to practice? You can continue to practice complaining or you can practice speaking in appreciation. Appreciation is the energy and frequency of abundance. When you are appreciating something, it is coming from a place of already having it because you are seeing it and admiring it in the now. In the energy of being grateful for a thing, you are fulfilled and satisfied and at peace with it, which is the opposite vibration of lack and not having the thing. It is the energy of abundance because witnessing it, you see there is plenty. This is the same in the language you use with others as it is with the language you use with yourself. If you give someone appreciation and gratitude for who they are or something they did, what do you usually get in response from the person? If you complain, blame, or shame someone for not doing what you wanted or not doing it the way you wanted it done, what do you usually get in response? Just notice and appreciate.

As awakened beings, we are here to remember and align to the highest vibrational match of our divinity by being conscious, sovereign creators and an embodied, integrated soul. When it comes to the language we use overall, I want to give you something to contemplate. If we are living in impeccable integrity with ourselves in the remembrance of our Divinity, then we wouldn't ever be speaking any limitations about ourselves because we already know from within that it would be out of alignment with who we really are.

What about FUCK?

Yes, I said "fuck." Now check in. Does that word trigger you, or are you completely at peace with it? There is a reason we get to go here if you ultimately are committed to living free. Why? What would your freedom have to do with the word "fuck"?

Living in full freedom, it is important to be completely transparent, with nothing to hide and nothing to prove. I could just ignore or hide this part, as many have told me for years along my path to not go there, not do that, or not share certain things because it would turn people off. And...it might. Again, you are always in choice, and I always want you to do what serves you the most and is in highest alignment for you. There is a very important reason we get to check in with how you are operating with words.

With that and before I go on...I simply want you to get curious about this question: If a word is used by someone, or in any circumstance or situation, and it bothers you, what or who is in control of your experience? Are you in control, or is the person, circumstance, or even the word that bothers you dictating your feelings, experience, and reality? We can expand this to see beyond words that trigger, people, actions, behaviors, and all aspects of life that can bring up a trigger for us. I want to focus in on this here and now as we are dissecting language and the unconscious ways we block manifesting what we want. Back to the word "fuck."

I'll preface this by saying that if it does bother you, I was there too.

I was traveling on a bus, and group of younger guys were laughing, having the time of their lives, and talking. Not a bad thing, yet the word that continued to fly out of their mouths was "fuck." I remember feeling so bothered, annoyed, and disgusted with it. The entire time I kept thinking how it was so inappropriate and offensive. I couldn't wait to get off of the bus.

The word dictated my experience and trapped me in a vibrational loop of judgment, rejection, separation, and even shame, all blocking my ability to manifest and receive what I wanted. See, I chose to buy into a story that took me out of peace, love, and joy and took me into disgust, judgment, and projection onto others. I now know that anything that you have resistance to creates a contraction. Contraction is a frequency of energy that blocks you from receiving. I want you to really pause and take that in because that is a clear, easy way to see if the energy is working for you or completely blocking you from receiving what you desire. Again, whatever you have resistance to is an energy of push away, fight, block, rejection, and ultimately creating separation. When you are in that blocking, disconnecting energy you become that low-vibrational energy of separation. These are old programs and old ways of being human that keep us in suffering. That is conditional love that is saying I only accept you if you do what I believe versus accepting you for all you are. Remember that unconditional love is the inclusion of all things, not the exclusion of anything.

How can you receive more peace, love, joy, and abundance if you have an obstructive energy around you? Yes, you do get to protect your energy by choosing what is best for you, who you surround yourself with, what you choose to focus on, and being in the energy that you love and supports you, but what we want to get clear on is how you can unconsciously be in an energy of guarding, pushing, fighting, or contraction. When you put out that frequency, it will magnify and return to you. The answer is becoming neutral.

I'll share a personal story to give you better understanding of what I mean by arriving at neutral so that you are able to honor all people, all experiences, and all feelings and ultimately align to the energy that will always serve you.

Being raised in Utah and in a strict religious environment, my entire life was one of wearing a mask, acting and operating in a way that was deemed appropriate by others. As I began my own internal journey of breaking beyond parameters, stories, and constructs that I had learned, I had an interesting experience that allowed me to see where I was scared to go and who I was afraid of being.

And...it had everything to do with the word "fuck" and what it represented.

As all things in front of us are there for our greatest, highest good and the perfect experiences for our own ascension; my experience with this word became the start of one of my greatest gifts of freedom.

I had become the Body-Mind Mentor on ABC4 TV weekly and began speaking on stages in Utah. I had committed to being an open tool and was practicing trusting my internal guidance when it came to being the greatest, highest good for the crowd I was speaking to. I stopped planning or preparing; I had committed to walking up on stage and allowing the knowing of my experience and the best information for that specific group to come through and serve. I had some amazing experiences already that had shown me that I could never plan out what was best, and I got to trust the process of life and myself by allowing. This took me down a journey of loving and accepting myself no matter how it appeared or showed up, which, of course, confirmed for me that it always was for my greatest benefit as well as the benefit of all those involved.

On one occasion, I was on stage, channeling information that was streaming through me. I literally would feel the directional guidance of exactly what the crowd was seeking, their questions, and exactly where I got to go to support the individuals I was doing breakthrough work with from the stage.

And then suddenly, the word "fuck" wanted to come through me....

I was saying something, and then the word barely became present in my mind before it went to flow through my mouth. Suddenly, I stopped the flow of my words. I held back. I felt my whole system want to shut down and do a double take because it interrupted the steady stream coming through me.

After that event, I got curious: *If I am committed to being an open channel of truth, why did I stop and hold back?*

Using the 5 Steps tool, I began to see what was really operating and I could see that I was afraid...

I was afraid of being judged, rejected, and misperceived. The thoughts coming up were that if I used that word, those listening would automatically shut down, be turned off, and even think that I was a bad person. Then they would miss the actual message, truth, and opportunity for freedom I was sharing. I knew these were just thoughts and projections based on my own experiences and belief systems. I saw that they came from the paradigm and programs I was raised in as well as the environment I lived in. So, I took the next step and began to question those beliefs and paradigms. *Where did that belief that this particular word, "fuck," or any other word was bad or wrong come from? Obviously, from our society and especially from a religious society that created a context of control by teaching what is deemed good or bad, wrong or right, and acceptable or not. Why, then, did this word want to come through me? If I was really afraid of using it and didn't want to use it because it had never before been a part of my language and I had deep associations of not being right or OK, then why would it want to come though, especially as I'm channeling freedom and enlightenment and tuning into our truths?*

Ahhhh, I see... Did you hear it? That's it exactly...

Freedom, enlightenment, and tuning into our TRUTHS.

What I heard was that maybe God, or Source Consciousness, or whatever construct you want to use for this was sending this through me for that very reason. God wanted me to say "fuck"? Can that really be true? Well, what if God doesn't see it as we've chosen to perceive it? It is simply a word that our society has attached a constraint upon, which creates an internal feeling. What if God knew for that very reason it would trigger everything inside that was based upon those beliefs and programs?

It would be a clear representation to see where we were hiding, still separating ourselves from others by being in judgment or rejection, and where we were withholding love. Could saying a word really do all that?

What else was available? I saw how I was perfectly receiving the experiences for my own healing of any limitations inside that were in the way of my ultimate freedom. Of course, then, this was the perfect thing to show up for me to see what inside me still got to be healed and loved.

I saw my own fears that I would be rejected, judged, and misperceived that were holding me back from speaking freely. If I couldn't get beyond that, what was I declaring to my core self and the Multiverse as to the life I was choosing to live and who I was choosing to be? I would be saying, "Hide, mask yourself, care what others think, and don't be the true you." I would also be playing along with the exact structure and paradigms everyone else was upholding to stay within the box and boundaries that everyone else approved of. Fuck that...

I'm certainly not here to be normal or play small, conform, or color in the lines of the picture of someone else's reality. What I am here for is to discover all of me and be a channel of unapologetic expression and light for myself and others. I am here to be free by being all of me and come into my own truths, remembrance, and exemplify it for those who are also seeking.

I also tuned into the energy that I felt when the word wanted to come through me. It felt like fiery passion. If I was to say, "She is a fuckin' bitch," the energy projected would be negative; if I was to say, "Fuck yes," it could come through as a high-energy expression of excitement and passion. I recognized there were so many examples of individuals who clearly used the word this way.

What was really stopping me from speaking freely was my own fear and if I let that stop me, I would only be reaffirming those exact constructs and beliefs to live in my comfort zone of fears, wear a mask, do what was acceptable, and agree to only allow the level of freedom, abundance, joy, and happiness to be received that reflected that same amount of what I was giving myself and what was comfortable in that current comfort zone. I was the only one who could put those limitations on myself and I was also the only one who could step beyond it into a new level of expression, truth, love, joy, passion, and play.

I committed, at a new level of inner-standing and being a clear channel of unapologetic expression, to stand for truth. At the next event I was speaking at, suddenly, "fuck" clearly came through, and I let it fly. My body felt a bit of fear as it came out, and I saw some of the crowd react in surprise. In the back of my mind, I noticed those ideas I was afraid of that had stopped me the first time pop up, and yet using the 5 Steps, I had already addressed these and now could see them as untrue. At this particular event, I even noticed my dear friend's mother in the crowd, and the look on her face would've been a reason to refrain, again coming from a place of wanting her acceptance. Instead, I breathed into it and continued to speak the free unapologetic truth that was coming through me. I knew that I was simply there in service as the perfect mirror for each individual to see what was going on inside of them and that whatever they thought, projected or perceived actually had nothing to do with me.

My experience completely surprised me and again reaffirmed for me that beyond fear is freedom. After the event, my friend's sweet older mother came up to me and said, "You know, when you swore, it really shocked me and would've turned me off, but I could hear what you were saying. We are all perfect, whole, and complete in whoever we are and whatever we are experiencing. I could feel God coming from your words. Thank you for teaching me where I judge and where I stop loving."

Tears filled my eyes as I felt the appreciation for following my truth. After, as I was swarmed by individuals wanting to talk to me, the message my friend's mother gave me was repeated in different words, ways, and experiences many times over by the participants in the crowd. What had come through was the message of freedom and love beyond any constraints and ideas. I couldn't authentically be an example of freedom unless I *was* freedom. Yes, there were some who also said, "If you could just not swear, then...." and I thanked them for their perceptions and didn't attach to what their view and perfect experience was.

Originally, I had the fear that if anything like that came out of me, I would lose people who would have otherwise attended my programs. Again, as I broke that thought down and looked at the truth, I knew that what was important to me was serving people and teaching freedom, and that is the only reason I desired them to be able to be in the programs in the first place. It wasn't about the money; the money was simply a byproduct and reflection of the amount of value I created and how much I served. It didn't make any sense to have those people in my programs. I discovered another reason it perfectly served me to be fully and unapologetically me; it was the perfect filtering system for those who were really ready and open to move beyond the stories and work with me or my team. I was teaching people to stand fully as themselves and shed the masks we put on for society. If they weren't ready to move beyond those constraints, and would lose their shit over me using a word, and were not able to see the message beyond it, and would stay stuck based on that, then they probably weren't ready for me anyways. I realized that I only wanted to work with those who were ready and who I was free to be myself with because freedom wasn't holding back, playing small, or wearing a mask.

This is where you get to tune into the energy of a particular word. Know that if it doesn't feel good for you and your associations, you don't have to use it. However, if it triggers and bothers you or if it is controlling your experience when someone else uses it, there is some curiosity to dive into so that you become neutral with it and realize it's just a word. A word doesn't hold power over you or determine who you are, and you can honor others to live, speak, and experience the life they want in their perfect process, just as you are worthy of yours.

The point of me sharing my own personal experience is for you is to see more TRUTH about what could be unconsciously holding you back. Whatever the word may be, if you have a trigger associated with it, it's a clear reflection of what inside gets to be looked at so you can come to a place of freedom with it. This doesn't mean that you get to a place where you want to say "fuck"; it means you tune into why you would have any stories, judgements, or perceptions that would have you placing judgment on someone else or an experience instead of being at peace with allowing it to exist.

One of my greatest freedoms was from inner-standing "*All things have a right to exist.*"

If you judge someone for being outspoken, loud, and expressive, it is because you are afraid of being those things or feel triggered by that person because something inside you says that those qualities are scary; you can't behave like that; or that its only safe for you to hide or play small versus being seen. By the same token, you can look at how you do what it is you are judging. How are you too expressive, loud, or outspoken? In some way, there is a reflection for you, showing you what you aren't willing to accept within and aren't loving about yourself. That is it. Pure and simple.

I am committed to always using just one filter before anything comes out of my mouth. That is the filter of radical responsibility to always take full ownership of everything I choose to speak, perceive, and therefore feel. All that is required for you to be the creator of your reality is for you to tune into the energy for you. If you catch yourself in a story about how someone else is being, acting, looks like, or even what words they are using, catch it .You can use the 5 Steps to support you to take radical responsibility of what you are experiencing and you can heal it and come to neutral around it. You can honor them to do what serves them best, and you can honor you in your freedom to do what serves you best. Isn't that beautiful? Nothing to fight, nothing to control, nothing to guard or protect yourself from. Just honoring and allowing each of us to create and receive the reality we choose. It also makes life super easy when we drop the fight and become the vibration of unconditional acceptance and love.

So, let's tune into any other aspects around your language and the behaviors that are creating your world. Do you say everything you want to say? Do you acknowledge, allow, and embrace every emotion that comes through you or give a voice to it to be seen and heard? Do you love yourself in all of the places you consider dark as well as light? Can you love the messy and the messenger in all forms and at all times?

If the answer is "no," I'm so grateful you are here right now and willing to look at what is blocking your ideal life of freedom. This is exactly why you did choose to be here for this to perfectly be showing up for you. You are obviously committed to be on the path to seek and create greater for yourself. The path to making it a "yes" starts with the awareness and radical responsibility for how your perceptions, beliefs, programming, language, and feeling systems are connected to the body, which becomes the energy and vibration you are operating and existing in.

Just trying to "convince" yourself of something different will never work. Now that you've fully dove into the consciousness of your language and are aware of what you are choosing to align your experiences in life to by how you also choose to think and speak, you are ready for the final piece. We can now look at the very last operating system, which I consider the most important because it overrides them all. With this last piece in place, you will be capable of energetically vibrating out a clear message to easily manifest what you truly want.

Then, we will have all the pieces in place for you to use the most effective tool I've ever used and I continue to use, teach, and live by to always shift from unconscious to conscious, creating new neural pathways, reprogramming, and easily aligning to receive an even greater, more fulfilled, amazing life.

6

The Emotional Feeling Body

Your body is holding onto and storing every piece of emotional and energetic memory in your cells from every experience you've ever had. Your body will never lie and will give you direct access to everything that has been hiding.

Operating System #4:
Your Emotions

This is the most potent operating system, not to be ignored because it is more powerful than everything else that is creating an energy and vibration coming from you. What your cells and your body is giving out is 500,000 times stronger than a single thought. The feelings and emotions you've had or are having are the biggest contributing factors to everything you are attracting, creating, and therefore receiving.

Why does this really matter when it comes to getting what you want?

The TRUTH is what you want can only be RECEIVED when you are willing to RECEIVE the feeling of it. You can't manifest, create, or attract it when you don't first have the energy that matches that vibration to pull it to you and receive it. Surface self-empowerment tells you to visualize what you want, think about it, and focus on it. Part of that is true, but what you feel in your body and its frequency and vibration will always overrule the vibration of the word, thought, idea, or belief. You can't receive it by thinking about it because it is a less powerful vibration than what you actually feel and believe in your body.

THIS is the biggest gap to manifesting and receiving a different life experience. If I say, "I am abundant," and my body feels heavy, as if I don't believe it, then it doesn't matter how many times I say, "I am abundant" and claim it, affirm it, or declare it. What overrides the positive vibration of the word "abundant" is your feeling towards it—that could be a limiting belief connected to the word, that you are not it or that you don't have it or have a reference point for it because you've never had it. See, we get to go deeper and feel what we actually want.

Matching the Physical Symptom with the Emotional Issue

Let's look more closely at how the body is sharing with us exactly what is going on.

If your world is in chaos and you're feeling out of alignment, remember that the body never lies. Go internal. Ask yourself not only what you're feeling but where you're feeling it to help you determine the root emotion. In my experience working with clients and applying the insight of world-renowned healer Louise Hays as well as many others I studied under as I learned the depths of the body connections to all our internal pathways, I've learned there are common ways your body manifests emotional issues. Every area of the body and every illness has an emotional connection.

For instance, if you are feeling anxiety, it is connected to not trusting the process or flow of life. If you have a cold or are congested, it is associated with too much going on at once or mental confusion.

Anything to do with your back represents the support of life from finances to emotional support, depending on the specific area. The lower back connects to money and concerns over a lack of financial support; the middle back connects to guilt or feelings of being stuck in the past; and the upper back connects to a lack of emotional support, feeling unloved, or holding back love.

The knee connects to your ego, stubbornness, or pride, and discomfort in the knee relates to being inflexible. Heaviness in the lungs connects to grief. Stiffness in the feet and ankles connect to a struggle to move forward. Constriction in the throat connects to feelings of losing your avenue of expression. Shoulders represent our ability to carry out experiences in life joyously.

All diseases are simply dis-ease with life and all diseases showing up are just showing us what is in disconnect and ready to be healed and loved. They indicate where a person is out of flow with life. Symptoms of these diseases are stuck emotional energies, which create trauma in the body. Diabetes will show up as a result of a lack of joy in life. My dad had diabetes since he was 19; he lived in a belief system that said he had to struggle and sacrifice to survive. Weight issues connect to fear and a need for protection. Weight issues also signify running away from feelings, insecurity, and self-rejection. Fatigue connects to resistance or boredom. Anything with the liver has to do with chronic complaining fault finding, feeling bad, and the storage of anger. High blood pressure connects to the suppression of anger. Cancer connects to deep hurt, longstanding resentment, or having secrets of grief eating at the self.

When uncovering an emotion, I always pinpoint the area where I am feeling sensation or discomfort to determine what is going on. If you don't know how the specific emotion relates to the physical symptom, I've found there is an easier way to get clear by looking at the basic core emotions corresponding with these main areas of the body.

- Head/Neck and Shoulders = Connected to anger and inflexibility; if discomfort manifests in the back of your neck or head, the emotion can be related to a past event

- Heavy Eyes and Chest = Sadness

- Stomach or Sacral = Connects to fear and the inability to digest new ideas or assimilate them

- Pelvis = Sexual patterns, block in creation energy

- Feeling tingly all over = Yay! You're feeling lightness and joy!

Always look at what is internally going on when you have a physical symptom. I'll say it again and again that energy doesn't lie. It will always give you clear feedback. The body will be a key signal for you to see that something is going on.

I also take notice of whether whatever showing up is on the right or left side of the body—the right side representing the masculine, or the "doing" energy that is striving to move forward, and the left side of the body representing the feminine aspect, or the "receiving" energy. When I got out of bed the day after being offered to be on national TV every single week as The Body-Mind Mentor, nutrition, fitness, mindset expert, I discovered I couldn't put any pressure on my right foot and it was in intense pain when I tried to do so. I hadn't done anything prior other than go to bed. As I went internal with the 5 Steps, I discovered a whole bunch of fears my little girl inside had of what would happen if we "moved forward" in being on TV. The right side of the body, moving forward, and foot reflected moving forward in life. We can also utilize this to see what we are in resistance to doing, moving forward in, or receiving.

My Body Taught Me How to Overcome Breast Cancer

I was 24 when I was diagnosed with breast cancer. The moment I found out, I called only two people: my former—who I was still married to at the time—and my mother.

"I have breast cancer." As I spoke those words out loud to my mother on the phone after walking out of the doctor's office, everything froze, time stopped, and what happened next changed me forever. In that instant, I saw a movie play out in my mind as I felt the magnitude and energy of those words. They carried a gray energy and a weakening vibration that felt sick and heavy.

Instantly, this movie visual in my mind showed me those words blasting out a vibration that cascaded over the entire planet and then expanded into the entire Universe. It was like watching the impact of an atomic bomb suddenly wiping out everything in its path and continuing to grow and expand until everything is obliterated. I saw what life would be like from that moment on if I continued to speak out that exact declaration. I saw everyone in my world interact with me as if I was a victim who was sick.

Ring! Ring! I picked up the phone. It was my sister and, in a concerned voice, the first thing she asked was, "How ya doing, hun?" In this vision, I saw myself being sick and the dramatic impact it would have on my little boy, Skyler, who was only one year old at the time. *What will happen if I don't choose to heal my body?* I saw what the reality would be if I chose to focus on the sickness and how it would expand to everyone else only focusing on that with me too.

Intuitively, I was guided to ask myself, *What am I feeling?* I noticed I felt fear that I would die, I wouldn't see my little boy grow up or be there for him, and that I'd repeat the pattern for him that I was raised in. I grew up with a dad who was sick, and we were always aware of his diabetes and its effects. From it came a belief my body was something I had to fight, and I had been fighting it since I was young. I could see that this very experience was a byproduct of that.

Then I asked myself a very powerful question. *What do I want?* I found a whole shit ton of internal struggle from that simple question. I knew that, of course, consciously that I didn't want that life. I wanted to live for myself and my son. I wanted to be healthy and strong. The epiphany that changed the direction of my existence came from seeing that there was an unconscious desire to stay in the comfort of the sickness instead of choosing to give myself permission to have a healthy life.

That sounds crazy, right? Stay in the comfort of the sickness instead of living in health? That's all I had ever known, and it had been my identity. Yes, I saw it. See, I knew, in that moment, telling more people—putting those words out into the Universe repeatedly—would not serve me. It would only give power to that energy. As I was guided to ask myself these questions, I saw what was going on underneath. What did I want? I wanted health consciously, yet unconsciously that was not what came up. What I found was that the victim who only knew how to survive and struggle her entire life wanted to announce she had breast cancer. I recognized that this is how she felt good enough and validated. I noticed a strong urge within to share the struggle and let people know that this is what I was now going to be dealing with. Then, the words my brother had once said, when I was confronted with yet another extremely challenging life experience, rang in my ears: "Marci... you are the strongest person I know. If anyone can handle this, you can." Wow... That would've been taken as a compliment in the past, yet I was seeing it clearly now for the very first time. It's like my little girl inside, so tired of all the struggle and fear, cried out, saying, "NO! I'm so tired of being the one who has to handle all the pain and the struggle, take on the responsibility, overcome, and survive."

I didn't want to be the victim who had to keep surviving and proving I was enough by how much I'd suffered. I could see how this belief system came from being raised in a religion that said life was hard, full of struggles, sacrifices, and tests, which, depending on how well you endured them (not overcome them, endured them), and that is how you would be rewarded a mansion in Heaven. My entire life I'd witnessed this in my family; every area of life was bombarded with struggle, sacrifice, and suffering with the focus to simply survive. I was clear that if I didn't choose to act and respond differently, then I would keep experiencing hardship, struggle, and pain and just be playing out the identity of a victim and a martyr.

What did I want? After calling myself on my own bullshit to break it down and see it clearly, I decided in that moment I did want to live for myself, my little boy, and I wanted to be healthy and give myself permission to choose something different. This moment was a monumental wakeup for me, as I had all of this happen in a flash of timelessness in this dimensional reality. I had received a Divine Gift that lead me to choose to take my power back, and this divine guidance I'd been led through to come through it was the creation of the 5 Steps to Freedom, which became the most transformative foundational tool for myself as well as those I coach in my programs today. It took me from being on an unconscious path to recreating the same experience to choosing consciously with aligned frequency and action to move into what I really wanted.

I had a powerful vision and experience that I felt in my entire being that whatever I thought about, focused on, spoke, and felt would be my experience. In that moment, I made a commitment to myself that I would no longer speak my victimhood. I told my mother on that same phone call that I realized that whatever I focused on I would continue to experience and that I was now choosing health. I was making a commitment to not speak or focus on the cancer; to instead only discuss and focus on my health.

I had realized that my mom was someone I shared my complaining and victim life with. It is what we talked about when she would call and ask how I was doing. I'd complain I didn't sleep, which lead to complaining about being exhausted, stressed, and any other things that weren't working. I realized I had been doing this all along, and it was time to create a different relationship experience with my mother for the sake of my own life, my son, and her life as well. I told her then and there that if we were going to talk and continue to have a relationship during this time, then we got to agree to focus only on how I was healthier every day and how joyous my life was. I also asked her to not share this information with anyone so there was no one else aware of the sickness. I also asked her to keep it sacred and basically swore her to secrecy of its existence. Only she and my husband at the time knew about it, and I wanted it to stay that way because my vision showed me clearly that this choice would create everything else. I explained to her this was the commitment I desired from her; otherwise, we would get to put our phone calls and communication on hold during this time frame in my life and take a break from communicating while I focused on healing. She was stunned at what just happened in that brief moment of time, yet she agreed.

I knew the first step to healing was to take radical responsibility getting clear on why I created the breast cancer. I dived into the emotional connections to the breasts. Breast cancer was associated with a refusal to nourish the self and receive mothering and nourishment—instead, putting everyone else first.

It made complete sense. I'd been living my life wearing a mask, always doing whatever I thought others wanted to make them happy. I had been putting myself last and didn't even have a voice or opinion for many years.

I had to take radical responsibility for the fact that I created this illness, living my entire life in trauma, drama, and struggle. My body didn't work because, from the time I was little, my belief system said it didn't. I had been suppressing all my emotions. I had created an identify that said I was a victim who had survived. I was scraping by as a perfectionist, afraid of failure yet continually sabotaging my success.

This experience was one of the many that took me deeper into the internal world where my mess became the message I could share. I got to make the changes, embrace new beliefs and perceptions, and choose new behaviors that aligned to a new level of self-worth to create different results in my life. I continued to focus on my health, catching myself in my negative thoughts and patterns and tuning into them in ways I'd never fathomed before. I began living a moment at a time and creating the micro alignments and shifts that would change the macro of my life experience. I began to practice the tool of the 5 Steps over and over and over again, which supported me in moving through the resistance I found and led me to creating freedom.

One year and zero medical treatment later, I went in for testing. My breast cancer was gone.

It hasn't stopped there. I've continued to overcome physical challenges by upping my inner discovery and learning how to go from a body I fought and struggled with all the time to a body that always remains healthy with ease. Things have still shown up on my journey, only revealing layers that were ready to be healed and loved, and using the tools and being in alignment with the energy, I've always quickly been able to heal myself of any dis-ease or symptom that ever arose. I knew it simply was a reflection of being ready to blast through the next layers to receive even more. Most of all, I always remember and know that each symptom that ever shows up is only a gift of feedback of what else inside still gets to be loved.

In this culture, when we address sickness, we often study the symptoms instead of getting to the root cause, which is the emotions and the energy they carry that are existing inside you. To create health, we get to create a healthy internal environment.

Because of how we've been trained to operate, how we're expected to behave, and what we focus on if we are sick, you can see why we've stayed in the struggle and only continued to create more and more of it. We only continue to feed what is creating the internal environment to continue to be a place where disease can proliferate and grow. Sickness is simply showing us where the vibrations in the body are out of harmony. When we focus on healing the root cause and your emotions, then we come back into vibrational alignment. If you truly go within and choose to be with all of you to heal what is simply wanting your presence, then your body will align to the healthy body that operates perfectly as it was designed.

Your Body Is Getting Younger Every Day

Another valuable shift for me with the body was coming into the truth of how my body is truly designed instead of believing what you constantly hear in the collective. I chose to forget everything I'd ever been conditioned to believe about aging and discovered my body is a regenerating machine. Here is the ultimate truth I chose to find: you are a divine miracle, and your body an innate machine made up of systems operating in harmony and the vessel or vehicle to allow you to experience the world around you.

This started for me when my boys were still very young, and I started noticing I was getting wrinkles in my forehead. At that same time, I was also starting to tap into deeper levels of in-ner-standing of the body, seeing it for what it truly was. I began to look for evidence, but all I could find was what society told me: the body stops working. We get old. Things hurt and break down. I decided to choose a new perception. I did some research and found that we constantly generate new cells and every year we regenerate all new organs. Clearly, we are actually getting younger everyday if everything is constantly reborn and renewed.

I also discovered that I could communicate with my cells and give them clear direction to design the exact body of health and experience of health I wanted. I created nighttime cellular design and morning cellular design meditations for myself, and that is now also a part of my programs. I give myself exact direction, which sits in my subconscious system all night long and all day.

Along with this practice and communication to my body, I started only speaking, thinking, and feeling like I was 20 years old because that was the number that came up and what felt good to me. This may have been because when I was 19, I had a heart attack, and I never really felt like I experienced being 20. I wanted to experience truly feeling youthful and full of energy and the vibrancy available at 20. This number 20 became my mantra and awareness.

After a short time of aligning to this, I began to forget my real age and when someone asked me, I literally had to stop and think about it because 20 instantly is what wanted to come out, and it's how I felt. I also began to use the phrase "years young" when someone asked me how old I was. I'd reply I am this many years young, and I began asking people how young they were if I wanted to know their age. I consciously shifted my focus onto youth and vitality. In time I began to truly feel as though time and age didn't apply to my system anymore.

What happened—and you can see it in the pictures and evi-dence of my past—is that my wrinkles disappeared, and I began looking younger and younger. Years went by, and I continued to look younger than I did when I first began to apply this.

It brought me to question even more of my beliefs about my body. How else was I making it hard? I began to question all of my beliefs from the past that said it took a certain amount of exercise or eating a certain way to maintain the results that I had. Of course, I believe in taking care of myself, honoring my vessel and what supports it. However, I discovered more ways to drop the fight and find absolute peace with my body. As I traveled the world in deep-dive experiences, I wouldn't work out for a week straight, yet I would actually get even more lean because I had designed my cells and body to remain in health.

This was my own personal experience of applying all operating systems to be focused on and creating a youthful, healthy body with ease. I had turned back the clock of time and tapped into universal anti-aging timelessness as the authority of my body system.

Knowing my body is designed to operate perfectly and in optimal health as my divinity, I've continued to stay lean, toned, and healthier than I was years ago when I was teaching nutrition and fitness alone. The more I understood, the more I tapped into my internal discovery, got curious, and became in ultimate alignment with my light body.

On top of this, I know now that the more we clear the stuck energy from our cells, emotional traumas, and what is creating "weight" or the heavy density of low-vibrational experiences is what causes our body to become "lighter," and that has only allowed me to look and feel lighter, adding to the timelessness. As people would ask what I "do," I honestly could only reply the truth of my experience, which is I continue to become more and more of a light being, and to be in enlightenment is to be in light. Dr. Bruce Lipton also shares science around how our cells are always either moving towards growth or protection mechanisms. He shared a great insight that for our bodies get to eliminate stress, worry, or anything that would put it in protection mode to be able to get to neutral. Yet, for our cells to move towards growth, they require a high frequency such as love, joy, and happiness. Yes, it all began to click the more I chose to be the high frequency of my Divinity I was designed to be, and knowing these truths and practicing them, I only continued to become lighter and freer.

Have You Cut Yourself Off from Your Emotions?

You have learned that your physical body is tied to your emotional operating system. In order to fully get to a state of freedom, you now can give yourself freedom by determining what it is you're feeling when it arises.

Do you ever stop to ask yourself what you are feeling and why you are feeling that way? Most likely, you might not even be aware of what you are really feeling, or even care to know why because from a very young age this was the exact thing you were taught to avoid, run from, shut down, ignore, move past, change, put aside, and suppress. You might unconsciously—or even consciously—believe that feelings are bad because they are a form of weakness, vulnerability, and pain. You may believe that your feelings don't make you look good and take you out of control.

Imagine, as a child, you run to your parent or an adult crying. What happens, and what is the common response you receive?

"What's wrong? Shhhh, shhhh, shhhh... Calm down. Stop crying. Why are you crying?"

In other words... EMOTION is bad and wrong.

This kind of message is where it began for most of us. Even before we could consciously remember, as a baby and as a young child, when we expressed emotions that didn't seem to please others around us, we received a message that it meant something was wrong. We take on the clear message that something has to be wrong to be express emotion, to feel it fully, or to be vocal about what we are feeling or seeing. To express sadness, anger, discontentment, fear, or anything other than what seemed to fit into acceptable emotions came with it the direction to stop it, shut it down, calm down, or in some way fix it to stop the emotion. This led to an entire shutdown of the way we were designed to create and operate. Shut it down, don't cry, don't be heard, don't be seen, don't feel, don't have emotion, and don't express, and stay in the paradigm of what is acceptable. We received this message over and over again as we were trained to shut down what we were feeling, to cover it up, and to hold back, and it is how we are now operating unconsciously today.

Feeling is a multifaceted system. It includes the emotions, thoughts, words, body language, body sensations, and the subconscious mind. The subconscious mind is a powerful force because it doesn't include the logistical mind and the ability to make sense of anything. It always comes down to what we heard, what we saw, what we felt, and therefore what we learned, decided on, or chose from those things. This means that we can be operating out of unconscious beliefs, patterns, and conditioning.

All of this creates a massive disconnection from living and being because you are not actually BEING at all. You are acting, pretending, and operating subconsciously in a mask of what you were told is how you are supposed to be, look, act, and behave.

The Consequences of Repression

Let's just evaluate this and the possibilities for a moment. Imagine you are a child playing at a playground. You fall down and get hurt, or maybe you get pushed by another child or another child says something to you. You go running to your parent. You are feeling an intense emotion, crying, and your parent responds, "Shhh, shhh, shhh... What's wrong? Calm down" or even "It's OK," to try to suppress the crying. In this case, you are not being taught to discover what is there; you are being taught to stop what is there because feeling it means something is wrong.

Now, of course, this was just the language we were taught. The parent or caretaker could've had every intention to make you feel better and support you, and it was just what they learned as well. All of us have always been doing the best we knew how at the time based on all we learned, so practice remembering that as you tune into these memories and connections of where this started for you.

What followed for you to stop crying and feel better could've been any number of things that then became a part of your belief system. Your parent could've said, "Some kids are mean. Just don't play with those kids." They could've told you to "stop being a baby" and "get up and push back." They could've told you to just avoid that child and go play somewhere else. Most likely the feedback you received wasn't inquiry into your own world and what you were feeling or why; it was a projection from whoever was sharing of their own world, their beliefs, patterns, and behaviors of dealing with people. You could've decided that people are mean and looked for people to be mean and the world to be mean or unsafe. You may have unconsciously decided that you couldn't trust others or their intentions and that people were out to get you, and therefore now you act out accordingly to protect and guard yourself from people.

When you repress your emotions, you skip the interaction with the self as source. There is no allowance or permission to feel what it is, why it is there, and where it came from, nor is there curiosity about what it means, if it's true, or what other possibilities there are for you to see.

On top of this, instead of the feeling moving through your system and being released, your body actually contracts and locks the fear, shame, and rejection you feel from the message that what you're feeling is wrong and needs to stop. When you don't allow yourself to feel whatever you are feeling, what you are actually declaring to yourself at the core level as well as what you are giving out to the Universal field is: "I'm not worthy." Think about this vibration going out and how it is being expressed every time you continue to react in this same unconscious way. If you don't allow yourself to feel and experience, what does this say about being able to have whatever it is you want? It is a clear declaration that you're not worthy of having whatever you want because you're not even worthy of feeling what you feel. Whenever you suppress your emotions, hold back your expression, and hide away from being seen or heard, you are clearly saying, "I'm not worthy to be here, to exist, to take up space, or to have an opinion and voice." We only pile on more and more of the emotional garbage that has our unconscious frequency vibrating, "I'm not worthy of the love, abundance, play, fun, and ease I truly want."

THIS is why it is so important for you to now understand that you can begin feeling your feelings as you move forward. This is how you are designed to create, and so we get to discover, clear, and release the layers that you've held onto and stored as well as now stop the process of only adding more layers on. Taking radical responsibility is the way we align to a different experience if that is what you choose.

What would your experience be if you freely felt what came up and questioned it all? What if you gave yourself the permission to feel the emotion as well as look at what it's really about and what was really going on for you? Even just allowing this space and curiosity at a deeper level sends a different message to your internal system as well as the energetic field around you. It says, "I AM WORTHY to fully feel, express, be seen, be heard, and have my own opinion and understanding about what is true for me and what I really see, feel, and decide I want."

Now imagine yourself on the playground again, but this time you're able to run up to your parent, caretaker, or the adult in your life and have them receive you and respond with open arms: "Ahh, sweetie...." Then, you get embraced with the allowance and discovery of the question: "What are you feeling?"

What if you felt safe to express: "I'm feeling sad"; "I'm feeling hurt"; "I'm feeling angry"; or even "I don't know what I'm feeling"? What if it was allowed to be felt, heard, seen, expressed, and discovered to move through your body? What if you learned to communicate what you were feeling and felt completely safe to be heard and seen in what you were experiencing? What if it was normal to be given permission by others and yourself to navigate through all you were feeling and all that it had to reveal to you in its process? What if feeling and expressing everything your body was telling you was how we all lived? What if this was our NORMAL way of being, communicating, feeling, and expressing and how we were trained to live? It is and can be again, allowing you and everyone you interact with freedom to fully be and in turn to fully create. Aligned to your divinity, you can be the example of the New Human and allow us to experience the New Earth where we unconditionally love, accept and honor all things.

You Get to Look Back to Move Forward

In every single moment, the energy of WHO YOU ARE is what you are creating and why you have exactly what you have now. It will continue to generate what you get by how you continue to respond and be. It is easy to see why we have had a huge gap and disconnect in manifesting what we really want and remembering who we truly are. Keep reminding yourself that "*It is not who you are; it is just what you learned.*" It can be unlearned, and you can remember and return to easily being all that you are.

Take a moment and reflect on what you would consider traumatic experiences from your childhood, or those experiences that became traumatic due to the belief you took on at the time and how it affected your life. In school did you have a moment where you felt stupid in front of the class and decided you were stupid? How did that affect your entire life experience up until now? Maybe you did everything you could to prove you weren't stupid, or maybe you bought into the idea that you couldn't do things because you were stupid. Did someone tell you that you weren't good at something that you loved to do, and so you gave up on doing what you loved or giving yourself permission to ever explore new things and try them on because you were afraid you'd simply not be good at them?

For a moment, pause, contemplate and sit with this.

Can you go back to a memory, experience, or vision of a time when you were a young child and you felt it wasn't safe to feel, cry, express, be heard, seen, or have emotion?

How about a time when you were being your authentic self—who was playful, creative, or spontaneous in your own unique, innocent way—and some of the big people or those around you made you feel silly, wrong, embarrassed, ridiculed, or persecuted?

Where were you?

Who was there?

How old were you?

What was happening?

As you feel into these memories, remember that you are sitting safely wherever you are, now, here in this moment, simply in thought and discovery. You've already come through this, and today you are simply looking back and feeling it for the purpose of liberation from it; by feeling into this, you are now able to release any stuck energy around it because you now have the gift of clarity to see it for what it really is, and the 5 Steps will guide you fully through this. We are just starting to awaken and become aware here and now.

What if in the experience, you gave yourself permission to explore and get curious? Most likely this was never modeled for you, yet your innate being knows you are here to simply discover and express your fullest divinity. Remember that as a baby, you crawled around on the floor, getting curious about everything, even how to use your body and how to move and discover what you loved to do and play with. You are here to get curious about all of it and to find what you innately love, your unique gifts, your dharma, passions, and ways of being that fulfill you and allow you to live in peace, bliss, abundance, and joy now and always as you expand into your greatest joys and adventure that is this holy human journey.

Our emotions and feelings clearly tell us what is happening and allow us to see the thoughts going on in our heads, which then influence the perceptions we choose, the behaviors we then act out in, and our overall programs and results.

Sky Guy's Story

The 5 Steps to Freedom tool became and still is the greatest tool I use for myself, with my growth partners, and in all relationships and scenarios in life to move through all unconscious programming and into responding and choosing what I want to experience as a divine sovereign creator. We'll go into this in depth, yet here I want to give an example of how easy and fast this can be for you to begin to feel what you are feeling and the freedom it brings.

In my Freedom Coaching audios, I use many real-life examples with my babes, and I'll share one here about Sky Guy to give some context to how this can be possible, even from a very young age.

Skyler, my oldest, was around six years old at the time. I picked him up from school and when he got strapped into his seat, I asked, "What was great about your day?" We have a habit we've created after school of asking two questions: "What was something you did for someone else today to make them feel supported, important, or loved?" and "What was great about your day?"

I incorporated this with my growth partners so we could look for success in life and celebrate success each day. This is so their minds become trained to look for the good in all things and to focus on what's been awesome to then continue to find more of it as well as to look for opportunities to give out energy and love to others. They always love reporting back with creative ways they did this and all the things they could list that made their days awesome and great.

What automatically happens in this process is it brings up whatever else is going on that gets to be felt, heard, seen, and expressed to allow clarity and peace because we talk about all things. I could instantly tell that Sky's energy seemed off. Most of the time, we are trained to ignore what is really there, just go through the motions and pretend it's OK or bypass it. His answers were really basic and standard, yet his energy was speaking loud and clear as a red flag to ask more questions. I could've assumed he was just tired or mellow from a long day at school and ignored it, but I have learned that the quality of your life is determined by the quality of powerful questions you ask, and that energy never lies.

Our standard and normal is to feel awesome, and any time we don't feel awesome and we feel resistance, we chose as a commitment to look at it deeper, and that means going internal.

I asked Sky, "What are you feeling, babes?"

"Nothing. I'm just tired," he said.

"Oh, OK... Is there something else on your mind or your heart?"

"No, I'm good."

This is usually where we, as parents, partners, or friends, stop. We stop because we think that this is normal, and that "I'm good," "It's OK," and just going through the motions of life are normal.

I phrased my questions for more clarity to assist him in feeling even more safe to express versus holding it in because "I'm OK" was not what we settled for or tolerated or what he usually chose. Even though his words were saying it, his body language and energy were not expressing a peaceful, happy tired. At this stage in their lives, my boys freely express without it having to be coaxed out of them, yet this is where we were at in our journey of practicing acknowledging and voicing all things.

I said to Sky, "Babes, I notice it feels like your energy is kind of down. Would you want to share what the thoughts are that are going on in your head right now?"

Suddenly, his eyes welled up with tears. He finally said, "I'm stupid, Mom, and nobody likes me."

"Ahh, love. Wow," I said. Thank you for sharing that with me and that you are feeling that way. Where did that come from, sweetness?"

He began to tell me that he was drawing a picture in art class, and a girl came up to him and said his picture was stupid.

"Ahh, I see. That's interesting," I said. "What did you choose to think and feel because she said that?"

"That my pictures are stupid and that I'm stupid and nobody will like me"

"Hmmm, I can understand that, babes, and how you could feel that way having that thought, love. Can we get curious about it? Are you willing to look with me at the thoughts to see if they are really true or what else could be true? Can we look at it, babes?"

He agreed softly, "OK"

I began with, "Do you sometimes like things that your brother doesn't like?"

"Well, yeah..."

"Is it OK that you like different things than him?"

"Yeah."

"So, is it OK that this little girl has her own opinion of what she likes and doesn't like?"

"Well, yeah."

"So, is it OK then that she doesn't like your picture and that you do like your picture? Do you like everything that everyone else does, or do you have things that you like and don't like? Is it OK for us to be different?"

The energy started to lift, and the lightbulb turned on. I then asked, "Are you drawing the picture for her or for you because you like to draw?"

"Well, for me because I like to draw."

"Great. So, drawing makes you happy, and you are doing it for you."

"Yeah."

"Then, if you are drawing because you like it and it makes you happy, my love, and you are the only one that can make you happy, does it even matter what she or anyone else thinks about your painting or drawings?"

"Well, no. I guess not."

"What does matter then?"

He started to sit a little taller as he answered, "That I like it and that I'm happy."

"Yeah, babes. You got it. You are doing it for you, and she is worthy to do and like whatever works for her, right? We're all different and can accept that she gets to choose whatever kind of life she wants and the things she likes to do, and you get to choose the same for you."

His energy completely changed.

My next question to him was: "Now, what are you choosing to believe about your drawings?

His response: "That they are great because I like them."

"Awesome, love, and what do you believe about yourself? Are you really stupid just because someone else has a different opinion or likes something different than you?"

"No."

"Does it really matter then what she or others think about you?"

"No."

"What does matter?"

"What I think about myself and that I'm happy."

"Yes, babes. You got it."

"What would you like to create now and would feel good for you? What would allow you to feel happy again because you are worthy of feeling happy and only you can create it?"

He chose to pick a song from his playlist because that was one of things that helped him create a new vibe and change his state. He grabbed the iPod, checked his favorite songs list, picked one, and we jammed out the rest of the way home. He then was in power to create the rest of his day to look exactly as he wanted and to return to feeling awesome versus going through the motions and just feeling OK. This was a demonstration of the tool you're going to be using that allows you to easily move beyond unconsciously reacting to consciously responding.

What if we recognized this as our natural process, which is to feel, evaluate, and express, which then allows the emotion to move its full course through the system and come to a place of understanding, peace, and clarity? Freedom is to fully be you and to allow yourself to express and experience everything.

My growth partners (aka my boys) always talk about how only WE can determine and create our own happiness and only WE can make ourselves happy. After breaking things down that they can see clearly, they realize that when people are mean, it has nothing to do with them at all; in fact, it reflects that these people don't love themselves. My boys stopped caring what others thought at a young age because they saw the truth and reality of the situation. If they did care, it hurt, or they were triggered, then it was perfect feedback to evaluate and for us to lean in and heal. They continue to be my greatest mentors and examples to me as perfect mirrors and reflections, and I'm so incredibly grateful for them.

The key here is to see that the FEELING is what gives you FREEDOM. By leaning into it, allowing it, and embracing it, you can see everything clearly and respond accordingly. **You will** always find a message of freedom in the mess, and what looks dark and scary will always hold your greatest gifts of light. The discovery of it awaits you, and the gift of it is there to be received.

Most people, actually it's been shown that about 98%, will stop after just two or three tries of going after what they want. The few who move beyond those "tries" most likely do so because they don't see them as failures, rejections, or evidence that they can't; they choose to see it as feedback to get more curious of how else they can. If something doesn't appear in your life as awesome, you can now welcome it with open arms of love and get curious about why it is appearing as a reflection in front of you and how you can receive even greater from it.

What happens when we don't express?

In this example with Sky, he would've taken on some crucial beliefs about himself and his identity, as well as some behaviors that would then greatly alter his life experience. He most likely would've created his world to support the idea that he was stupid and people don't like him, and that would've continued to show up for his life experience.

This Gift Isn't Just for You

I hope you can see that if we use the gift we've been given of exactly how we are designed to operate and be, as infinite creators by simply looking at what we are feeling and why, and are open to evaluating it, leaning into the feeling and what is in front of us, we will always give ourselves freedom and continue to experience greater and greater. It is and can be that simple. There is nothing outside of you that can give you your freedom; it will always be inside you and can only come by you. You are the medicine you are seeking for your freedom and healing.

Remember, you can only receive from others also to the same level and degree you are willing to give to yourself. Your relationship with yourself, and what you feel and believe about yourself, will always be a clear reflection of your external world. Choosing to express fully and give yourself permission to start being seen and heard will directly correlate with you giving yourself permission to receive.

You aren't just doing this for yourself to create the world and reality you want; you are actually serving, supporting, and assisting others to do the same when you choose to. Real authenticity and transparency is that there is nothing to hide and nothing to prove. Fully being yourself is the greatest gift of vulnerability that you can give anyone else, and that is true bravery. Being fully seen, heard, and expressed and sharing all of you is courage. Bravery isn't the person who is pretending, hiding, and holding back to look or act like they have it all together. See, when you are fully exposed and expressed, there is nothing to hide and nothing to prove; it is actually the safest place to be. It is pure freedom, and it makes it so easy. So, please, do realize that by you choosing to stand in your full authenticity, you can only be an example for others to do the same; you are sharing with them the greatest gift you could ever give to anyone else. Standing in whatever you think and feel is heartfelt honesty—doesn't that sound amazing? It is amazing, and it can be what we all experience. Realize that it is only because we've had attachments and stories around expressing and feeling everything that we've learned to hide and mask our emotions, which has kept us guarded, hiding, closed down, and separate from all the gifts we have for each other and the support that is available all around us to receive and have it all.

FEELING is FREEDOM, and that can be your new model you adopt and live by if you choose.

Are you ready for the new model and new way of being?

Discovery Opportunity #2:
Feel Your Feelings

Now is the time to get really honest as you look back at your life and answer these questions:

1. Up to this point, how much have you allowed yourself to feel?

2. What belief systems and programming did you pick up about feelings?

3. If you tend to mask your emotions, how has that impacted your life? What have you not allowed yourself to be, experience, or have as a result?

4. Now, take a few moments to practice tuning into your body and notice how you're feeling right now or any sensations you can become aware of and bring attention to.

I recommend writing it down so you can begin to acknowledge it. Practice being as specific as you can so you aren't just using the old program to glance at it with your mind. As you now give yourself permission to feel the slightest feelings in your body, you unlock more of your abilities to see what is going on, heal, create, and receive.

- Are there any physical symptoms you can pinpoint?

- What core emotions (anger, sadness, joy, fear, sexual) are connected to the physical symptom?

- Explore and ask yourself why you might be feeling the way you are. For example, "What could I be angry, sad, scared about?" (Depending on emotion you are targeting)

This is just to simply witness, allow more, and practice. Know that all of this will get clearer and easier as you move into the 5 Steps to Freedom.

Your Shifting Essentials

The Foundational Pre-Steps
to Effectively Utilize the 5 Steps

In this experience, I will cover the 5 Steps that can lead you to a heightened level of awareness. Awareness, after all, creates freedom to now choose what you want to consciously create. It's like looking at a map: half of reading a map is knowing where you want to go, but the other half is knowing where you're at. On the path to an amazing, magical, bliss filled life, that means taking responsibility for your experiences and having accountability for what you have created.

I will show you how—but first, there is a foundation of support we want to put in place.

7

Pre-Step 1: You Can Always Start with a Breath

Working with and through Your Emotions

The first thing that happens when you feel a negative emotion, get triggered, or experience discomfort is a physical and unconscious reaction. Your body contracts. You unknowingly become tense, and your body tightens; you may contract or hunch over, shrink down, pull in your shoulders, lower your head, or clinch up. Your breath then becomes shorter and more rapid, or you may hold your breath.

Contraction locks and holds everything into our system. The goal is to continually release those stuck energies that create limiting vibrations in the current moment so not to add more, as well as learn to continually release all that has already been withheld in our bodies. When we contract, we are actually blocking everything we want and putting up a wall.

This is why you will be learning and implementing the easy 5-step shifting tool, so you can always move right through whatever comes your way and get connected to where it came from and release it. You will always be clearing it instead of contracting and adding more of it.

To avoid a body-mind meltdown that can cause even more disconnect and disease, here's what you can do when negative emotion creeps into your peripheral: BREATHE. Breathe because your breath is the flow of life—life-force energy; it is through breath that we can move energy instantaneously. So, instead of contracting, holding your breath, or allowing it to become shallow, which will only create stuck energy, you can support yourself and stimulate flow by allowing yourself to breathe into it. Breathe with intention, see yourself directing the breath and energy through your body, and notice how effortlessly your body moves the air and energy through you.

Breathing is the most vital action we take in our lives; interestingly enough, it is also the most unconscious action that we take. When we are stressed or anxious, we tend to take shorter, more frequent breaths, which further spreads these negative mental states. It automatically activates the sympathetic nervous system, which cranks up stress hormones like cortisol, increases your blood pressure, and ups your anxiety—all of which promote the fight-or-flight response. When you choose to slow down your breath and make a conscious effort of taking deeper breaths, you get a very different response automatically in your body system. Your body begins to relax, as it is receiving a message that everything is OK. Breathing slowly and consciously activates the parasympathetic nervous system, which can bring a calmness and relaxation into the physical body as the response. When you do find yourself triggered or experiencing any emotion you don't like, simply start taking deeper breaths.

Each deep inhalation circulates oxygen in your bloodstream through your entire body. This is a flow system to move feelings and energy so it doesn't become stuck, and as you increase the amount of oxygen flowing in your body, the pranic body comes alive, as you are giving it life-force energy.

This will become an important tool to support you whenever you are triggered because moving your body's energy will bring you to the present. If we are present, we can react consciously to create what we want instead of unconsciously reacting in our smaller, scared, limited self that only keeps the cycle going.

Pay attention to how you are breathing right now. We are breathing unconsciously all day long; this is an example of how you are an effortless creator. As you feel any type of uncomfortable emotion or trigger, simply start to breathe. Deliberately direct the flow of breath, prana, or life force. This will ease the intensity of the trigger, bring you to the present moment as a creator, and allow you to move forward consciously. As you focus on deep breaths and the movement of the energy, you will automatically be able to further relax into what you are experiencing, allowing you to become more peaceful and accepting of it energetically, which will enable the mind, body, and energy to work for you as you take the next steps.

So, start now...even if you aren't triggered or experiencing something you see as negative. Anytime you practice breathing more deeply, it will influence how you are feeling as well as improve your mental clarity and your physical health.

Integrate Movement

The other advice I have for you to implement with your breath is to simply add some movement. If you are standing, you can simply begin to sway side to side as you breathe. If you are sitting, you can rock forward and back, side to side, or in whatever way feels good. If you have more room and access to space and feel safe to do so, whether you are in a crowd or by yourself, you can make bigger movements. The more you are moving, the faster the energy moves through your system. You might want to raise your arms above your head and then circle them down to your feet, around and up again. Whatever feels good and creates movement. It can be big or small; I've done this in subtle and not so subtle ways in very crowded places as I noticed a trigger come up. If you apply this technique along with the 5-step shifting tool, you will move quickly to emotional freedom.

Now remember, this is not the *solution*; we aren't breathing and moving to just move the intense energy to a calmer state and then run from it. We are breathing and moving to allow ourselves to get really present, softer, and in allowance to accept the emotions. This will open the doors to all that is available to heal.

Breathe and sway....

Breathe and sway....

Breathe and sway...

Then do it again and again as you allow its affects to settle in. You'll notice after you begin breathing, the intensity in your body and of the emotion will most likely pass or settle down. We don't want to stop there, or it will just come back to the surface because it wants to be healed. Once you have breathed into it, you are ready to lean into it, revealing the issue that is ready to be witnessed and healed.

8

Pre-Step 2: Give Yourself Permission to Get Curious

The Power of Quality Questions to Guide Your Life

What determines the quality of your life is the quality of the questions you are willing to ask yourself. I am a collector of powerful quality questions, and it was through the guidance of powerful questions I discovered the easiest path to seeing exactly what was operating in the unconscious, which then made it easy to clear and create something different. The questions are a powerful way to see the bullshit operating and to fill in the gaps to see what is happening inside. Again, what the mind says is just a piece of it, and the questions allow us to see what's going on in the mental, physical, and emotional body.

If quality questions are so important, what's stopping you from asking them of yourself? One answer is distraction. Your comfort zone, for example, is full of distraction and validation. Instead of launching that new venture with your business or working to create more closeness in your relationship, maybe you turn on the television, get on social media, or choose another non-related activity instead.

The gift—and what you'll come away with as you work through the 5 Steps to shifting your reality—is realizing you're actually creating circumstances that keep you from moving forward by masking patterns and validating choices that don't serve you. Why? It's simple: you're asking the questions that don't support you in remembering who you are and becoming what you want because your brain is programmed to fixate on the problems not the paths to solutions.

For instance, if your internal dialogue starts with, *What if this doesn't work?*, then you're creating an experience born of fear-based energy. If you ask your mind a question it can solve instead of one doomed from the start, you'll get a different response. *What would be possible? How would this work? How can I create this? What would feel good? What is calling my soul forth and is the most nourishing for my soul? How can I experience more joy right now? How much greater can this moment get?* These kinds of questions open doors rather than closing them. Your automatic response is understandable—we've been trained in a shitty language system as well as the broken mindset to automatically go there—but now you can retrain and reprogram your mind to operate out of infinite possibilities.

Another challenge is that too often, we tend to look to others for validation of our choices. By doing this, we are telling ourselves that we aren't worthy of giving ourselves permission and that our decisions have to be approved by someone else. Only you can ever know what is best for you, and your life experience gets to look like whatever it is that serves and supports you the best. The opportunities are right there in front of you for you to move into greater and greater, and whatever you are putting out will show up for you. If you wait for permission based on someone else's approval, then that is your clear response to the Universe.

When I was the waitress barely scraping by, I had a friend tell me about this free event one evening about "moms living their purpose." I instantly felt that I had to be there. Onstage that night I watched the man who became my first mentor. He spoke about following your purpose and had several moms talk about their personal stories—about doing what they loved, giving themselves permission, and not buying into the story that they should just be good moms. They encouraged us not to allow our perceptions and belief systems to hold us back. What he offered at the end was a weekend two-day seminar on stepping into your purpose, which was $500. Now, I didn't have $500, and yet everything in me said I had to be there. Instead of saying to myself, *Oh well... I don't have $500, or I can't because I have $10 to my name and I have two kids to feed,* or any other reason that my brain could've created if I looked for the reasons why I couldn't, then I would still be a $2-per-hour waitress.

The first thing I did was go to the staff registering people and began to ask questions. "Do you require a down payment to get a spot now?" "What are all my options?" "Do you have a payment plan?" I told the staff I was going to be there, signed on the dotted line with an agreement I'd have the payments to them before the seminar, and I instantly began asking myself, *How can I earn an extra $500?*

I began getting curious about what I could sell, what I could do, what other ways could I create value for other people to earn this exchange of money as a value back? I decided I could apply this instantly to my waitressing job and attract great customers, give them great value, and make more in tips. I set an intention to make $130 a night in tips, which the norm was around $20 to $40 tops. I decided I might as well aim higher than I had seen because that's what I required. The very first night, I made $115, and each night following increased. I began selling my first fitness product I'd created, "The Whole Truth About Weight Loss," to my fellow staff I worked with and even the customers. Out of nowhere, customers at the table would begin to make comments about how they could see my "guns" or arm muscles, even though I was wearing a long sleeve, button up, man's white shirt and tie as the standard waitor and waittress attire. Suddenly, we'd be in a health conversation, and I'd end up selling them my DVDs, as it was exactly what they were looking for.

I ended up with exactly $500 to attend the event.

After the event, I knew I had to do something very different to create different results, as it was clear that for my entire life I had only known how to struggle and sacrifice. To move forward with the man who became my first mentor, it would cost me $15,000. A lot more than $500 and more than I'd ever made or spent. I'd never even bought myself a car for more than a few thousand dollars. And...I obviously had gotten those results by not valuing myself more than a car or investing in myself as my greatest asset.

See, so many people play a comparison game on the value of money. The money is simply the exchange tool that reflects your level of investment in yourself. It also mirrors the law of parallel returns—whatever you put energy into is exactly what you will get energy back in. If you put your time and energy into going to the gym, you'll get energy back in your body. I didn't have money. I was broke...and yet I knew that doing the same things that I had been doing, not investing in myself, wasn't going to get me something different. I also could see that I had the money results I did because that was my exact shit as a result and reflection of what I got to face.

Now, for a moment, consider what feedback I might've gotten from my family and friends about spending $15K on a coach. Being a single mom, with only $10 in the bank and with each paycheck barely getting by, I wanted to do *what?* They most likely would've thought that was pure crazy and even irresponsible; that it wasn't smart; that I wasn't being a good parent; maybe even that it was selfish; that I should just put my head down, go to work, and save up money.

My own internal questioning could have also sabotaged me the same way; if I said, *I can't do that. There is no way I can afford it. If I go through with it and still fail, where will that leave me?* Many people internally conclude they can't without even asking questions of how they can or what is possible.

Instead of looking outside myself for answers or asking negative internal questions, I asked questions to look for possibilities and to find a solution. "Do you take payments?" "What does that look like?" When I discovered what the first payment would be, I was far from having enough for even one payment. I got even more curious and looked at every possibility with wonderment and excitement in that faith-based energy, like I was playing a game. Instead of giving up, and with the right questions and energy matching, I found a way to come up with the first payment, giving myself permission and taking the step to create this new reality for myself.

Something I live by now that started from this moment is... **If you say you want something, and you aren't moving towards it in some way, then you are in a bullshit story, validation, or excuse as to why you can't have it.**

There are so many times we don't invest in ourselves and move towards what we want because of our unconscious programming, commitments, and an internal struggle. When our investments aren't that high and don't hold much value, it's not enough to move us beyond our comfort zones and unconscious commitments.

Being that highly invested in myself ensured I was going to pay attention and do everything to step beyond my comfort zone, even though it scared the crap out of me. I had my ass on the line to come up with the money to pay the payments as well as pay my bills and take care of my boys. I implemented what I learned even though it confronted everything, which allowed me to step into receiving and creating a different result. The law of parallel returns gave back according to the degree I'd invested in myself and took action to create a different life experience.

The trick here is to get curious. Imagine, for a moment, you're in line for a roller coaster. If your internal line of questioning is *What if it malfunctions? What if I get sick? What if the unknown over that first hill is scary and makes me uncomfortable?*, then the odds are you're not going to get on the roller coaster. You miss out on the ride, the adventure, the ups and downs, and what you learn along the journey as you get to the finish line all because you asked poor-quality questions.

If you approach that same roller coaster with all the soft, playful curiosity of a three year old playing a game—because, remember, that's how your subconscious mind reacts to situations—you'll face a very different experience. You'll do it with wonderment and curiosity. You'll be excited and you'll find possibilities to create the next step.

Quality questions are at the core of transforming your life. These are what intuitively came to me to guide me down a path to changing my life. That's why I've included the Discovery Opportunities throughout the book. As you continue to work through these exercises, you'll see how to reframe your internal conversation and ask quality, powerful questions to ultimately cut through your internal shit and to create internal clarity.

The Gift Is in the Shit

Speaking of your shit—chances are you've been looking at it through foggy, dirty glasses that were distorting how you see everything in your life. Yes, you think your shit is inconvenient and uncomfortable, and that's why it seems easier to avoid it, bypass it, or run from it. The truth is that your shit keeps you in your comfort zone and stunts your growth because it is something you've been avoiding.

Many people are hesitant to take a step in any direction other than the one they know because they're afraid to fail. So, instead, they don't move beyond what they have known as their comfort zone of reality, which only keeps them expereincing the very same.

That's your shit. It's a silent immobilizer holding you back from effortlessly creating the life you're meant to live. All of us have our own shit because it is unavoidable and inevitable as a part of our holy human journey to grow and evolve. What kind of person do you want to be? What are epic stories of people you hear about? Are they stories about people who stayed in their comfort zones and reaffirmed their personal shit, or people who chose to look it straight in the eye and face it? When you realize your shit is really just a story, perception, idea, or experience you had at a specific time now for you to evaluate and see clearly out of light, it can be simple and easy to create something different. It isn't really you at all; it's just the lens you once viewed life through, and it can change.

Here's the thing, though: your shit is actually your greatest gift.

If we didn't have uncomfortable things that arose, we would remain stagnant. The discomfort is feedback that tells us something isn't working so that we can then shift and change accordingly from that feedback to create something even greater. Our lives get greater and greater because of our shit. Embracing my shit, knowing it would always show up as I approached my comfort zone, allowed to move toward receiving an even greater experience and life.

Your world will shift drastically when you embrace and realize that you can't hide from your inner reality. You have probably tried at some point to run from it or ignore it, begged God to remove it, or wished someone would come change it. Hiding it in the closet only keeps it growing and creating more.

Embracing your shit as your greatest gift gives you the opportunity to look at it now clearly to create freedom. My own experience, and my experiences with many clients, has shown me that the Universe will always bring me something to reaffirm what I want when stepping into the next comfort zone. So, it truly is bringing you a gift that is asking you to clarify by how you respond with what you now really do want. What is showing up is simply a byproduct of what you've done in the past.

When you see it through the lens of gratitude and appreciation for revealing what there is in the way of more gifts, more opportunity, more love, and your ability to receive more, then you can welcome it with open arms. Embracing it rather than fighting it can change the entire game, the experience you have, and how easily you can now move through things.

We all have the same opportunity and we all have our own unique journey full of the things we chose so we could discover all we are and share our greatest gifts. Your circumstance is just that; it reflects what you are internally aligned to and living right now, and it can easily be changed when you change the frequency around it.

Finding the gift in your shit is how you'll bust out of your comfort zone to achieve true freedom. Instead of running from or wallowing in those uncomfortable moments, you can easily choose now to apply love there instead. This frequency will override the current frequency keeping you in limitation and allow you to dissolve, transmute, and heal it to open up a new experience. This can happen as fast or slow as you allow it by how much you choose to love, how much your heart can expand, and how much you are willing to lean in. Embracing it is acceptance energy, and fighting is hostile energy, keeping you in the struggle with it. You always have a choice; you can give yourself the liberation without the suffering.

Pain Without Drama or Suffering

Society largely views pain—both physical and emotional—as something negative. We're taught to run away from anything or anyone that might hurt us. By hiding from pain, though, we're simply choosing to live in our comfort zones. We're giving power to the pain, letting it grow and control us.

You can stop that cycle now and hear this truth: **Pain is our greatest gift; suffering is a choice.**

Yes, pain is and will continue to be hard if you believe the lie that it is hard, it is there to hurt you, and any other negative beliefs and associations you've attached to it. Pain is the piece that allows us to pay attention and find the gift in the shit. The shit, aka the pain you are experiencing, will always bring us our greatest insights and freedom. Again I'll remind you that PAIN is there for you to PAY ATTENTION.

PAIN = *Pay Attention Inside Now*

Shifting my association to pain as the greatest emotion that gave me feedback, I began to use it to "pay attention inside now" and to love, accept, and embrace it as one of my greatest gifts of feedback to get clear and precise with what exactly wasn't working and got to shift. The emotion allowed me to move mountains in minutes and massively create different results quickly in my life.

Pain is the most intense indication we have that a situation isn't working. For example, if pain shows up in a relationship, you're likely to leave without taking the time to address the behaviors or beliefs that caused that pain. What happens then? You move on to a new relationship, only to eventually find you've attracted the same type of partner. Same pain, new face. It's a cycle.

Feelings are feedback, and pain is feedback in its truest form. It's part of our human process—nothing more, nothing less. If there's drama associated with pain, it's because you've put it there. It is just an emotion like any other. Each emotion shares something with us, and pain is your greatest indicator of what gets to shift for your next level of happiness to evolve.

As you work through the 5 Steps and shift into awesomeness, you'll begin to realize you can have experiences that are different going forward. Pain is part of our process, and it will always be there. Seeing it as a gift can give you the perspective you need to break that cycle.

We'll explore this in detail as we work though the 5 Steps covered in this book. For now, though, know that shifting from shit to awesomeness as your norm will require you to get real with—and choose to embrace—the glorious gift that your pain holds.

9

Pre-Step 3:

Acceptance of All Things Is the Key

Let's tune back in as two children have the same experience of being afraid because they believe there's a monster under the bed.

The first child's parents rush into the room at the sound of his cries, yelling, "What's wrong?" As the child shares that he is afraid because there is a monster under the bed, the parents, probably tired and frustrated, react in anger, frustration, ridicule, or disappointment and reject the child's fear. They might scream, "There are no monsters under the bed," go back to bed, and shut the door. They might devalue the child's feelings and say, "There is no such thing as monsters," or "You are being silly and stupid," or any number of things that prevent him from being heard.

From that experience alone, there are many things the child saw, heard, and felt, and there are a number of lessons he could have learned from that experience—that he is alone and unsupported; that he can't trust others not to hurt him; that it's not

OK to speak up or express how he feels; that fear is supposed to be suppressed; or that he is unloved and should be afraid of being anything other than what the people or things in his life are telling him to be.

The second child has parents who are aware that feelings and emotions are just feedback of what someone is thinking and seeing or believing and experiencing. They aren't wrong, they aren't bad, they aren't even necessarily true—they just are an experience.

In response to the second child's cries, her parents rush into her room and calmly and softly ask, "What are you feeling?"

The child replies, "I'm scared."

The parents respond, "Ahh, sweetie, why are you feeling that way?"

The child is then free to speak her emotions. She can share that she feels afraid because she believes there's a monster under her bed, that she is going to be hurt, that she is unsafe, that she is in danger—or whatever is connected to this emotion, which is powerful insight.

In response, her parents say, "Ahh, love, thank you for letting me know that you are feeling unsafe right now" and/or "Thank you for letting me know that is why you are feeling this way. I can understand how you could feel that way with those thoughts. Can we look under the bed together?" And they do. They also go through the 5 Steps to create a new belief system, form new perceptions, and help her integrate this process into her actions so the child doesn't keep repeating the fear and cycle.

What is important here to see is that acceptance of all things is the key to moving through them; ACCEPTANCE of ALL things creates an allowance and willingness take the next steps to HEALING it.

We get to give ourselves permission to fully feel our way to Freedom and that means we get to always **FEEL it to HEAL it**, and we can only do that by accepting what is in front of us instead of fighting it.

As soon as we tell ourselves that saying, thinking, feeling, experiencing or expressing something is not OK, our subconscious mind shuts down and goes directly into survival patterns and mechanisms we've learned instead of staying open and allowing the discovery of what is available. It opens and becomes available when we feel safe to explore.

Remember that your subconscious mind operates like a child. Your life is being run by that same inner child. It has already developed all the patterns and behaviors to stay safe, and the ego mind knows all the tricks to keep it safe. If you ask yourself a powerful question and the response that comes up is "I don't know," that is a response of guarding, protecting, and shutting down because it feels unsafe to go beyond that, to discover what is available on the other side of knowing. If we know, we might find something that scares us and so "I don't' know" keeps us out of responsibility and moving forward, safe in creating a block of what we do know.

"I don't know" or getting stuck at the actual opening of the discovery point is where most people stop because deep down there is an attachment and association of fear connected to it. Fear of being vulnerable, seen, and heard and fear of what is beyond this comfort zone.

If we get even softer with ourselves like a three year old child and we act as if we are playing a game instead of looking to find an answer to something that we are afraid of, our entire body system relaxes and allows us to open up to find the answer that is fun and exciting.

If "I don't know" still comes up as the answer, we can accept and love that too, and then open the space to continue. We clearly can see it now for what it is, a sign that fear exists on the other side and it's wanting to stay where it feels safe. Yet, we know now that RECEIVING is always on the other side of resistance.

Keeping this in mind, internally, responding to "I don't know" might look like, *Ah, OK. I can understand that. Right now, just breathe and notice that we are totally safe in this room. We are always protected and supported, and right now we are just playing a game of curiosity.* If you breathe for a moment and let your three-year-old self come out to play, reminding yourself that you are just playing a curiosity game, then you can re-phrase or ask yourself the question again in another way. *What else could we be feeling around that? What would that look like? What could that be? Why else?*

If we always ACCEPT whatever shows up and practice continually getting curious about it, then we can discover why we have that thought, idea, belief, story, or perception about our experience in the first place.

Let's drop back a bit into a much broader view of acceptance that will hopefully assist you in seeing why approaching the 5 Steps in the energy of love and acceptance is also one of the greatest keys to living a life of peace and experiencing a flow of life free from triggers. It is because there is no longer anything to fight, anything to prove, validate, hide, or run from. It becomes easy and liberating when you simply accept all things.

How this might apply in your life is that it can be challenging to not judge something about yourself or others when you have a story of what is right or wrong. Whatever you are pointing your finger at, judging, or projecting on is simply a reflection of what you haven't owned or accepted within yourself and don't love. If you don't like something about someone else, it is because you haven't owned the aspect of it within yourself that triggers you. You might be triggered by someone that has owned their sexual expression and you catch yourself thinking "that's too much" or putting a judgment on that person because you haven't owned your own sexuality, self-expression, or ability to receive pleasure, and so therefore you judge it. Everything is a mirror of what's inside. What I continued to remind myself of through all my own processes of both catching myself being the judger and the one being judged is that there can never be "Too Much" in your Wholeness. Your wholeness is ALL parts of you.

The next level I'd love you to breathe into and allow yourself to get curious about is that you are all things.

What does that mean? It means, as a human, you reflect the whole. If a human has the ability to express any trait, then you as a human have the capacity and ability to display every single trait that exists. See, every strand of your DNA carries the entire evolution history of life within it; every cell carries the intelligence of the entire body, just as every atom that is in your body contains the exact reflection of the matter comprised of the cosmos. The microcosm is a reflection of the macrocosm. Each cell that is you reflects the whole.

The Cosmic Law of Reality is that what is in ONE will always be in the WHOLE, and what is in the WHOLE will always be in ONE. Just like there are laws of the Universe, we have universal qualities and traits that exist within each of us as a human blueprint.

What you've been taught, though, is most likely a very different story and has created a very different view and perception of the way things are. You've been taught that you are different, and yet the reality is that you contain everything inside you that you see in others. The greatest lie is that of separation, which leads you to see yourself as separate or different from anyone else because you are a reflection and replication of the same universal truths, matter, and framework. We are all ONE while simultaneously also having a separate identity we choose. You will always be capable of choice, of exuding the traits you choose to express, of choosing what aspects you want to discover, to share, and to exemplify to the world as your unique self. You are, however, the very same framework and vessel of possibilities that exists and is in each of us, and in everything.

Comparison Is the Thief of All Joy

Just as you have a right to experience whatever it is you want, others have a right to experience whatever it is they want. If we didn't have all these different aspects, then our journey here to study human consciousness would be pretty boring. We wouldn't learn much if we only allowed one way of being, one way of living, one way of believing, one way of learning or experiencing life.

Even identical twins come with countless variations. Siblings raised in the very same home with the same parents have completely different perceptions of their childhood and experiences. Each human is composed of more than 37 trillion-plus unique cells. Think about the amazingness of this and how magical and unique you are. You have your own voice box, fingerprints, and toe prints that are all uniquely only yours. Along with this, you have your specific perceptions, experiences, beliefs, patterns, programming, behaviors, personality, divine gifts, and abilities that are—again—only yours. No person can ever be like another, just like living a joyous and fulfilled life will never look only one way. There are many ways to the top of the mountain, and one path and experience is very different from the next.

When we're living and thriving as creators, of course, everyone's normal is different. When we try to create just like someone else, our energy gets stuck; we create and live in resistance because it isn't us, our innate blueprint, or who we are. We have been raised in a society that has created parameters and boxes to fit into that base your happiness on factors depending on others. This only makes you a victim to life's circumstances instead of the creator of your experiences. What does being a successful businessperson look like? What about being a loving, present parent? Is there any recipe for what makes a perfect relationship? Deep down you already know the answer to that because no two people are alike. The answer is no; it never has to look a certain way— that was just a lie and story you were told. You can learn tools to support and assist you in creating the life you want, and it can always only come from you to decipher exactly how the experience gets to look like for you.

To think that you are different, better than, or even less adequate than is just the story of judgment and comparison you chose to buy into. The TRUTH isn't that I'm not like you, and you aren't like me.

THE TRUTH IS ...

I Am You.

You Are Me.

We Are They.

They are Them.

Them are We.

And that is why....

ALL Things Have a Right to Exist

We are what we see because we could not see it if it didn't exist within us; if we didn't hold it within our capacity, then there would be no recognition or understanding of it as a possibility.

Are you open to the idea that, if you were raised in an environment where sexual abuse was how your family showed love, you could possibly act out sexual abuse? In what way have you ever abused someone? In what ways do you or have you ever abused yourself? Have you ever beat yourself up or shamed yourself for sabotaging with food, not achieving a goal, or losing your temper, or do you bombard yourself with inner negative self-talk instead so that no one sees it from the outside? How are you abusive with sex, or how have you ever been abusive with sex? Do you withhold it from your partner out of spite when you are angry? Do you keep yourself from fully allowing, expressing, asking for what you want, and experiencing it fully because you don't feel worthy of receiving pleasure? Have you ever thought about acting out some sort of abuse? Can you see that we actually all contain every single quality and have the capacity to exude every single trait in some way? We are all simply experiencing or exemplifying each quality to the level or degree we choose. Everything is and always will be a reflection of what you are learning about yourself, your own creative power, and the abilities you are operating from right now.

Pointing at others and looking at them as if they are different is how we validated the lie of separation. You are and will always be every trait and quality that exists because you are human. You carry these infinite possibilities within you that you are worthy of expressing in whatever way and form that you choose.

One of my core values and how I would describe myself is being extremely authentic, transparent, and vulnerable, as would most others in describing me. I am, at the very same time, manipulative, a liar, and a fraud. How can that be? And more importantly, why would I admit that I am a fraud when you are reading this book that is coming through me? That doesn't seem like the best plan if I want you to like me, listen to this message, or feel like you can trust me? That is just it. I don't have a plan; there is nothing to pretend to be, as true transparency means there is nothing to hide and nothing to prove. I don't have an agenda, attachment, or expectation of you or require anything from you. I share these truths because I am called to, because I am free with the truth of knowing I am all things, and sharing that is giving the greatest gift I have to give, which is being the most authentic, transparent, and vulnerable person I can be. Even so, while I desire to stand and declare truth, I still am human, with scared little girl parts of me that are fundamental to my experience and journey. I still have things that trigger my "not enough-ness," and my egoic and scared self wants to act out in manipulation with myself to bring up old fears and even patterns that would make me want to run and hide. This is how at the same time I am standing in truth, I can also experience feeling like a fraud, wanting to hide, and not feeling like I'm enough. When I choose—instead of believing the fear—to breathe into it and apply love and acceptance of it, I then release its hold on me.

Noticing that there is a fear of being judged, rejected, or even seen and felt is just part of all that is in me. Hiding that would be the very essence of manipulation to myself and others. Being fully authentic with all of me and my journey, there is nothing to hide, and that is pure freedom.

I discovered for myself that it is the very opposite of what we have been taught and are trained in when it comes to our emotions, feelings, and expression. This is why I am not trying to hide from the scared little girl; I am actually seeking to find more and more of her. I'm seeking to discover more of the ways that I am triggered to want to run, or retreat, or guard, or defend into my smallness. I'm seeking to discover more circumstances in which judgements come up that make me feel separate from others; this enables clear feedback about what I haven't owned within myself, what else inside me I am still carrying judgment for, and what else inside gets to be healed and loved. I know that the resistance I find is what is blocking me from even more connection, love, peace, joy, abundance, pleasure, and all things I desire to experience even more of.

If I pretended I was anything but all things, I would only be continuing with the very lies that build a prison of suffering.

Suffering is always a choice.

Just like thriving is a choice.

This is one of the common ways as a humanity we create and spread our own suffering.

When we claim it, we can change it.

Once we accept that we are all things, we can then see how a trait can serve us and also work against us in allowing the creation of what we want to manifest. That is all it is when you don't attach any other story to it. We can then choose how to utilize all the traits we are for our and others' greatest good. When we see others exude certain traits yet know that those same traits exist within, how can we judge others for having or expressing those traits? Doing so only keeps us in denial of ourselves. Instead, we can honor the other person choosing to be that expression and having that experience; it is their choice as a worthy being to learn in that way here and now. Just as we deserve and have the right to experience whatever it is we want, everyone is worthy of experiencing whatever it is they want also. There is no double standard. You want others to accept who you are; you accept others fully for who they are. It doesn't mean you condone the behavior; you simply release any attachment to it because it has nothing to do with you.

When we can look at what someone is choosing as a trait to exemplify as a byproduct of what that person has experienced, been raised in, was programmed in, and is actually choosing for their greatest and highest learning here at this time, then we find understanding. That is all that is required. It is actually through understanding that we can find forgiveness. Judgments will always be there; there is no need to shame yourself for having a judgment. The opportunity is to catch it and turn it back on yourself to utilize it as feedback of where it came from and why it even came up because you know the truth is that what you judged is a reflection of you.

Maybe your mind wants to jump in here and use logic to prove whatever perception you have is right and true. The thing is, logic will always validate whatever perception you are looking to find. We see this everywhere that war exists. One side believes they are right, and their logic proves it to be true. On the opposite side, they have their own logic proving why they are right. Proving yourself right only comes from the energy of scarcity, that there isn't enough to go around, there isn't the allowance of all things to exist, and it comes from the scared self that has to prove they are right out of fear of losing the identity they cling to, and the intolerance of something only reflects the fear of being the exact thing it judges or fights against.

Let's use again the example of sexual abuse. Maybe you see someone who has perpetrated or even experienced it as lesser than you. You see that person as a being who needs to be saved or doesn't know enough; the truth is that they are a fully aware and divine being that chose that experience and role. You experiencing something else in life doesn't make you greater. It just means your highest self chose and is choosing a different life experience now for your understanding. At one time, in your life now and in other lifetimes as well, you were also the abuser, and to judge it still now only means you haven't accepted, owned, and loved that part of you that can operate in a shadow frequency of abuse. To reject that part of you, just as you reject someone else experiencing it, only makes it show back up in in your life consistently, right in your face, because it is the thing that you have resistance to.

It doesn't mean you allow or accept it to be done to you; it means you stop attracting it when you stop fighting, judging, blaming, or shaming it. You can simply honor yourself and your worthiness and at the same time have no judgment for someone who is experiencing that for their life lesson at this time. You are not the same person you were five years ago, just as whoever you might be judging who or is triggering you is in their perfect process and journey right now too. Remember that resistance energy only blocks manifestation because you are vibrating an energy of blocking, guarding, and separation. If you are in resistance to your neighbor who triggers you, or any person or organization and their way of believing or being for that matter, the resistance to them is blocking your ability to receive even more joy, bliss, pleasure, abundance, peace, love, and play...more of everything you want.

You can only receive to the degree you love yourself and are open to receive. Whatever you don't love or don't have a clean energy of neutrality with in others reflects what you aren't OK with and willing to love in yourself. If you can only love so much, you can only receive that much. If you are only open to receiving in certain ways and through certain avenues and people, then you are closed off to the infinite possibilities.

This is what I mean by **ACCEPTANCE of ALL things.**

I did give a clear warning at the beginning of the book that you might be challenged or triggered by what we lean into. And I still want you to question all things for yourself, see what resonates with you, and honor yourself in choosing what serves you best. I have no attachment to what you choose or what you think, believe, or feel about me, or I clearly wouldn't have told you I am just as much a fraud as I am someone who stands for transparency and authenticity and speaks truth. I'm just as much a bitch as I am an angel. I love every inch of my darkness as much as I love my light. I am at complete peace with all parts of me, and because I am not suppressing or hiding from any part of me, I am free and at choice to utilize all of me for my highest good.

To accept all things in your own discovery of what you reveal will be how you can heal it. We have to feel it to heal it, and if we can't accept that it is even there, we only keep hiding, rejecting, and running from it. Doing that won't ever give you the opportunity to heal.

Now you can relax. It's easy when you realize there is nothing to judge; there is nothing that ever happened that was wrong or could ever be a wrong decision, experience, or even choice in your life because it was what you perfectly chose and it was perfectly attracted to you from the very energy you were and are vibrating. There is nothing that could ever be bad or needs to be shamed.

There is nothing to blame. It was all and just is an experience. This experience came with thoughts, ideas, feelings, and behaviors that have all been for your perfect growth process. Being able to allow and accept it then allows you to move through all the emotions to feel and heal.

Divinity isn't what we have deemed perfection. Divinity is wholeness, and to be divine is to be whole, and to be whole is to be everything that we are. It is in the acceptance of our ALLness and oneness with all things, all beings, and all experiences that we can come back to unity and be open to receiving all that is.

When you can grasp and understand this, peace and freedom are also in your reach because you can now let go of any and all resistance, you can surrender to the flow of life, you can let go of trying to control anyone or anything, and you can become the receiver of all things you desire, as your energy is free. Your frequency is clear when you free yourself from these perceptions and behaviors of the past and cease to be a victim to resistance. When you can embrace resistance and become the frequency of divine, unconditional love and peace, you become and you are the acceptance of all things.

Something that always assists me in the moments I want to view others or the circumstances in front of me with judgment or out of struggle is this...

I remember that this very thing in front of me must be my soul's kindest act for me right now in my experience. I remember that every interaction is for a reason, and this very thing is the greatest gift I could receive right now for my healing, growth, expansion, freedom, and remembrance of my Soul's Sacred Contract. The person in front of me I might be challenged with is a gift to hoist me up on the slippery mountainside of ascension where I was stuck or stagnant. This experience or person brought itself to boost me up to a greater view and perception of possibility for myself and what I could be experiencing in life as I chose to let that pain go that they triggered and allowed me to see what was existing within.

These ideas and language might be completely foreign to you or even stretch your mental programming to consider a new perception beyond what we've talked about, as you are the creator now and you can open up the realm of what your highest self already knows and has preset for you.

The Sacred Contract and Purpose of You

There are Universal questions we all seek answers to: "Why am I here?" "What is my mission or purpose in life?" "What should I be doing with my life?" "Why is this happening?" We are all seeking purpose. Well, let's sum it up and make it easy. YOU are the purpose. Everything in your life, moment by moment, is for the purpose of your own discovery. You don't have to go searching somewhere outside of you. Think about it this way: when you have a struggle that shows up in your life, you want to overcome that struggle, you want to find a solution, to fix it, heal it, and find peace with it, right? It takes you on a journey of seeking and discovering. That journey of what was a struggle, or a mess, if you will, eventually becomes what you know and have learned to solve, and the mess becomes a message or a gift you have to share with others who are seeking the same freedom. Everything showing up in your life is for the purpose of your discovery and leading you to your gifts, your dharma, and what fulfills you.

Now, it makes sense that the mind wants an answer because we as humans are impatient and we want to plan it all out and control it. We want to know what we should do, where we should go, who we should work with, and what we should focus on. This type of constant questioning can leave you in a state of stress and create physical symptoms and sicknesses as well. Notice also the energy of that. It comes from a scared, low-vibrational self that needs to arrive at a story that says, "I've achieved this and I'm now good enough" or "I have these results or credibility and now I have validation." Doesn't this—only loving yourself based on conditionalities—look like a program of suffering? That is domesticated, conditional love that you are now applying to yourself, and these self-domesticating patterns create suffering. It's understandable because it's how we've been programmed, but it's important to get to a place of trusting and loving yourself enough to give yourself permission to do and experience what feels good for you and is right for you. It's important to let go of all the parameters, boxes, stories, and perceptions that only create your own suffering. All of it is, of course, a part of the beautiful holy human journey. You will always come to this faster, though, if you relax into it, surrender, and allow it. Confusion of your purpose and direction in life bring havoc to all areas of your existence because you are living in that panicked energy. We want to be operating at a place where our energy is in alignment to receive and see what's available instead of blocking it, fighting it, or "trying" to figure it out.

It is understandable that the mind wants to make sense of things for us to be at peace with what is happening so it can receive what is there. Our spirit body also wants to be able to connect to and feel this deeper truth of the bigger picture when things can seem far from effortless.

We know the logical mind doesn't really exist, yet the universal truths do. So, what will assist us in accepting our shit, challenges, and learning opportunities in front of us and not get stuck in the illusion, stories, and constructs of the mind from our human experience?

We get to journey back before we were even human.

Most of us have had some incident happen that we labeled as bad, and then later, as we looked back on it, we thought, *Thank God that happened. It led me in a whole other direction in my life, allowed*

127

me to meet so and so, to find this teaching, person, understanding, or experience. Looking back at these moments is like looking at fractals of your history, fractals of the person you are that found, remembered, and became empowered with who you are here to be. You can see how important that interaction was. This is also what I mean by whatever is in front of you is what you set up as the kindest act for yourself.

You've also probably experienced people in your life who you felt you "recognized" in some way; you knew them or felt like they were familiar to you even though you'd just met. How can it be that someone you just met made you feel like you'd known them forever? These divine recognitions are part of the Soul's Sacred Contract.

If we actually understood that our experience of time, space, relationships, and experiences was predetermined and very carefully selected by ourselves along with supportive divine guides, then what would there be to fight or question about this moment we are in?

Grasping this divine clarity that our entire life has been constructed by us for our benefit and that we've accumulated the wounds, the experiences, and the people we have for a reason is of great importance. There are no accidents, and the Universe is always in divine order. If you had this awareness, could you let go of trying to control and relax into the remembrance that everything is always happening for you? You are always in the right place at the right time and experiencing what is perfection for your journey right now. You are always divinely guided, step by step, by this Universal intelligence, and that is happening effortlessly and endlessly for you. As you trust this, your intuition becomes clearer and you can begin to receive it easier and easier as you drop the resistance around whatever is showing up. If you saw life through these eyes all the time, you would absolutely respond differently to your reality. How much easier would it be to choose the next step without the added story, pain, or suffering?

My divorce with my former is the best way I can articulate and share with you how much this different perception and knowing assisted me, supported me, and completely changed my world.

When I finally awoke to this awareness and could see my former for who he really was—one of my Divine Besties, who volunteered to have this experience with me for me to learn what I wanted to—I could only see him out of pure love, gratitude and appreciation from that moment on.

The first time I got a glimpse of this understanding was reading a very simple version of it in the children's book *A Little Soul and the Sun* to my kids. I had begun teaching my kids the conscious concepts I was learning and had looked for children's books to impart some of these messages. This book is by Neale Donald Walsch, who is well known and famous for *Conversations with God* series.

From that story, I took away a vision of the place where we existed before coming to this holy human experience and life school journey. You can fill in the blank of wherever that might be that resonates for you. I was sitting and contemplating what I wanted to experience and understand. In this place, everyone was seen as light and the truth of who they are. Imagine a beautiful place that is full of rainbows, unicorns, fairies, and pixie dust if you will. I saw myself wanting to be a vessel and expression of freedom and liberation and wanting to bring energetic shifts of perceptions, laws, and truths to bring healing to the planet, a rise of frequency to our humanity, and a remembrance of the divinity that we are. Obviously, to come to a place of knowing those truths and being able to share them meant that I would require my own journey of experiences, souls to interact with for these lessons, and my own healing to embody these truths and be able to truly pass on these codes. I would require not just someone but many, many, many someones to experience life with and forgive.

I had this vision of my former as one of my Divine Besties approach me and say, "I know you want to experience these things to understand ultimate forgiveness and what that looks like, feels like, and the process of it to arrive at the experience of it. I love you so much. I would be happy to be one of the individuals that comes into your life to give you such an experience." He would wrap his high-vibrational being with a darker frequency and energy to have an action or behavior that would bring about an experience of forgiveness, and he was willing to do that for me.

In the same contract, and through this act and our exchange in relationship, he would also get his perfect lessons to assist him in exactly what he was wanting to learn, understand, and experience for his highest self to emerge. We were going to be assisting each other into our highest knowing and ascension, and what we were going to "do" to each other wasn't personal, in fact, it was an energy and act of love.

Can we now also see why judging an act or behavior through our human eyes or understanding only keeps us in limitation? If the act of "cheating on me" that my former gave to me hadn't happened, where would I be now? I can look back at my entire life experience from that moment on and am so encompassed with love, gratitude, and appreciation because I see where that event led and took me in becoming who I am today. That experience is what guided me to find the answer and solution for my own peace, understanding, and yes, receiving exactly what I wanted, which was to learn and come to an experience of ultimate forgiveness.

Can we now see that good or bad doesn't really exist because what we would've labeled as bad, or what society has judged as wrong, was actually, on a spiritual plane, the greatest gift of kindness and love for my soul's highest potential and evolution I could be given. There is no such thing as bad or wrong in what you call the "darkness" and nothing to fear because darkness is just a different calibration of frequency and energy.

I used to be afraid of certain things and certain experiences, but giving something fear just gives it more power, and when I realized there was nothing to be afraid of, that it was just something that operated in a different energy frequency and had no power over me, those things I was afraid of or gave power to fell away. As did my judgments for any and all things, as I realized everything was and is just the perfect experience or perfect interaction and is in perfect universal order for everything my highest self and the highest self of every person involved is seeking and has chosen for our journeys of evolution and remembrance.

Begin to just look back at your life and see these fractals of time and experiences and the evidence of this. You are now and always have been receiving what you so carefully preplanned and cocreated with the collaboration of divine guidance based on the contracts you chose to fulfill and the divine potential that is you. You scripted what you wanted to experience, learn, grow in, and serve the world with, and you created many individual agreements and subcontracts with others that love and care about you to be a part of your experience. This includes your closest friends and your greatest adversaries, along with those small interactions in time that triggered you. Some have been with you many times before and even now in parallel lifetimes to support you in your ascension over and over again.

Every relationship and every experience are opportunities that were set to guide you in your growth and continually shapeshift your life to the remembrance of what you felt called in this time and reality to experience and become. You asked for these experiences and these people to show up for you. You agreed to meet certain people at certain places and times in life for this very reason. You are connecting consistently with your Divine Family, who are here to support you, and this is why you have a sense of recognition and remembrance with them. You've most likely shown up for each other many, many, many times before and traveled together through many lifetime exchanges in support of each other to reach your spiritual growth and potential.

I came from a religion that didn't believe we ever had any more than one lifetime, and that might be what feels true for you as well right now. Whether you believe it was for this lifetime as your only one, or you believe you have countless lifetimes to experience, evolve, and grow through the traits and journeys of being human, can you simply open up and expand to see it being for your greatest and highest good?

Along with this perfect divine order, you do and always will have the power of choice. You can choose however you wish to experience the growth and learning of all that comes to you. If you choose to take on blame, shame, judgement, and hurt during an experience, then you are learning through blame, shame, judgment and hurt. In the same experience, you can choose to learn out of forgiveness, love, and healing. You can appreciate those that you have interacted with for what they taught you and for keeping their contract, or you can hold anger and hatred towards them and continue to project a victimhood mentality. Each thing is neutral because it offers the opportunity of experience based on what you choose. Whatever way you choose to experience it, you are learning. There is no right or wrong; just choice.

I'll do my best to share the way Caroline Myss explains choice, which I love. You chose to come here and learn how to use a certain tool. Let's say it is a knife. If you choose to grab this tool first by the blade, you will be cut, you'll bleed, and you'll experience pain. You will most likely see this neutral tool as a weapon, something that hurts, and may even feel afraid of the tool. Experiencing pain, you could choose to then project that hurt onto others and use this weapon to harm others because it is what you are choosing to learn and how you are seeing this tool currently.

Let's say you choose to grab the knife by the handle and discover how it can be used from this perception and experience.

You begin to learn that you can cut food and feed people with it; you can use it to carve, cut, and create art; you can use it to be a tool for building, for shelter, for ways that you can serve, support, and help others with this tool.

You could say that this object that is neutral represents life and the polarity we have available with all things. Polarity will always exist, as we have the sun and the moon, darkness and light, energy that manifests into form that will always be channeled into what you could describe as a positive or a negative effect.

At any point in your life you can decide to drop the tool you've been using if it is causing you pain and flip it so that it functions to serve you. You can see that everyone has just been reading your script and everything is created from your energy, your choices, and what you asked to learn. When you are committed to your own freedom and liberation, the option that remains open for you is to see every experience out of love.

Having these foundational truths allows you to move through the 5 Steps with much more ease because we have awakened to a greater consciousness and inner-standing that we can now bypass getting stuck in so many low-vibrational patterns. There is one more really important way of "being" that I adopted as my new model of how to operate and supported me in completely changing my world.

The New Model Is the Embodiment of Being

What does that even mean? It means we've forgotten how to "BE." How to be in harmony with all of ourselves, every emotion, every person, every experience, and all of life. We are being called to upgrade to operate from a consciousness, vibration, and way of "being" human that is and always will be for the greatest and highest good of everyone. The New Human that can lead the way for us to receive the New Earth that is available.

We've been operating from our heads instead of our hearts. We've been trying to plan it out, strive, force, and control all of life by "thinking" it through instead of "feeling" it through, surrendering to the flow of life and allowing the energy to guide us to the greatest gifts to be received. Only focused on "doing," we forgot how to "be" and therefore receive. We ran right past everything we wanted because we only knew this masculine, structural way of "doing" as the main example we've had for creating everything from building a business to experiencing relationships.

Although I was on a journey of consciousness and energy in all the ways we've discussed, I had only seen these structures and examples that said this the way to create anything. Not having a reference point for any other way of "doing," I held onto my "warrior" archetype, continuing to show up as a fuckin' warrior and strive towards my goals and creating success this way, unconscious to how ineffective it was. The first coach I invested in was a man who ran a Men's Warrior Program, and I was the only female ever to be accepted. That is how much of a fuckin' warrior I was at the time. He would use me as an example to all these powerful men, saying that if I could do what I was doing as a single mother with two little boys, then what was their excuse? I was again validated for fighting the fight I had practiced my whole life: the skill of overcoming the obstacle ahead. I am so grateful for everything I perfectly learned in this stage for my healing, and it all shifted for me when one day I realized I was tired of being on the battlefield and always in the fight. Why was I choosing to create life to be a fight? Why was I fighting to achieve goals and for success?

I saw clearly at a new level that the energy of it and life experience wasn't what I wanted to continue in. I decided it was time to step off the battlefield and to embrace my worthiness as the Divinity I am and have always been. I allowed myself to embrace what I called The Enlightened Empress as I began letting life deliver and bring to me everything I desired and required, operating from flow, ease, and grace as my new way of "being." This was when life massively shifted for me as I began opening up more and more of my feminine flow to dance with life, follow the energy, and create and discover more of my gifts and capabilities to continually receive. This is when ease and grace, bliss and flow, became my natural way of being.

I got to harmonize both the masculine and feminine aspects within to operate in divine flow of give and receive. I follow what feels good, what is the most nourishing for my soul, then create through inspired action to receive again in ease and grace. It was after this that I was able to serve and coach many of the high-level men who had also gone through that program and to serve both men and women in high-level leadership, to teach them the next levels of dropping the fight, creating their businesses and lives led by spirit, to receive greater than they knew was possible with ease.

Now being even more aware, we can witness whatever we struggle to be at peace with or have a desire to control and we can remember that only allows it to control us. It is, of course, being revealed to heal, love, and become at peace with. To clarify, we do get to take action and move forward in life, and we can remember how to do that through the masculine aspect in harmony and balance, which is through taking inspired action from feeling the energy guiding us instead of forced action based on thought. Forcing a certain way is a lot like guessing what the view of the whole valley looks like while standing directly at the bottom of the mountain you want to climb. You just can't see it all when you are on one end of the path. There are many ways up the mountain and infinite possibilities of how to get to the top, how to experience the journey, and what we'll discover along the way, along with many glorious views to behold when we let go of the plans, attachments, expectations, stories, and ideas and follow the energy to receive.

We get to let go and surrender for the allowance of our innate gifts and pathways leading us to the greatest joys, grandest adventures and freedoms that are beyond what we currently can see. The feminine flows with life and energy like water that is moving and dancing down a river. When it comes to a rock, it just glides and flows around it to continue to dance and play. The 5 Steps tool teaches us to allow the energy to guide us as we discover "the rocks" that show up. The resistance in the path is only diverting us to be able to shift and access even greater.

Your Highest Self, Source, Great Spirit, Divine Mother, The Multiverse (or whatever language you want to use) can see the entire layout that isn't just the view from the top of the mountain you want to climb. It sees the entire spectrum of the cosmos and how to bring all things to you that will light up your very being to utilize your innate abilities. My own experience time and time again, along with all the clients I've coached, is that it is always greater than we could've ever imagined or ever had in our current scope of possibilities. That's just how fuckin' cool being connected to all of life and all you are really is. We are here in collaboration as co-creators through divine interdependence with all of life.

Why else? We've discussed how feelings and what we are vibrating at a cellular level is 500,000 times more powerful, and so we are using an inkling of the effort with a magnified result. We do have a brain in our heart referred to as heart intelligence, which allows us to expand our human consciousness. When we bring the mind, body, heart, spirit, and all parts of us together, we are operating fully as the powerful sovereign creators we are. The heart field extends around us in every direction and interacts with all of life through feeling. As we begin to operate from our feeling bodies, we remember how we were designed to create as we move and flow with energy in each present moment. Through the examples in this book we can see that being present with whatever is in front of us is always exactly what we require for our greatest expansion to step beyond the comfort zone and receive even more.

Have you ever heard that saying "Yesterday is history. Tomorrow is a mystery. Today is a gift; that's why they call it the present"? I love that, and it is so true that the gift is living in this very moment.

For myself, it was a challenge at first to wrap my head around letting go, surrendering, dropping the plans, and how just "allowing" was going to get me anywhere. That's just it, though; I was trying to use my head and still think it through. I came to inner-stand that the greatest gifts were always in the present moment. I began to find the magic and miracles, blissing and blessings always available everywhere and in everything around me. I committed to peace as my priority in every moment because I knew it would only reveal what I wasn't at peace with and allow me to receive even more.

My daily mantra I practiced and aligned to until it became my new belief system and way of experiencing all of life was this: "I joyfully serve the divine and all of humanity, while the Universe and Divine effortlessly takes care of all the details, while I float in a constant state of bliss, receiving all I desire and require." I would envision myself floating in bliss, fully supported, being and carried by the energy of Divine Source (or whatever you label it as) and an energy moving ahead of me setting all things up for my ease and grace. This is now how I experience life.

You came here for the awe, wonderment, and discovery of it all. There are going to be days when you feel so filled with energy to create and produce through inspired action, and then there will be days where you absolutely get to just self love, let go of all plans, ideas, and attachments, recalibrate, and just be. Every single day and experience is meant to be its own divine, beautiful adventure and gift. It isn't meant to look the same, just like you are always moving, flowing, shifting, and expanding. Surrender and allow the adventure.

How do you align to that? It was through my journey and consistently using the 5 Steps to Freedom tool that I was able to consistently clear stuck emotional energy or imprints within me, shed programs no longer serving me, and I simply became lighter. Enlightenment is to be in light. The lighter I became within, the more I remembered my wholeness and allowed myself to align to this knowing of my worthiness. Aligned to this, I could truly now believe and allow myself to always be fully supported by the infinite abundance of the Universe, worthy to receive with ease.

When we are working in accordance with our divine nature to create and the laws of the multiverse, we effortlessly bring formless into form with our direction of energy. This is where we become Alchemists of Light, which is really the best way to describe what I actually do. I teach people to become alchemists. As an alchemist, or you could call it a magician of energy, you know there isn't anything to fight or prove; you simply have the ability to turn dirt into gold, wounds into strengths, and to transmute anything in resistance to the greatest gifts for you to receive.

This is the way of the New Human, who embodies their Wholeness through loving all they are. It is operating from this place of alignment in the highest vibration with all of life that we can experience a New Earth and a greater world than we've ever been able to imagine. In this new way of be-ing, we shed lower vibrational experiences such as lack, scarcity, sickness, disease, or separation, and they truly can become a thing only in old memories we just don't resonate with anymore. This is my vision of the world we get to live in. We create peace for the planet when we each begin to be peace.

"Perfect peace and joy is our inheritance and divine birthright. We only are asked to give up our belief in lack."

If you'd like even more support on this topic, check out any of my shows on "Force vs. Flow" on the *Awakened Being: Conversations to Create Change* at marcilock.com/show.

Now that we have these foundations to support us, let's dive into the "how to's" for using this easy and simple tool for our greatest liberation, abundance, and bliss now: the 5 Steps to Freedom.

5 Steps to Freedom: Quick Reference Guide

1. What am I feeling right now?

Where is it in my body? (head, chest, stomach, pelvis, etc.)

I notice I feel... (rejected, hurt, sad, like I'm not good enough, etc.)

2. Why? What am I focused on?

Why am I feeling this way? What's the story, thought, perception, belief, or trigger that came up, or what I am putting my attention on?

(Why? Because when that was said to me, I felt stupid and not good enough. What this brought up for me is a feeling from my childhood that what I do is never good enough)

Connect as much as possible with why that feeling came up and what it is connected to.

3. What do I really want right now?

I want... (an epic relationship, to feel safe, connection, to feel supported, to express myself, to experience even more love, freedom, to be happy, feel joyful, etc.)

If this is what I want...is what I am believing, focusing on, or doing going to get me that? Are the thoughts I'm believing and perceptions I'm having even really true? What other perceptions and possibilities could exist?

What is the feedback I now get to use to get what I want in this circumstance?

4. What is the NEW belief, perception, and focus I am choosing to get what I want?

To have what I want, what would I now get to believe?

What would the new belief, perception, and focus now get to be to give me what I want?

Change the perception to come from FAITH energy. See the possibility or belief out of excitement, wonder, and curiosity.

5. What is the ACTION I get to take NOW to give myself what I want?

AND... How can it be fun and easy?

In this circumstance, what action would I get to do that is in alignment with and will move me towards what I want?

What is the next step?

Ask for what you want to create the solution.

CHANGE YOUR VIBE and STATE to match an energy of feeling good and take the ACTION to now create what you want.

We'll now go deeper into each step to create even more clarity in moving through each shift.

10

When, How & What to Expect with the 5 Steps to Freedom

I LOVE simplicity, and I love making the complex seem and become simple. Using the 5-Step shifting tool makes everything so easy.

We know that we can't just think our way through life. It just doesn't show up according to our mental plans because it is impossible to see the entire view of a single moment, and there are always infinite possibilities that exceed what we can imagine. The 5 Steps can bring infinite solutions, ideas, opportunities, and answers that illuminate the dark and lead you to new possibilities and paths, which will give you the next step up that mountain you are exploring. Each step walks you through the shift to align, create, and receive what you really want.

The 5 Steps transformed my world and my life, and I've witnessed its effects on thousands of lives, as it is a foundational piece of my programs and a tool I consistently utilize in all of my life. I shared earlier that the 5 Steps were a gift. I can't even claim to have created them because this tool came through me and

I received it intuitively as I began to get curious and seek answers for my own life.

So, let's make this simple, shall we?

When do you use the 5 Steps to Freedom?

That's easy! Anytime you don't feel peace, love, joy or awesomeness. More specifically, anytime you experience an emotion that you don't want to be feeling. That's it. If you catch yourself feeling anything you don't enjoy, or you notice you are in an "unwanted" experience that is not aligned to your true nature, then it's time to quickly go inside and through the 5 Steps. The other time to be aware it's time to "5 Step it," is if you notice you are in a pattern or behavior that is sabotaging and not in alignment with the result you say you really want. Doing the 5 Steps is how we will reprogram the new patterns and realign back to our natural state of experiencing peace, joy, and bliss as our norm and reality.

The reason this is so beneficial and powerful in transforming your reality is because each and every single time you do it, you retrain your mind, clarify what is really going on, reconnect with your true self and desires, align to new neural pathways, and construct new perceptions, beliefs, and behaviors that all become the pathway of least resistance as your new norm. This allows a natural shift for it to become who you are, how you operate, and how you see and feel about the world. It truly is a pathway to freedom from operating unconsciously and reacting subconsciously to being in the driver's seat and consciously creating your life.

Operating through what I knew, I couldn't have a frame of reference or internal representation and experience to connect my subconscious to believe or feel something else, so it would continue to stay in the same box I built. Each one of these steps allows you to move forward as you create a new frame of reference and an internal representation within you for a new overriding frequency that is greater than what you had, so you create new ways of operating, which result in lasting changes.

The first suggestion that I have for you, which you can implement right away, is to have this tool available for yourself EVERYWHERE. Take a picture of the 5 Steps and have it on your phone, print it out and put it up where you can see it, have it in your purse, in your desk at work, in your car, and hang it up on your fridge, even on your bathroom mirror. In order to train your brain, you must repattern your way of RESPONDING and operating. My brain naturally thinks and operates this way now. I don't even have to try; it just goes there versus going where it did in the past.

The entire goal here is to take massive action in your life and become proactive in creating these changes so you can timeline hop into a new reality as quickly as possible.

As you begin catching yourself in awareness, witnessing it, and noticing yourself out of alignment with a feeling or experience that is not the level of awesome you want to be feeling, you'll most likely start feeling like you are using the 5 Steps ALL THE TIME. Seriously, this is so normal. When anyone starts, the number one thing I hear is, "I feel like now I'm just doing the 5 Steps all the time because I am catching everything I was doing that I didn't see before."

And I say...YES to that! Hallelujah! Let's celebrate the success that really is, and please know that this is a very, very, very good thing to notice because it means you are in awareness. You are catching the low-vibrational patterns that used to just slip right by and were creating your unconscious reality.

It might feel overwhelming or like you are now processing all the time, yet I want you to please realize that this is so incredibly fantastic. Each time you actually go through the process of the 5 Steps, you are reaffirming the new pathway and recoding and imprinting new behaviors, which are changing your reality to the one you want to be living. You are now catching and shifting so much, and that is why it can also change so quickly. Catching and shifting creates your new norm, so you want to embrace this and do it as much as possible. See it as an accomplishment that you are catching yourself and shifting to aligned patterns and a conscious state of peace, love, joy, and awesomeness.

Giving yourself permission to do it is the key. If you don't use the tool to change your reality, nothing will change. Look at each time you have an opportunity as taking an inch towards the goal. Now can you see how far you truly can go, even in one single day, when you focus on one inch in front of you at a time. Otherwise, you'll just continue to stay in a pattern that sees a mountain blocking your ideal reality. It is possible to move mountains quickly and shift those blocks every single day when you continue to focus inch by inch. As you do, you'll find you look up, and those inches have added up to miles. Suddenly, you've climbed a mountain and are surprised at how quickly your reality truly is changing to the life experience you desire.

Using this tool can require just a quick 30 seconds, or it can be a situation where you might say, *OK, later tonight when I can be more present with this, I'm going to go through this deeper and give myself the opportunity to really clear it.* It will become an even quicker and easier process for you the more you practice it, and you'll eventually do it less and less as it just becomes how you naturally respond. You'll also begin cleaning up the energy in your life so that what you will experience only more peace, acceptance, bliss, and ease as your norm.

I want to also emphasize the importance of going through each of the steps. One of the things I hear the most from those who have felt stuck and like they aren't getting results as quickly is that they continually stop at Step 2 or 3. They feel the emotions and connect to why they are feeling them and simply decide to stay in that. I get it; it is understandable, as that is feeling more than most people have ever allowed themselves to. I will also consistently tell you that I want you to feel all your feelings because that is saying we are worthy of all of the experiences we want, and feeling it is how we will heal it. You are worthy and can be in feeling your feelings as long as required and as much as you want. That means you also can be in choice of how long you want to stay in something and when you want to give yourself permission to move to freedom. Most of us have been trained to feel and go straight into unconscious patterns that don't align us to what we really want and keep the vibrational frequency stuck in the same experience.

There might be moments where you think, *Fuck it. I'm still feeling. I want to sabotage,* and in these cases your little boy or girl inside is simply scared of what you will find or even of being freed from the comfort zone that really isn't comfortable. That's OK too. You'll have some of those experiences and will get to ask yourself: *How much more suffering do I want to endure? Am I ready to move beyond this pattern, heal this, and give myself freedom?* I have individuals share with me that what they used to be stuck in emotionally for a month became a week, a week became a day, a day became a few hours, and eventually it was something they could consciously see and move through within minutes.

This is why It is important to note that to come to peace, to find a solution, and to create change, you get to go through all the steps. This is also important because the last step is what brings you into the action to align your frequency with a high vibration and to create a new pattern and experience. If we don't create a new feeling and experience that overrides our old pattern and engrained feelings or frequency, then we still are reaffirming what we discovered, which keeps us stuck in limitation.

Remember, the way you're responding now is your path of least resistance—whether it's a pattern to instantly respond in anger, frustration, or sadness. That is what has become your trained response you know, and that is the most familiar and easy to you. If you choose to react in the same way, all you are doing is recreating the same shit that will continue to show up. You are now creating a new framework of how you will operate, which will become your new trained response.

This allows you to be in power as a sovereign creator, operating and responding consciously, moment by moment, instead of being a victim to circumstance. You have never been a victim to anything, and now you can see and implement your power of choice instead of being controlled by your unconscious shit.

So many people who are using the 5 Steps suddenly one day realize that they are experiencing what they had wanted. It isn't necessarily a big "ah-ha" as people misperceive is required for a big shift. Yes, you will definitely have deep "ah-ha" discoveries, yet it is the micro alignments day by day that compound and create massive change. *The mastery is in the micro alignment.* I truly have had people say, "Oh my gosh, I'm doing the 5 Steps all the time, I'm seeing everything, and it can feel *overwhelming* and like I have so much work to do." Then, these same people say, "I don't know when it happened; I just realize now I am loving every day of my life. I am feeling such peace and ease around my relationships. I even easily make money now." They can't really pinpoint a moment when it "clicked" because in each moment you are now micro aligning, imprinting it into the way you operate and "clicking" it in. They all continually work together and add up to recalibrate your system into accepting and believing that you are worthy. It gets to be easy, and each micro step compounds until that becomes the macro, which becomes the way you are operating, living, and vibrating.

Remember, before you go through each of the 5 Steps, keep the three pre-steps in mind. The moment something shows up, begin to breathe, with movement if possible, to move the energy and get present with yourself to go inside. Give yourself permission to get curious and ask questions, then soften into acceptance of all you are experiencing and discovering. Remember that whatever is in front of you is the greatest gift for you to now heal and receive the life experience waiting beyond it.

11

Step #1:

What Am I Feeling Right Now?

What exactly am I feeling right now?
Where am I experiencing it in my body?

Creating Awareness in Your Body

When you feel something unpleasant creeping in, it helps to pinpoint what sensations your body is experiencing and where. Remember, if you're angry, you may feel it in your head, neck, or shoulders; if you're sad, your eyes may sting or feel heavy, or you may feel heaviness in your chest. You may feel fear lodged in your stomach or blocking your sexual energy in your pelvis. We want to arrive at a place where you feel peaceful or even tingling and lightness throughout your body, which is joy. Until then, we want to really tune into your feelings and what is in your body that is ready for you to fully witness, accept, and allow its healing.

Step 1 is all about creating an awareness around what you are feeling and giving it a right to exist. By posing the question, "What Am I Feeling?", you take yourself from operating from your head and into your body. Remember, you have been taught to "think it through" and not even recognize what feelings and emotions are happening in your body. This bypassing and ignoring of the emotions and energy is what has been creating everything else you are experiencing. It is the root of what is going on. You might be used to going straight into using your head and asking yourself questions like: *What should I do?* Or *What do I have to do?* This only keeps you disconnected because you are trying to use your head and completely cut off how you feel. This also keeps you in a place where you feel like you have to try, force, and fight. This energy comes from a place of lack because it reaffirms there is something missing and something you have to do that is outside of you.

When we ask the questions, "What am I really feeling?" and "What else is really happening?", we are giving ourselves permission for it to be OK to feel whatever it is that we are feeling. This gives it a voice, a name, and a space to allow it to come up from the shadows and exist. In doing this, you are also teaching yourself the new pattern of allowing, opening up to, and getting curious about things instead of the instant pattern of shutting down. Just applying this can instantly work miracles on your core inner beliefs if you haven't allowed yourself to ever really feel your feelings.

In the "old normal," experiencing an emotion is when your neuropatterns would instantly kick in and your body would be thrown into reaction-mode. With your unconscious mind in the driver's seat, you repeat the same patterns and get the same results—a classic example of subconscious self-sabotage at the hands of emotion. A physical example of this is how we turn to food, alcohol, or any other distracting behavior, such as numbing out with social media, TV, or anything that sabotages the result we really want. Emotional eating, which most of us have done at some point, is a clear example. What happens is when your body experiences stress and is so desperate for relief, you eat to ignore and suppress what you are really feeling because your focused on the food instead of the stress, anxiety, or other feeling that makes your inner child uncomfortable. You are seeking a feeling of relief from the food or other feeling you connect that food with. We know that this doesn't give you what you desire; it only distracts you from resolving the issue and keeps you in the cycle.

How do you stop this shit cycle? Truly pinpoint what you're feeling so that you seek the connections to the trigger and the reason for it. You are stopping the self-sabotage pattern before it starts by just asking this first powerful question, giving yourself permission to really tune into your body and what is there, and taking the next inch and powerful step to move towards healing and resolve it to shift back into feeling good and awesomeness as your norm.

The Hack to Open Up to Your Emotions

The transformational phrase I trained myself with was "Ahhh." It might sound silly, yet it works every time. "Ahhh" or "Ahhh, sweetie," instantly allows me to drop into my heart and apply love to the situation. It reminds me to see the little girl inside who is hurting and be soft with her. It also became an instant reaction and way of seeing others every time I was confronted with someone else in a trigger. I'd look at them and think *Ahhh* and see a little boy or girl hurting. I'd apply the same thing as I learned to be able to allow and hold space for all emotions and all experiences to exist. I became a field of divine unconditional love, support, and acceptance in all relationships by practicing "Ahhh." Other words I use are "Interesting..." to remind myself to get curious. "Interesting..." I attracted that, I had that perception,

I had that experience, and then I'd go exploring. One I started using in the beginning of my journey was "It's perfect" to encourage myself to see everything as perfect and remember that whatever I'm experiencing, I'm doing it perfectly.

You have the power to get in touch with your emotions at any given moment. Sometimes identifying your feelings is easy, but it might feel more challenging if this is new or if you are going deeper into really allowing yourself to fully feel. For example, you may start to feel and know things just don't feel "quite right," or you notice something that happened didn't "feel good," or your body doesn't "feel good," yet you can't quite put your finger on those emotions. Maybe you realize you're not in the energy of love and that you just feel "off."

If you realize something just feels "off" and yet you don't have a name for it, you can still give it a voice or name by saying, "I notice I just feel 'blah.'" or "I notice I feel 'off.'" Then, see if you can drop into more presence with yourself, breathe, and open up even more by asking yourself, *What is really going on, and what am I feeling underneath this?* Do your best to continue to open up more layers and find more specifics. You can always tune into where that sensation is in your body to target more of the core emotion.

I mentioned the core areas where we feel emotion in Chapter 6 and at the beginning of this chapter. You can also get access to these as a reference to support you in the book resources guide at book.marcilock.com/resources.

For example, if you are feeling the sensation in your head, anger is the common core emotion linked to the head, then you can try approaching the emotion with curiosity and asking, "What could I be angry about?"

Remember that every physical symptom is a byproduct of an emotion. Your head does not just ache out of the blue for no reason, even though you've been taught to pass right by it and validate it by saying it's because you've been working all day, or due to the noise from the kids playing, or whatever reason you want to look for. The truth is, the physical expression is coming from an emotion inside.

There are countless times when suddenly I realized my head had some slight discomfort or was giving me even a bigger signal and was hurting. *Hmmm...interesting*, I'd instantly think and ask myself, *What could I be angry about?* I hadn't felt like I was feeling anger or an emotion, and yet my body told me something was going on. The body never lies, and it will always be your first signal there is an emotion going on below the surface. As soon as I get curious and tune into why I could be angry, and sometimes it takes a few times asking and being with it, clarity always shows up.

I may end up laughing, thinking, *Wow, I didn't realize that pissed me off or I had some attachment or expectation around that or I didn't realize that kind of bothered me and I bypassed it because of this....*

This is key to finding the subtle little things that wouldn't otherwise be discovered, addressed, or validated. For instance, if something slightly bothered me that someone said, and I didn't even realize it or acknowledge it, it is most likely a pattern or program that is operating and waiting to be recognized. This discomfort came from a deep core belief and wound that I didn't want to bring up; or I didn't want to address it with the person because I didn't want to bother them; or I feared that they wouldn't like me. In this case, I might have unconsciously or spiritually bypassed it with an "It's not a big deal."

If I get curious about the feeling and ask myself what it is, I then can go through the steps and see if it was just an old attachment for me, a story, or if it was a projection. After that, this could truly be "not a big deal" because I can clear it from it having any negative energy attached to seeing it for what it is and realize it was just my own old attachment and perception. I also get the opportunity through the 5 Steps to reprogram, recode, and imprint the new belief and action to heal it.

If I'm not clear, and I am now noticing that there is more to this to get to peace, a solution, and clarity within, I get to move into aligned actions and ask questions to the person who I felt triggered by. This gives me an opportunity to take responsibility for clear, conscious communication with the person and remain in a clear and positive energy with them that is going to declare what I want to be experiencing to the Universe. Leaving this unclear energy and ignoring it will only keep me in disconnect and separation, and I will continue to attract and receive what I don't want.

Like I mentioned in Chapter 6, the other thing that can support you when looking at where the emotion is showing up in your body is to look at the specific symptom. You can look it up on a body-symptom app that shows the emotional connection. My favorite app I use on my phone when I, my clients, or my boys are experiencing any physical symptom is called "Heal your body A-Z" by Louise Hays. It comes with a long alphabetical list of symptoms that show the emotional connection and gives you a mantra or new belief to apply. You'll be applying the new belief in Step 4, so this can also support you there.

First, start by looking at the negative emotional connection that the app suggests. Ask yourself, *Does that resonate? How could I be feeling that? Did anything happen that could've triggered that feeling?*

One night, Sky had a bloody nose show up before bed. I asked him what he was feeling, and he didn't have an answer; he didn't know. I looked up the connection to bloody nose, and it read, "A need for recognition. Feeling unrecognized and unnoticed. Crying for love."

I then utilized that knowledge to reframe my questions to him and get more curious. "Babes, was there anything that happened today at school that made you feel 'not good enough' and like you weren't recognized or noticed?"

He said, "No."

I said, "Just sit with that for a minute and think about if anything made you feel like you weren't good enough today."

"Ahhhh." He lit up. "I know." And that is when he shared that he was picked last on the team for a game at school. He felt like he wasn't good enough and that he was ignored, not recognized, and not noticed. The little baby boy inside was crying out for love and wanted to feel like he was good enough.

What would have happened if we didn't have the physical symptom to show us that something was there? He would have locked that feeling into his body—that belief that he just wasn't good enough—and it would've imprinted and layered into his system, and then, vibrating and believing that, he would continue to attract and create more experiences to validate it.

After we walked through it and cleared the perceptions, he aligned to his new belief that he is special and unique; that no one else can ever be him. We looked at how he has his own strengths just like everyone else. As we came to his action step (Step 5), the action we took was re-affirming and looking at all the ways he was good enough, special, and unique and all the ways he could recognize that about himself (giving it to yourself first, not expecting it from something outside of you) so that he could really believe the new thought and feel it to be true. His next step was to breathe and feel this new belief in him as he repeated these mantras, reaffirming it: "I love and approve of myself"; "I recognize my own true worth"; and "I am wonderful" along with other affirmations he had created for himself.

Another scenario to be aware of is one where you are in an experience of complete awesomeness. Let's say you are sitting with your love and suddenly, you feel something show up in your body.

It's great if you can catch this because you don't have to have some shit show up to allow yourself to move through the comfort zone to your next level of awesomeness. Most people don't catch it here, and so they create shit or sabotage the experience to create what they truly believe they are worthy of. You can lash out, get edgy, or do anything when uncomfortable to bring this awesome experience to a painful one without being aware. This is why practicing noticing your slightest feelings and these cues is so valuable.

In this example of sitting with your lover, let's say it's a newer relationship and you're blissed out, laughing, and having a great time. Suddenly, he or she tells you they love you. A beautiful moment, and yet you instantly begin to feel discomfort—a tightening in your stomach and a heaviness in your body. In the past, the uncomfortable feeling would've triggered you to create a reason to bolt if one of your survival patterns was to "leave" the situation because the energy felt too overwhelming to deal with. So, you suddenly find an excuse you have to leave, and you shut down the ability to go deeper into love, to allow yourself to receive even more love, and to move into the next level of receiving.

Another response could be that this uncomfortable feeling begins to fester and grow inside you, and you then project that feeling out; creating what you believe deep down to be true, you suddenly become annoyed, start a fight, and reaffirm the very core beliefs that were rising up because they were triggered. Maybe your belief was "I'm not worthy of Love"; "Love doesn't last"; "Love hurts," or one of countless others that reflects what your true relationship to relationship and love is.

The gift is the body is telling you where your comfort zone is and what's in front of you to heal so you now can expand beyond it.

If in this scenario you instantly notice that your stomach got tight. You could ask yourself, *What am I afraid of?*

Wow, you can instantly notice, *I'm afraid I'll be hurt,* or *they'll leave,* or any other reason that fear would come up from hearing "I love you."

You might've felt tightness in your chest, reflecting sadness. *I notice I'm feeling sad. What could I be sad about?* As you move into

157

Step 2, exploring the why, you might discover that you felt sadness because in the past, every experience of a love relationship ended in pain or hurt. Once you learn how to move through these shifts, you'll see how easy it can be to get clear with the feeling and even the person involved. You'll be able to move through it so you don't unconsciously prove yourself right and destroy a relationship because deep down a feeling wants to be seen, heard, and healed.

In these moments that can feel difficult, the key is curiosity. Approach your feelings with love and curiosity, letting that light energy lift you away from the fear and judgement that surround your emotions. Know this: progress comes from CONTINUING to ask the right questions that will allow you to continue to unfold and open up to the discovery. It is a practice of allowing yourself to go deeper, remembering that you are safe, and applying love to the situation. If you stop at Step 1 or 2, you made progress, and that was apparently enough at the time. You also get to continually breathe into it, give yourself permission to lean in, feel more, see through the disguise you gave it as fear, and discover the freedom that is waiting for you. All fear is just waiting for you to transmute it back to love. You can choose how soon you are willing to allow yourself to go there. It is always your own perfect process.

Anytime you identify an emotion—even a vague one—approach it from a place of wonderment. *Interesting,* you might think. *I notice I'm feeling sad in this situation. I can feel it in my body because my chest feels tight.* Or, *Interesting. I notice I'm feeling scared. I can feel it in my body because my stomach is upset.* Or even, *Hmm, I notice I'm feeling shitty again and I'm frustrated by that because I thought that wasn't supposed to happen anymore.*

Your experience may be rather easy. You might ask yourself the question "What am I feeling?" and know what you're feeling. When you know what you're feeling and can have a clear name and label for it, you apply the conscious language of taking full responsibility for what you are feeling as well as allowing it to be fully seen by pointing to yourself and saying, "I notice I feel hurt, rejected, pissed off, frustrated..." or any specific name for the feeling you are feeling. Pointing to yourself is a reminder you can't point outwards or project onto anyone else; **no one "MADE" you feel something—you chose to feel it.** If you are triggered, it is based on what's going on inside of YOU. Eventually, you won't have to point to yourself and will just say it in your head, but this will assist you and train you to begin taking full responsibility as the creator.

If you notice you just don't "feel," then that is OK too. You might be completely shut off from feeling emotions. I would still urge you to go through the 5 Steps around that. "What am I feeling?" *Numb....* "Why? Why have I shut down feeling?"

Once I had a gentleman in one of my masterminds who said he literally couldn't feel and he hadn't really had feeling for over 12 years. He had a business and a beautiful wife and family, yet he felt like he went through life numb and not really allowing himself to experience the joys in life because he didn't know how to feel.

I took him through the 5 Steps, and within minutes, we discovered exactly why he had shut down his emotions. He was raised in a military family and was constantly moving when he was growing up; it was after his second or third move as a young child that he decided that if he let himself feel, he would just get hurt. He had to say goodbye to friends over and over and, not feeling like he could have connections to things in life, he decided it was easier to not feel or become attached to anything. He had been practicing not feeling for a very long time, and now he could see it for what it was and practice the new beliefs, perceptions, and actions to reconnect him to life. He started to cry, looking at all he had shut himself off from, and he said he hadn't cried in over 12 years.

We can also see that how we choose to rewrite our story or reframe all of our experiences can be very powerful. Someone in the same experience could've decided they were so blessed that they got to live in so many places, see so many different cultures, meet a variety of friends, and be exposed to so many different ways of life. They could've decided their parents blessed them with this adventurous life full of opportunities. I'll share with you a process that will take you through a deep experience of shifting the timeline as if it happened the way you now choose and ways that you can completely change your DNA and what's happening in your body to reflect that. It is a time hop into a new reality because you can change what you experienced in your body at a cellular level, and that completely changes your reality now.

If you haven't been feeling, now you can see that you can start to practice. Breathe and say to yourself something that resonates with you, for example: "I am worthy of feeling my feelings"; "It is safe for me to feel"; "I am worthy of feeling"; "My feelings give me freedom"; "I love feeling what life is expressing to me" or "My feelings are my greatest gift."

You can begin to tell yourself this new truth and practice by using the check-in technique I'll be giving you later, where you will stop to see what is happening in your body. Realize that if we don't allow ourselves to feel and to receive the feedback of what's really going on, we just keep spiraling in the same reality. Choosing to block and ignore our feelings only continues the low-vibration and frequency that tells us we are not worthy. The actors around us will continue to support that vibration by reading the same script we have set because we never choose to move beyond this script and into a new level of receiving something different.

So, please, pay attention to any feelings that come up in the slightest that don't feel good. This is your cue to begin the pre-steps and go within. Getting in touch with your feelings means receiving back the power of all parts of you and opening up to even more. If you're consistently stuck in negative emotions or running away from pain because it's uncomfortable, you're just telling the Universe you're not ready for more. That you aren't ready to experience light and love. That you aren't worthy enough to live your life fully in the awesome you choose. And that's bullshit. Because you are.

Facing your feelings allows you to fully process them. Only then can you truly let go of those negative emotions and expand. During this process, you become less reactive. You allow yourself to move in and through even difficult moments with ease, the first step in the journey to complete alignment. Experiencing negative emotions like those above is just part of our process. Now that you've identified and faced your feelings, you get to understand and use that as feedback.

Discovery Opportunity #3:
Explore the Unconscious

1. Is there a time you can connect to now when you gave your power away or made a decision that you can see has formed your life?

2. Tune into each operating system now (Thoughts, Perceptions, Language, Feelings). How have you been continuing to live out this decision? What are the things you think, the things you look for, the words you speak, and the emotions you feel that are creating this to still be true for you?

3. In what ways have you been holding back from being all of you? List out the behaviors that are keeping you small, hidden, waiting, or sabotaging you from being in full expression of all you are.

4. Where have you been looking for permission outside of you? What are you seeking to be able to now feel this permission? What are you wanting to give yourself permission to now experience?

12

Step #2:

Asking Why?

Why?
What am I focused on?
What's the story, thought, perception, belief, or trigger I
am putting attention on?

Know Why You're Feeling It

Giving yourself permission to feel your feelings without judging them is the first step to allowing yourself to utilize it as feedback and to know why you are feeling them. It all comes back to your pre-seven-year-old mind, that little child. You've been living under belief patterns you developed at a young age, and your adult emotions and reactions to situations are byproducts of those subconscious perceptions of what you believe your experience should look like. When your experiences don't look like that, you most likely judge, blame, or shame yourself. You sink and settle into old reactionary patterns and get stuck repeating the same old shit.

Here's the crazy thing, though—those reactions are simply the results of triggers. They actually have nothing to do with the present moment and everything to do with ones that came long before. This core concept can assist you to shift your perceptions and open up a whole new world of clarity around your emotions. Also realize that you can now catch and break down those imprints when you become conscious of them.

To pinpoint "WHY" you felt the way you did, begin to notice and become curious as to what set it off or "triggered" you.

What Is a Trigger & Why Is It Important?

A trigger can be anything that brings up discomfort for you. It can be a word, an image, an action, a smell, someone's body language, a place—literally anything that is connected to an emotion, thought, belief, experience, or story.

A certain flower smell instantly takes me to the memory of my father's and best friend's funerals, which occurred in the same week. If I walked into a store and they had that specific flower smell, it would transport me back in time. That unconscious trigger would cause my body to feel heavy, sad, and connected old beliefs that people always die, love doesn't last, and it's not safe to love. Then, as a result of that trigger, I might go into unconscious patterns to guard, such as looking to create a fight with those around me, to push others away, and block myself from receiving more connection and love. All of this from smelling flowers when walking into a grocery store.

The gift you are learning is to notice and recreate a new association and experience. Now, since I've healed the associations, it doesn't even affect me, and even if the smell did bring me back in time to that quick remembrance of experiences, I have only love and gratitude for them. That means now it instead is utilized as a form of empowerment that instantly takes me to a new association of appreciation for all of those I love and seizing all the relationships I have in my life now.

The old trigger becomes a form of strength. Your wounds and what you may have seen as your weaknesses will become your greatest strengths, your mess will become your message, and your darkness will become your light. The commitment to yourself in getting there is to practice noticing the moment you give your power away to something else and choose to take conscious radical responsibility to shift it.

Years ago, when I first started dating after my divorce to my former, I remember this guy I was dating texted me and asked if I wanted to go somewhere with him. I texted back, "Sure." In the following texts, I noticed a completely different energy, almost cold and irritable, retracting from where he just was, as if he was now trying to push me away; he seemed to suddenly be shutting down the conversation in a hurry and trying to cancel the whole idea he just presented. I felt the energy shift because energy never lies, and so I asked, "Hey, I notice it felt like the energy just shifted a bit. Is there something I said or something that happened that brought something up for you that you didn't like?"

Most people aren't used to complete authenticity and straight-up talk, and you'll discover it is extremely refreshing and makes life so easy. It took him a minute as well as me asking a few questions to guide him to finding more clarity, yet when he did, this is what he discovered: When I said the word "sure," he instantly put up his guard, wanted to shut down, retreat, and push me away. Why? Why would he feel that way? Well, he connected it to when he was married. His experience of the word was when his wife used to say "sure," she didn't really want to do something and acted bothered. His association to the word "sure" was a misleading way of saying yes when you mean no and don't really want to. What did that bring up for him? As you can imagine, it brought up rejection, as if I didn't really want to go; it brought up feelings and images of a failed marriage in his eyes, not being good enough, and all sorts of internal connections to shit.

The moment he finally shared why he felt like suddenly running with me, through my eyes I saw him as a hurt and scared little boy, and my response was... "Ahh, thank you for sharing that with me. I can totally understand why you could feel that way based on your past experience." Then I clarified for him what was true for me. The word "sure" to me meant, "yes," "cool," "sounds great," or "sure, I'd love that."

If I wasn't present to the energy shifting and feeling it even in my body and willing to speak to it, then what could've possibly happened? He probably would've kept trying to do things to push me away, acted like a douche, lashing out, and I clearly wouldn't have opted in for further exploring the relationship.

Also, note that if I hadn't done my own conscious work, then all this would have ended up being an experience of one wounded child bouncing back and forth off of another. His wounded child reaction would then trigger my rejected, wounded little girl, and back and forth we would go until we parted ways, only to reaffirm the same shit deep down and move on to repeat it again with subsequent relationships in our lives.

Triggers are catalysts because they cause reactions. They start something, often leading you to make choices based on information you have in the moment. In other words, triggers cause you to be reactionary, stealing your power of perspective in situations because it creates an illusion in front of you and an emotional internal representation to the past. Your past has you projecting the same illusion into your future based on what you think this moment means from your past. You aren't operating in the present and are only choosing to be a victim to your past. Can you see the chaos involved when you aren't in this very moment, the moment that is happening right now?

It's important to remember you are not the only one operating from this perspective—in fact, most people are walking around operating unconsciously, and we already talked about how 95 percent of what we are doing is memorized when you aren't operating consciously and living in the present moment. When triggers block us from truly understanding and accepting each other, we get stuck in a vicious cycle. That is why we practice seeing ourselves as a little child when we are triggered, as well as any other individual involved. Their fear, screams, or words are simply reflections of how hurt and scared their inner child is and what they are deciding in that little child state.

We all have these beautiful triggers. Your kiddos will most likely model the same type of response mechanisms you've created. They can be carrying the same type of triggers and a commonality of how they react to them from beliefs and experiences they've taken on from the environment they've shared with you. In fact, it's easy for me to identify when my babes get triggered because I can recognize their energy shifts and see the survival patterns show up. They are beautiful reflections for me to see where I do the same things because I know they are mini replicas of me and I can see in them the same patterns that I got to heal and continue to evolve from.

Remember, nothing was wrong before when you were in that place of negativity. All your characteristics and tendencies are your truths because they FEEL true to you based on your beliefs, perceptions, and experiences. What you will get to see and get curious about is what is really true and what just feels true based on past associations as soon as you allow yourself.

When I first was really becoming aware of what I was unconsciously reacting to, I caught myself raising my voice, shouting, and getting frustrated with my kids. I realized that obviously wasn't what I wanted to be doing or be experiencing with them. As I'd go through the 5 Steps, I'd begin to see where I had started to get triggered prior, what emotions I was feeling in my body, and the thoughts and beliefs that were there and I didn't address, which eventually lead me to lash out. Because I was willing to look at it, I was able to see it clearly and simply move through it with the whole 5 Steps. I was then clear on how to align myself to it. I had a new belief, perception, and action I would be practicing and would be able to more easily notice and feel these emotions coming on, which made it possible for me to address them right away.

It obviously was never about my boys; it was about what was building up inside me that made me feel out of control and on edge and therefore I'd end up projecting what I was feeling outside of myself and onto them. Of course, I only wanted to give love, support, and acceptance to my boys, and that had to start first within myself. I then got to apply radical responsibility to create what I wanted in my real-world environment.

That next time I started feeling frustration begin to show up, I would go through the 5 Steps quickly to get clear on why it was even happening, what I wanted, and the action to take. It was as simple as this with my boys: "Hey guys, I'm noticing I'm feeling a bit overwhelmed right now and frustrated. I notice the loud noise is affecting me. What I want is to focus on getting this project done. Would you guys be willing to go play downstairs or outside for a while so I can focus on getting this done and then we can go play together?"

My boys would say, "Sure, Mom," or we'd communicate through options and solutions that felt good and worked for all of us. I stopped having bitch mom moments, which I never wanted anyways; that only created hours of drama and issues to be resolved. Operating consciously and communicating makes life so easy and effective, you will never want to go back into hiding, stories, or wearing a mask and projecting.

Pain is one of our greatest gifts to continue to find these triggers that are the starting point to creating something new. I taught my boys from the time they were young that triggers and our pain moments with each other were our gifts to look at as feedback so we could create even greater together. Anytime we did or still do ever experience any resistance with each other, butt heads, or have any energy or experience that doesn't feel good together or creates disconnect, we always get to look at and celebrate it. We know that the gift is in the shit, and so we are committed to always, always, always looking at what happened to evaluate where we each got triggered and why, as well as what was really true and what we now get to see, believe, and practice to have a greater experience together.

If you had a moment you consider "bad" or not your finest response, it doesn't mean the rest of your day has to be ruined and it certainly doesn't mean anything about who you are. It just reflects the patterns you've learned, the core wounds inside that felt threatened, and what gets to be seen, loved, and healed.

The next simple inch and step you can take is to take interest and get curious in how that process looked and unfolded for you. We aren't going to judge or shame it—just look back on it from a peaceful place. What were your triggers? What did that experience look like for you? What behaviors and perceptions can you change going forward? The simple and easy tool is just to go through the 5 Steps around it and take yourself to clarity and freedom.

So, if you totally fucked it up today when you were triggered, and you didn't get to respond as consciously as you would've liked...guess what? That too serves you and is a gift. I love to think of it this way. I see my interactions with others showing me the layers and the depths I am capable of going like it is a game. If someone says something to you, and you lose your shit, we know the feedback is several-fold deep; you see what triggered you, why, and all the other things that the 5 Steps will reveal, allowing you to heal what's been hiding and now be able to align to a different reality and experience.

Now, let's say you are practicing the behaviors to align to a new belief. Suddenly, a trigger shows up and you simply notice it, breathe, and consciously respond differently to it. Then, let's say this person who might've triggered you takes it just one step further, and then...you lose your shit.

The shit show was a perfect one.

What you just got was the perfect feedback of how many layers or levels you could go before you lost your shit; how much you have mastered your consciousness or mastered your ability to respond consciously. I had a divine teacher in my life share with me this analogy I then adopted of seeing relationships as this game with them as my PETs, my personal emotional trainers, reflecting back to me my level of ability to respond with love, softness, acceptance, compassion, and understanding. They also continue to assist me to see and reveal what else inside me still gets to be loved and healed so I can become that reflection back in those situations. I am getting practice to continually see my ability to respond consciously instead of reacting. Now, I see it all as beautiful feedback.

Whatever showed up, whether it was yelling at your kids or lashing out at your spouse, employee, or loved one, guarding and pushing away, hiding, or sabotaging the life you want in any way, remember, your darkness, too, serves you just as much as your light. Learn from them both. Love them both.

The Conscious Response to your Unconscious Reaction

There is another response system we get to look at so you aren't sabotaging your efforts. If you get triggered, and your response is, *Dammit... Shit!* or *Fuck... I did it again,* or any other response that is giving off an energy of negativity, judgement, shame, or blame, then all you are doing is reaffirming to your core self that you suck and aren't worthy.

Along with this, remember that what you resist persists; wherever you put your energy will grow and expand. Responding with an energy that says it was bad or wrong only projects that very message and energy into the Universe for it to come right back at you to fight again. This is another place of learning to respond consciously and master your consciousness. It isn't anything to be upset over, and no extra drama is required. Even after the shit has been strewn all over, you can bring yourself back to gratitude and appreciation for it. Replace the words that come out as negative judgements with the words "interesting" or "it's perfect," as you are already practicing catching the triggers as they come up.

You can have a big dramatic shit show, and after the dust has settled, you can remind yourself that it taught you exactly what you needed to see, and you experienced it perfectly. If you lose your shit, you are losing your shit perfectly. Just acceptance of what is or has happened puts you in the right energy and understanding to be able to learn from it and heal it. If you judge and blame yourself for it, creating a story that if you do that, you aren't perfect, then so be it; your wish is your command, and you'll continue to experience struggle in your life, striving to be something other than you are. You will only continue to create the resistance showing up over and over again, reaffirming your belief of who you are and your reality.

The goal isn't to avoid triggers either because then we stay stagnant and in our same comfort zone. Having a trigger doesn't mean you have to lose control from it until you shed it either. It just means there was something that brought up a discomfort, pain, annoyance, frustration, or feeling that took you out of alignment with your natural state of love, joy, and bliss.

The practice to overcome it is first in learning to not react to the trigger or become a victim of it. You are worthy of your experience, and so is the other person or persons involved. Just allow yourself to notice the feeling that comes up without choosing to react, and remember you get to breathe and choose a conscious response instead. You can rid yourself of triggers—and the negative emotions they stir up—when you identify them first and then create completely different beliefs, feelings, and responses to them.

So, what if you don't know why something triggered you? Let's say that you noticed a feeling of heaviness come up in your chest, and/or you notice that you are feeling sad or some irritability but can't pinpoint a cause; then what?

Apply the other cue statements from Step 2, which are "What am I focused on?" and "What's the story, thought, perception, belief, or trigger I am putting attention on?"

When you stop and give attention to what was just flashing through your mind, what you might've just thought about, saw, or heard, even for just a moment, you'll discover the beautiful subtleties that slipped past, probably many times before. As I traveled the world and was in the most beautiful paradises, experiencing my dream life, I'd all of a sudden feel a subtle heaviness show up in my chest or stomach or another physical symptom. I'd simply get curious, and that would allow me to find something that wanted to be heard and seen and had been waiting to surface to allow it to heal. Then, what was available was even more joy, bliss, prosperity and awesomeness to receive. It could've been a quick thought about my boys back home, and maybe, even just for an instant, I had a thought attached that, such as, *I must not be a good mom because I'm away.* Obviously, this came from an old association or story that I'm not a good mom unless I did everything a certain way, which stemmed from a religious upbringing and limiting-belief programming. Even though I consciously knew that it wasn't true and had shifted these stories years ago, it could still be a trigger, which revealed that it required some more love or levels of acceptance to really align to and hold that new belief.

If I allowed that thought to slip by and have its voice without bringing presence to it, clarifying the real truth, and releasing the emotional frequency attached to the limitation, then the old belief is validated and will continue to live on. This is only going to build and create more shit to deal with in the future and require even more time, effort, and energy. Instead, we can quickly pay attention and save time, effort, and energy and only create flow moving forward by catching the unconscious.

I choose to see it and get present to my little girl inside that had a judgment towards herself. *Ahh, sweetie, what are you feeling?* The journey with the 5 Steps can quickly be moved through to see it. *Why? Oh, that came up from that old belief that I have to look a certain way and have to be around my children all the time to be a good parent. Oh! Haha. Silly human stories.* These old stories just want to say hello sometimes to see what you really believe now to be true. Once seen, it can be shifted to align to what was really true—that I love my boys dearly and was desiring to connect with them. Then, I could create that without adding the drama, accepting the old ideas and lies, or creating my own suffering.

"How you CHOOSE to RESPOND is what you get NEXT."

Get Off the Merry-Go-Round

Realize that the journey to enlightenment is to be "in LIGHT" and to align to a life of joy. If the entire process of healing and clearing meant that you had to dig through or remember every single experience, have the exact vision of what went down, and know clearly what happened that created a limitation for you, then we'd be stuck in the processing game forever. You could continue to stay in the "look at the shit" cycle for your entire life.

This isn't the purpose of asking "Why?" Yes, we want to create as much clarity as possible so we have all the information and feedback we can to utilize, clear, and heal. From one instance, so many gold nuggets can show you many beliefs and patterns and how these are showing up in all areas of your life. That is why we want to get as curious as possible and connect as many dots as possible so that we are healing as much as possible.

Our goal, however, is to discover for ourselves the root beliefs or decisions we made that we are operating out of and heal them, not dwell on them. Everyone in some way has almost all five of those root core beliefs: I'm not good enough; I'm not worthy; I'm not loved/loveable; I don't trust myself, others, or life; or I'm not deserving. You most likely have your one or two that are your main core wounds that most of your life's creations are built around and reflections of all of them arising in your life at some point. If you find that something triggered you and you don't have any specifics around it as to why, such as a memory or reason why you might be feeling this way, then you get to give yourself the opportunity to look deeper. So often, if we don't see it right away, then we just want to think it isn't working and move on. The truth is you've never allowed yourself to be with yourself even deeper and given the space for what is there to arise. Soften, and ask your inner self again, as if you are talking to a three year old and playing a game, "Why could I be feeling this way?" I've discovered huge programs and beliefs creating major sabotage and disconnect in someone's ability to receive money, love, and freedom all come into clarity when they just allowed themselves to go a little deeper and find what had been there under the surface all along.

Now, if nothing does come up for you, then you want to continue to move forward. You might just be aware of and connect that whatever you are feeling is from those old core wounds and belief systems of the past. This could look like... "Why I'm feeling this way is because of that old belief system that I have to be perfect to be loved, that I think things have to look a certain way, or that I am afraid of not being enough."

Connect it to as much of a "why" as possible in order to connect the dots to move forward and choose what you do want to experience and what new beliefs will become your new programs to operate from in the next steps.

The Power Comes from Powerfully Owning It

To apply this shift effectively, it is important to understand conscious language as it relates to both yourself and others. You don't want to get caught up in a blame-game/finger-pointing shit show based on how you were programmed to communicate.

You can easily begin to spot the words that take ownership of the situation out of your hands, such as you "you," "make," or any other word that points to someone else and reflects it was done to you, which is giving away your power.

Let's recap and look at some examples of how to practice taking full responsibility and applying conscious language.

- Step 1: What am I feeling? Point to yourself and say, "I notice I feel _____," paying attention to where emotions are manifesting in the body and taking responsibility of what you are choosing to feel. If you find yourself saying, "You made me feel this way," that is pointing at someone else and putting the blame on them instead of owning how you are choosing to feel. If this happens, you have an opportunity to catch it and come back to radical responsibility for what you are choosing.

- Step 2: Why do I feel this way? Build on your phrase from Step 1. For example, "I notice I feel _____ when _____."

The "when" can be shared in any way in which you are taking full responsibility. What you get to avoid is: "...when you did that"; "When you said that, it made me..."; "You hurt me when..."; "You made me sad, frustrated, angry, etc., when..."

You can instead practice responsibility by reframing your statement with you as the person with the power and full responsibility:

"I notice I felt sad when I heard that (statement/word), and I instantly felt like I wasn't good enough."

"What I took on from that is that *I'm not enough*"

"I had the thought: *I suck, and I wasn't good enough.*"

"It took me back to a memory in my past where I felt not good enough"

"It brought up a past belief for me that I'm not good enough."

"It reminds me of my past experiences when I felt like I wasn't enough."

"I notice I feel this way because I have an attachment to that word/action/image because of my past experience of..."

Isn't this glorious? You can see that you are catching your stories, thoughts, programs, patterns, and social agreements that the other person probably didn't even know about and, of course, wasn't intending. By seeing what the trigger was connected to, it shows us "why" we had the trigger and that it actually has nothing to do with the other person at all. Now you are capable of completely shifting because it comes back to you. In relationship, you can receive and give the most beautiful gift of vulnerability with those you love and get a greater understanding and connection to them. It really does and will open up way more connection and love as you practice.

Please be aware that what you might experience is a defense mechanism from the other person. You might say everything perfectly consciously, and yet the other person might think that you are complaining about them and think they did something wrong because you or they are triggered. If that is the case, again, you can simply receive it, see it as their story they are feeling to be true, just like you were having yours, and honor it.

As we begin to communicate consciously and drop our masks, we are retraining and reprogramming out of defensive communication and blaming. You get to be the example of the type of communication you receive by giving it first. Even if you are operating consciously, the person you are communicating with might not have the blessing of the same inner-standing as you. No matter how much they might point the finger and use the words "you made me feel" or " you did that to me," you can continue to breathe, allow, and master each level of the game and your consciousness by responding in love instead of losing your shit and creating more struggle.

Most people experience a bit of resistance as they are learning to apply what can be like a new language, just as if you were learning to tie your shoes for the first time. The more you apply the 5 Steps and practice, the easier it becomes; the pathways become set, and it becomes how you see things clearly and what you think and now operate from. Life will get massively easier, and your vibration will remain high when you aren't pulled into drama and don't create it either.

If you want even more support, clarity, and examples to work through your languaging and the tools to building and creating a new paradigm of conscious, awakened, and epic relationships, then I'd suggest diving deeper with me in my coaching "Awakened Relationships." You can find this on marcilock.com or follow the direct links on the book resources page.

Questionable & Unquestionable Truths

To assist you deeper in back-and-forth communication, there is something very important to have awareness around, and that is the difference between questionable and unquestionable truths. Everything is really a subjective truth because all things are true based on your perception and what you are looking for.

What we've learned and how we've been trained in our communication skills usually has us unconsciously running to claim the award for the victim position. We have learned to defend ourselves, point the finger, and then "prove" that we are "right." Does this sound like a sovereign creator or a victim? When you can see consciously that by doing this you are racing for the victim trophy, it might have you stop and consider a different way of being.

We know what is really going on is that inside is just a scared little boy or girl showing up who is afraid of what is happening because of some past programs, lies, and limitations they are feeling or perceiving. How do we get past these unconscious auto-responses and reactions of feeling hurt, putting up our guard, and then defending, which only keeps us in an unconscious victim cycle?

It's time to understand what can be questioned and what cannot, or in other words, what can be respected and honored by not questioning it because it isn't ours to own. These are the two types of truths more easily described as questionable and unquestionable truths. Yes, of course, we know that you can create an argument over anything, and I've told you to question all things. What I want to bring light to is a higher level of consciousness as to why some things simply get to be received because everyone has the right to their own truth.

Just ponder these questions: Can you be in anyone else's body but your own? Can you be in anyone else's head but your own? Hopefully you got a "no" for both of those because even if you are psychic, super tapped into energy and all sorts of multidimensional capabilities, you truly aren't existing and living inside anyone but yourself.

So, we know that the only TRUTH we can ever claim to actually know is what is true for us. This means it is what is coming from our own head or our own body. That is an "unquestionable" truth.

This also means that we can never actually know what is true for someone else because we are not in their head or their body and cannot speak for them as to what they are feeling or thinking; therefore, whatever your interpretation is about the other person is "questionable." It is not concrete.

That means you can't decide what is absolutely true for someone else based on what you saw and felt. We actually have no idea how or what another human is experiencing. The only way forward, then, in the highest vibration and inner-standing is to allow, respect, honor, and trust the perfect process for others and give them the space they require to peacefully exist within their own truth.

If you feel or perceive something, it simply is "what it is" for you. What someone else is feeling or thinking simply is what is true for them at the time. There's no need to try and prove or defend it—that's just adding more struggle, suffering, and drama. No one can question what you think or feel inside of you, just as you can't tell someone what they think or feel because you do not exist inside of them. If you catch yourself using language such as, "you think I'm stupid," "you don't like me," or "you meant to hurt me," that is all projection and assumption based because you are not inside of the other person and you can't actually know that. What you can do is take radical responsibility that reflects in your language as you share authentically: "I notice that I feel stupid, or unlovable, or hurt when I heard or saw that." You can then question your thoughts and perceptions that you have with others to clarify what was also true for them and get rid of the drama and chaos of projections and assumptions if you do want to move beyond the illusions and discover what will really serve you in creating the relationships and life you desire.

This is where so much disconnect happens in relationships because we try to tell someone else what we believe they think, feel, believe, are or were doing, all of which is really just our projection onto them. We think we are defending ourselves by denying what they feel or think to be true, but that is just playing the victim and trying to prove that we are right. We know now that this is also just a scared little boy or girl that chose to see and experience what they did based out of their deep fears, beliefs, and hurts. This is an important piece that will save you from a lot of struggle and patterns that keep you on the dysfunctional merry-go-round.

Think about if you have ever denied someone of what they are thinking or feeling or if someone has ever done this to you. This might look like, "No, I didn't do that" or "No, that's not what I said." Notice how it feels when someone tells you "No," that what you are feeling is not what you are feeling, or questions what you think and feel to be true for you. It feels like you aren't being heard, seen, felt, or understood. When you choose to say "No, I didn't do that," you are only defending. It keeps the spiral of defending and proving continuing, keeping you in the cycle. Our little boys and little girls all just want to be heard, seen, understood, and loved for who we are.

Even if you really didn't say it or really didn't do it, according to your own truth or perception, you still can honor what is going on for them and appears or feels to be true. It is what is going on in their head and body, and they are the only ones who can speak their truth for themselves. All the tension, struggle, and drama we create is simply a failure to recognize all things are true and have a right to exist and each person's emotions are valid. We can take responsibility for our own feelings while not passing judgment on the feelings of others. This means we now honor each person to have the experience they are having and choose their truth and whatever it is they want to be learning and growing in. Their choices of what they do with it will create the result for their life just as how you choose to respond to the experience right in front of you will create yours for you as well.

A phrase I used to remind myself of when I'd catch that energy was that you can't fight a fight with a fight. This would remind me that giving fight or resistance energy was only going to create more fighting, trapping you in the very matrix of struggle and declaring you only want more of it. Resistance only creates more resistance, struggle, tension, and drama, so let's choose to do something different with it to get a different result. It's really simple, just appreciate it.

"Thank you."

"Thank you for letting me know that's what you thought I said or that's what you heard. I appreciate you sharing, and I can understand how you could feel that way based on that perception. I'd love to share what my experience was, what my intentions were, and what is true for me. What I meant by that phrase was…"

We can appreciate getting the feedback of where someone is coming from and what is actually going on behind the lens so we can then create clarity. If you love someone, wouldn't you want to know what they truly are perceiving and feeling? It doesn't do any good to tell them that what they are thinking or feeling isn't valid. Instead, you can choose to hear them and say, "Thank you for sharing. I can appreciate that" or "I can understand that," and validate what they thought and felt, assuring them that what has been shared has been heard and honored, that they are safe to feel and experience all things with you and that it has been received.

You can even get clearer by repeating what you think they are sharing and you are understanding: "What I hear you saying is that when I do that, to you it looks like this, and it brings up these feelings for you. Is that what you are saying and what you experienced?"

Then, you can share the next level of clarity and break down each of the fears, perceptions, or stories that came up by moving through the 5 Steps to arrive at understanding and the new actions that feel good for everyone, are in the highest good for everyone, and are in alignment with what you want to experience.

This is how you make this simple. You take radical responsibility for your own thoughts and feelings, and you honor and acknowledge whatever thoughts or feelings others are experiencing too.

The Blame Game Is a Cycle of Unhappiness

Seeing beyond the illusion and that everything is a reflection of what is happening inside can give us continual freedom. As my boys experienced what you might label as being bullied or kids being mean, I would share with them that whenever someone is mean, it was just a reflection that they weren't happy with themselves. Blame is another big beautiful red flag reflecting the unhappiness someone is experiencing inside. This is important because as you continue to expand into even more love, bliss, and joy and be the light you are creating for your world of happy, you'll get to see it for what it is and give yourself the freedom to continue to shine in all of your light and be who you are here to be.

Yes, one of the tools to healing and alignment we have is to take radical responsibility for everything showing up in our world and get curious as to why we attracted it and what feedback it gives us for even greater. If we look more closely at this though, we'd find that this would only keep us in a loop and cycle our whole lives, asking why we attracted that and taking responsibility for the way other people are showing up in the world. This would only be to create a continual story of our own suffering and unconscious codependency by having an attachment that you require the world and others to show up a certain way for your own happiness.

It can create suffering when you believe that you will finally "arrive" on your spiritual journey only when everyone and everything is showing up in your world in love, light, and peace. There is never a place to "arrive" at because you are always perfectly where you're required to be right now, just as everyone is in their perfect experience. As you align, your entire world will shift around, and that doesn't mean that all ways of life won't be continuing around you; you will just have a different response and interaction with them.

The next layer of your awakening calling you forth, my loves, is to know and experience that other people's ideas, expressions, behaviors, and ways of life or any outside circumstances are not what determine your state of happiness and way of being in the world. In other words, when you operate from your emotional wholeness, no one can take you out of your own happiness. Heaven is your state of being because there is no attachment to the experiences of other people; you simply honor them, and they don't take you out of your truth or the reality you choose. Life can only add to your happiness, but nothing can take your happiness from you.

Our journey is to alchemize and heal everything in resistance. I've experienced many individuals on their spiritual journeys refer to family members they had to "cut off" so they could be peaceful, happy, free, and discover their healing. Love is the inclusion of all things, not the exclusion of anything. These are beautiful spaces we can see calling us to even greater abilities to heal and love. If you ever catch yourself in the blame game, where you find other people are affecting you, it is only revealing what inside is now ready to be healed and loved. It is calling for you forward to give yourself your own healing and be able to fully be with and honor others without it taking you out of your own peace.

You might experience relationships in your life that will be a part of your lifelong journey, such as family members who haven't had the same gifts of awareness as you. It might be a common pattern of blame or unconscious tactics of manipulation or shaming that a parent or loved one uses out of their own deep hurt and cry for attention and love when they interact with you. Their projection onto you that you are responsible for their happiness based on if you are showing up the way they want you to is just an outward reflection of their unhappiness. This doesn't mean that their pattern has to change for you to be happy; that would only be adding another attachment into the mix. If it is affecting you, what is showing up is your attachment for them to change their behavior and allowing the experience they are having or patterns they exude to take you out of your state of joy.

If you saw it for what it was and looked closely, you'd see that if this is their pattern, then it is most likely operating in all aspects of their world. It isn't you making them unhappy; most likely everything is making them unhappy. This is a mentality of seeing life through the lens of being the victim who is not responsible. *If my co-workers did this, I'd be happy at my job…. If my partner acted this way, then I'd be happy in my relationship…. If I didn't have this issue, then I could do that….* We already revealed earlier how this is the common illusion society operates from of "Have-Do-Be." "If I had that, I could do that thing, and then I'd be happy." We already dissolved this illusion, and you know that you get to Be-Do-Have to ever get what you want. Be the vibration, do the things that someone in that vibration does, and you will match the frequencies to manifest, receive, and have it.

The healing available is to let go of all attachments and to see them out of their true divinity, knowing they are just reflecting the unhappiness and hurt child within. Your opportunity is to not react to the blame or shame and instead to consciously respond by being and holding a field of divine unconditional love, support, and acceptance. You can do this while standing in your own truth and honoring them for the experience they are choosing as their current truth.

Instead of blame, we can practice finding grace in all things. The greatest gift we can give ourselves and others to receive our own healing and liberation is to love what is right now. Love whatever life has delivered and brought for our perfect journey. When we can find ways to love what we would've deemed unlovable, unimaginable, and the worst experience we've ever had, we become the alchemists we are capable of as we turn it into our greatest experiences we could've ever received. This doesn't mean we have to take responsibility for the event; it does mean that we are always responsible for how we respond and what we decide to do with it. As you free yourself of whatever is creating your own suffering, you also then shine that light of liberation for others to also receive.

"I'm Sorry" Feeds the Blame Game Cycle

When you were a child, do you remember being told "Say you are sorry?" Saying sorry has most likely been something we've all been taught since the time we were little and it's how we learned to operate from blame. You might be wondering, *What's wrong with that? Isn't saying you are sorry a good thing?* Let's evaluate it and question all things. First, nothing is ever wrong because we all have a choice, all things have a right to exist, and there is no such thing as good, bad, wrong, or right. I'll keep reaffirming that for you so that you can see all things are simply an experience that have an energy and vibration. What we can look at is the result of that energy or vibration and question whether it is what we want.

Let's look at it in a few other ways and evaluate its effectiveness. What happens when you say, "I'm sorry"? Say it out loud and just notice what comes with that. You've most likely used it your entire life and you also might have great associations to it because to you it represents forgiveness, taking responsibility, or mending a situation. But I want to open the paradigm a bit wider to look beyond the surface interpretation we've been taught and see the actual energetic frequency that is coming through.

Remember that the frequency and energy of "shame" is the lowest vibrating energy that exists. Whenever shame frequency is involved, it is an instant blocker to manifesting and receiving. When you say "I'm sorry" to someone for something, whether or not you sincerely feel bad about it and are looking for a way to express it, what is happening underneath is causing more damage than you most likely realize. The reason we say "sorry" is to portray we feel bad about something or because we feel we have to say something to acknowledge a wrong.

Can you feel the heaviness of all of that? What it is really about? In this way, it is about shaming yourself for being bad and reaffirming to your core self that you did something wrong and have something to be sorry for. What do you think has been engrained in your system from a lifetime of saying sorry?

I mentioned above that when we are children, many times we are forced and trained to say we're sorry if something we did was deemed by one of the adults in our lives as bad or wrong. What we are learning is a bypass mechanism to not actually deal with the actual problem, pattern, or action that created something we didn't want to experience. We are taught "I'm sorry" and usually aren't taught any form of communication to create solutions because these words are supposed to fix it so that everyone can move on.

Standing over a child who took a toy from another and forcing the child to say, "I'm sorry" and give it back only shows the child that if he says, "I'm sorry," he isn't in trouble anymore; the negative attention is then dropped. He may also learn that if he does anything that someone doesn't like, he just says, "I'm sorry," and that's it, even if he doesn't feel remorse.

Have you met those people who say they are sorry for everything, or those who feel like everything is their fault, or people who have to make everyone around them happy and wear a mask so that they will be liked and not rejected? This is how many of us learned to interact with the world. This is another example of how we've learned to bypass what we really feel, hide, pretend, and show up how we think we will be accepted.

As I dove into the depths of operating in conscious relationships and got curious about what was really happening in situations, I began to look deeper at the energy of all things. I first started to notice this with my boys. I'd see one of them do something that upset the other, and then the other one would just say "sorry." Sometimes this was accompanied by a bit of an attitude, which could indicate that he didn't really feel sorry. I'd also see one of them actually feel sorry and say sorry, yet my other son would be feeling hurt and still acted distant, frustrated, and angry for a while. I evaluated that saying sorry didn't actually resolve anything.

Our opportunity is to simply question what we've been trained to do and see if it is really working for us. Is saying "I'm sorry" really fixing anything? What we learned and are teaching our kids isn't about taking responsibility or creating solutions; what we are reaffirming is that our children are bad or wrong and they have to act a certain way to make everyone happy, for people to like them, and to not get in trouble.

As parents, we often also attach a punishment with an action because again, that is what we were taught is how a child would then to learn how to behave. Let's go back to the example where the child took another's toy without asking. After giving it back and being forced to apologize, the parent makes the child stand in a corner and have a time out, separating him from his peers so he has to miss out on play. In one sense, you could say that you are teaching him to take responsibility and to learn how to treat people with respect and ask for something if he wants to use it.

What else could also be happening and going on for that child? What feelings are being absorbed into his system? What is he thinking, and what beliefs are being created or reinforced? Is he really learning how to interact with other children or create solutions? He is being told he did something bad and wrong (*I am bad and wrong. My mom is mad at me or my friend is mad at me*) and that he should feel shame and blame (*I'm missing out; I'm not worthy of play or fun; or I have to act a certain way for them to like me.*)

If a child is being forced to sit in the corner and miss out, is he feeling good feelings? No, and most likely he is feeling hurt, upset, angry, and like he is being wronged. Maybe the situation didn't even happen the way the adult perceived it. The entire time he is sitting there, he is soaking in all these feelings and may be concluding he has to be sneaky and manipulative to get what he wants and avoid getting in trouble because he didn't learn any solutions. He learned "sorry" and punishment. This type of discipline we've learned only creates more disconnect between you as the parent or guide and your children because they don't feel loved, accepted, and approved of by you; they may actually feel scolded, hurt, wronged, and afraid to be themselves.

The other thing I noticed with my boys is that if one of them brought up something that they didn't like, and the other one went into defense, instead of each of them sharing each other's perspectives, they would just say, "I want you to say you're sorry" or "Say you're sorry." It was obvious that with the training, "sorry" was an acknowledgment that the other person did something wrong, and it was a way of feeling validated or acknowledged that they felt hurt.

What I gathered from this is that we all really just want to be understood, heard, and seen and feel important. I had taught my boys to say they were sorry from the time they were little, just like I had learned. It was still the best I knew how at the time. As I began to open my awareness of the dysfunction in many of these trainings, programs, and patterns that were simply taught and repeated, I awakened to a new awareness of what was really going on underneath.

We began our journey of learning how to openly receive whatever someone was feeling, thinking, or upset about and to say "thank you" to acknowledge it, appreciate it, and then begin to create solutions. It took some time, as they wanted to say sorry and move on or wanted to hear sorry. We discussed that "sorry" doesn't solve the conflict; "sorry" is just saying that you did something wrong. We discussed that there is no such thing as bad or wrong because it always teaches us something. We can now see that when we do something or say something that results in another person feeling hurt, then it teaches us what isn't working and what we can now do to have an even greater experience together. We discussed that this understanding and sharing was a gift and that we now knew how to support each other even more and communicate better so that we could always have what we wanted together and could be happier.

We continued to practice leaning into any resistance as our gift of feedback and appreciating it. We created a way that my boys could practice the 5 Steps together so they could both be heard and understood and they could learn how to find a solution together. Whenever they had a disconnect, they would sit down in front of each other with their knees touching and hold hands, or if they were too angry to hold hands, they at least had their knees touching yoga style. One of them would hold a crystal, or selenite stick, or whatever item we had to signify it was that person's turn to talk. They'd practice saying, "I notice I feel..." and "when that was said or done, I felt like..."

Then they would state what it was that they wanted, which you'll learn more about in Step 3, such as, "I want to have a turn too," or "I want to feel like you love me and aren't thinking that I'm stupid," or whatever would come out that they want to feel or experience with each other.

Then it was the other person's turn, and they learned to start by appreciating the information they just received and saying, "Thank you."

"Thank you for letting me know you thought that, felt that, or it looked like that to you."

Then this person would get to clarify what they really meant and start back on Steps 1-3, sharing what they felt, why they felt it, and what they want to experience. They would take turns going back and forth until they fully saw and understood what the other person was thinking and feeling from the experience. They clarified with each other what was true for them, what they really meant, and what they wanted to feel and experience with each other. Then they could together move onto Step 4, which was to have a new belief, and Step 5, going into the action to create what they wanted. They also knew they would be practicing their new ways of interacting and communicating that they learned from the experience in the future instead of just repeating the old ways, which led to conflict. This only allowed our relationships to get greater and greater. They truly are best friends and true growth partners to each other.

Now, believe me, it wasn't always this smooth. As I guided them through this process, there were times when everyone would take a few minutes to breathe and evaluate what they were feeling on their own so that we could be clear in our communication and could be open to receive it in softness, calmly and effectively.

There were also many times we were just about to walk out the door for school and they were having negative energy between each other. I would say, "OK, what's going on, guys? What are you feeling?" We'd sit down and walk through all the perceptions and experiences, all the way to solution. The nanny would sit and wait, or I'd take them to school late, rearranging my entire day if necessary so that I could take the time then to go through the steps with them so we could arrive back to a state of feeling clarity and peace. How we are vibrating and feeling will always be my highest priority, and what they were vibrating would always take precedence over anything else because of the magnitude of its effects.

Sky's response a lot of times would be to say, "It's fine" and "It's not a big deal," yet I knew sitting with that energy all day was not fine and would be a big deal. It was only going to sit inside them all day and create deep imprinted beliefs and feelings, and those emotions would lead to sickness and even more shit showing up for my babes. So, instead, we'd drop everything and get clear, clear the energy, and come to understanding and peace so that they could go create an awesome day, have amazing experiences, reaffirm powerful beliefs about themselves, and be in a high vibration that served them and others as well.

190

It did take practicing this new pattern over and over and over again until it became smooth, the path of least resistance, and our nature. We practiced a new way of being because we knew that we got to create our experience and our reality. We are the source of our experience, and so we committed to going through the steps and getting better and better at our own expression and communication with others so that we could all be honored, feel good, and get what we wanted.

What happened along the way was that we began to really believe that all feelings are OK, all things have a right to exist, thoughts are just thoughts, and that doesn't mean they are true, and that we all are worthy and deserving of having whatever we want. We learned that we could communicate to arrive at a solution. It taught us to always evaluate things because we can't know what's true for someone else and because everyone is worthy of having their own thoughts, feelings, and experiences. We are all worthy of feeling good and being happy, and so we always find a solution to honor everyone and bring ourselves back into happiness and experiencing awesome.

Their dad, my former, once said to me, "I just have to say, the boys are so good at communicating with each other; it is so nice." He said that he didn't know what I did to teach our boys but he was always amazed to see how they could communicate and work through anything and that they were so good at it.

My boys are truly best friends, remain super close, and are amazing support systems and growth partners to each other. They still have their moments, their disagreements, and differences in perceptions about experiences with each other and also with me, yet we always know how to get clear on why we feel something and what we want to create instead.

Let's go back to the example of a child taking another's toy. Instead of walking over to the fighting children, scolding the one who took the toy, asking him to say he's sorry, and then putting him into the corner, what if we took a different approach?

You could walk over to the two children fighting, get on their level, and ask one of them, "What are you feeling?" Then, "Why are you feeling that way?" Once he responds, you could say, "Ahhhh, I can understand why you feel that way."

Then, you can ask the same questions and give the same validation to the other child, allowing both of them to be heard.

You could then teach them to communicate to find a solution: "So, what you are saying is that you also want a turn and to play with this toy, is that right? What are some ways we could do that? How could we make that happen? What kind of game could we make to both get a turn with the toy? What do you think would work for you both to get some time with it?"

"Do you think it feels good when we get to all play with the toys we want? Are there lots of toys here that we can all enjoy? What other ways could we create this? Maybe we could set a timer to take turns. What other toy or game would you love to play with while the other person has their turn?" Suddenly, they become engaged in a game of "how to create a solution," where the end goal is everyone getting a turn.

You could also get curious about what they could do next time if they want to play with something someone else is playing with. "What do you think you could do to let him know that you would like to also have a turn with this? Is there a way you could ask him or let him know that you'd like a turn? How could you nicely request it? How can we all have fun together and be happy?"

Asking questions curiously allows them to learn to create solutions. There are many more areas of support to allow children to learn to communicate with each other, but it starts here, and with your own inner child as well. It can be as easy as learning to move through the 5 Steps so we become aware of all we are experiencing and how to move towards what we want.

You might still be thinking, *When I say I'm sorry, I truly mean it. How can it be bad for me to say "I'm sorry" when that is what I am feeling?* You will always get to choose what is best for you and what will create the results you want in your life. Just consider the energy and vibration attached to it and if it ultimately holds the highest vibration for you to use. If we really are sorry, we can also learn to express that without attaching any energy or program of shame to ourselves or the lie that the experience was bad or wrong. Language holds extreme power in its frequency and what it puts out into the Universe to receive next.

Why would we do anything other than honor the experience that was a gift to teach you how the person you care about really feels and what hurt them? Appreciating it, acknowledging it, and honoring it is what they are seeking.

"Thank you, I appreciate you sharing that"; "I feel that"; "I can see that"; "I hear that"; "I acknowledge that"; "I feel so deeply that I caused you pain; that was not my intention"; or "I was not wanting to hurt you"; or "I didn't realize how much that was hurting you"; "I wasn't aware I hurt you"; "I wasn't intending to hurt you"; "I can see now how that hurt you, or how my actions could feel painful, or weren't clear"; or "I deeply appreciate this clarity and feedback, showing me where else I can grow and create an even greater experience" are all great responses that don't include "I'm sorry." You might find in a situation it resonates to say, "I apologize you felt that way, as it was not my intention." Tune into the energy for you of what you are saying and how you clearly honor the experience for each person. When I first heard the ho'oponopono prayer, which uses the words "I'm sorry" in it, I had to clarify that when using this prayer and the words "I'm sorry," that it was coming from a place of apologizing for any hurt or pain instead of a blame and shame energy and choose to align my feelings with it. You can choose the energy and be aware of what you are saying to yourself and putting out vibrationally.

Take full responsibility, appreciate it, and learn from it. Focus on what you want to create and how you will now create that with this person. That means to accept, acknowledge, appreciate, and embrace all of it to align the energy of gratitude and love for it as you now move into the actions of creating it as your way of being.

The CONTAINER of Unconditional Love, Support & Acceptance

The only "job," aka opportunity or even responsibility, you actually ever have in relationships is to hold the container of unconditional love, support, and acceptance. Yes, that can bring up a ton of questions, which only gives us greater insights into what stories we took on and are still projecting outside of us onto others.

I especially get bombarded with questions around this from parents, and it is understandable as to why, with perceptions that it is our responsibility to teach or raise our children to do or be certain things. Just notice again the stories, and even where you took on some of your own from your programming and what you got from the big people in your life telling you what they thought and believed, probably because they thought it was their responsibility to teach you.

I want to share this new idea and awakened paradigm of how relationships can be. How would you feel about all the relationships in your world if you felt completely loved, supported, and accepted for who you are and whatever you are experiencing? How would your relationships be operating if your spouse, lover, growth partners, family, and friends felt you loved, supported, and accepted them no matter what they were choosing to experience in life?

We are each here for our own unique discovery and expression of our fullest divinity. My children are not mine; they are the owners of their own domain and unique divine sovereign beings, and I am honored to be a growth partner on their journeys. I am honored that we chose each other in a sacred contract and relationship for this experience in our current human journey. I know they have been with me many times and in many ways, so how could I ever see them as less than all-knowing of their truth simply because of their physical ages?

My babes are just as much my mentors and teachers as I am theirs. They can learn from me by seeing who I chose to be and how I chose to live. I teach by being and not by telling them what to do or believe. I can share my thoughts and feelings with them, and I can get curious about theirs. I honor what feels true for them, what they are being called to learn and grow in, and what their truths for the highest and greatest good are. I get to honor their choices just as I honor my own. I choose to be a gardener who creates the space for their growth as well as my own greatest growth and evolution.

We don't operate under the paradigm of settle or sacrifice because that is simply a choice. We are committed to getting curious and finding solutions so that everyone is honored and supported in what feels good for them. That is the paradigm of parenting that is right for me, and you too get to choose what is right for you and your relationships. I choose the reality I exist in to reflect all that is available. My truth is to see all individuals as the divine beings that are, worthy of their own journey just as I am worthy of mine.

Let the Energy of Softness Be Your Guide

As you practice going deeper with yourself and with others through your communication and these steps to arrive at clarity, I want to remind you again to continue to practice getting soft. Whether you are interacting with just yourself or with another individual through these steps, you will create that space of unconditional love, support, and acceptance by sinking into your softness before you even begin.

Hold a safe container and space for open communication that is encompassed in an energy of authenticity, acceptance, support, and love like you would for a three year old. It is an energy that says: "Whatever you feel and think is OK, and together we can get curious about all of it and explore all options. After all, we are just playing a game."

As you practice listening to someone voice what they perceived or heard, you might notice an impulse to defend, prove, or to go into an old reaction. Remember, if a three year old fears there are monsters under the bed, you can understand it based on the point of view or understanding they have. The person in front of you is just sharing their monsters and what they are seeing that is true for them. As you breathe through it and practice holding the container of unconditional love, support, and acceptance for them to feel all things, you are allowing these feelings to surface, be held with love and then move through to be healed with ease.

Get soft because you really are dealing with both your little inner child and the inner child of whoever is involved.

The Power of Becoming Conscious

Once you become conscious and arrive at this level of clarity in this stage of the 5-step game—in other words, determine what you're feeling and why you're feeling it—you can begin to take control. Now you can disconnect from those beliefs because you're finally able to see the downright silliness of operating from perceptions formed in our pre-logical minds. How? It starts with unlearning, and this is how you un-learn those patterns and programs and begin to remember the truth of how you are designed to operate as a creator.

Allowing your emotions means you can heal and completely change the relationship between your current feelings and your existing beliefs. Unlearn them. De-story and deprogram your brain, body, and behaviors from responding the way you always did in the past, as now it is no longer true for you. In doing so, you will no longer be able to see and experience life from these old ways of being that now don't make sense for you or feel good and aren't in alignment with the life you want to be living.

This can now be caught and shifted in all the subtleties that are creating your world. If you're working on a project from home and suddenly you find yourself in the pantry about to dive into food and you weren't even hungry, or jumping onto social media for no reason at all, or you find yourself doing anything that is a complete distraction, it's because you were uncomfortable internally and whatever you were doing triggered something you want to avoid. As you lean into the steps, pinpoint what was operating unconsciously; this allows you to become completely conscious and clear to move forward, consciously imprinting new programs, stories, beliefs, and behaviors to create what you want to be experiencing.

Unlearning can be simple. Contrary to what you may be holding onto as a belief, not everything worth doing in life has to be hard. In fact, getting to the root of your emotions is as easy as you want it to be. Be open to receiving this new perspective. Lean into the process. Call yourself on your own bullshit, even and especially if it makes you uncomfortable. Choose to get comfortable in the discomfort because in that is where you will find and create your next level of freedom.

Being willing to look at and unlearn what isn't working means you're opening doors to what can work.

Discovery means you are willing to take the very next step and the very next inch in front of you and allow yourself to be led and guided to what is available around the corner.

Guess what else? You always have the right to change your mind. To flow, shift, and pull a complete 180 to discover what is right for you in this very moment. It doesn't matter where you are in the world, who you are with, or what you are doing, you will always have the right to shift, course correct, let your instincts be your guide, and step into alignment with your truth.

Life isn't limits; in fact, it is infinite possibilities, all available in each moment to give you the GIFT as a sovereign creator to infinite options and timelines to hop into right now, when and with whatever and whoever you choose. Life is a grand adventure of ALL things; you are your greatest adventure of discovery, and the purpose is you.

When you give yourself permission to simply BE with what is in front of you and in this present moment, and where the energy of life is calling you to now grow, you can always discover another layer in the purpose of being fully you.

You can and always will have the right to choose to shed all the stories, attachments, identities, expectations, and limitations holding you back from simply being fully alive here in this very moment called the present. Right now is worth living to the fullest. Choose to be here now in the experience of your now instead of waiting to be happy when you arrive at some other destination always outside of you in a future someday.

Arriving at the destination you "seek" and desire is simple. Discovery to anything and everything you want is simple. What creates the experience of happiness to be obtained no matter where you are at and no matter what you are "in" is also very simple.

It means choosing happiness right here and now in this destination. As it is, everything is always in divine order, you are always in the perfect place, time, and experience right in this moment. What you allow yourself to discover and choose to do with it will be a clear reflection of the frequency you choose to vibrate from and put out into the Universe. When you give yourself permission to discover, shift, change, flow, and own your own truth, then you vibrate I AM WORTHY and WHOLE and you magnetize the very things to you to that are a reflection of that worth.

Why do we see it as so hard then to get what we want when we are only required to take the very next inch forward in front of us? It is in the very next inch that contains all of the possibilities. I'll continue to re-affirm the new truths to imprint within you that it can be as easy or as hard as you choose to make it, all based on what you choose to think, believe, and feel about that next inch appearing in front of you.

It is simply a game of discovery, unraveling what no longer serves you, de-storying and deprogramming ways of being that are not aligned with your natural divine state and remembering all you truly are. Your greatest gifts are on the way to you right now, and you don't even know it. They only require you to follow your heart and take the next inch to meet and receive them.

Discovery Opportunity #4:
Get to the Root of Your Core Beliefs

1. To give yourself some extra clarity when you are moving through the 5 Steps, be proactive and take some time to come back to the idea of these five core beliefs. Do you feel loved/lovable? Do you think you're deserving of abundance, bliss, joy, or what you want in all areas of your life? Are you good enough? Are you worthy? Can you trust yourself? Can you trust life? If you answered no to any of these questions—write each of the core beliefs you realize you have down along

with any other limiting core beliefs holding you back in your life that you can recognize are there at this time.

2. Now, ask yourself why you feel that way. Remember, this process isn't about looking for every single event in your life that backs up that belief because that could consume your life. Instead, look and get curious as to the first times you experienced these beliefs and get curious as to the origin point if you can—if experiences pop in later in life, say thank you and continue to rewind and ask what happened before you were seven years old. Track and capture whatever you are discovering and be loving with yourself no matter your experience.

3. If you experience that there isn't a specific event that comes up as to where these beliefs, programs, or ideas came from, then it's time to get curious as to whether they are even yours. Are they yours, or can you see who or what was feeding these ideas, where you picked it up from, or who you took it on from unconsciously?

4. Once you've allowed space and presence for these roots to be revealed, continue to get curious to ask yourself if the belief or experience you perceived was or is really true, what other perceptions are possible, and what else could've been true in that experience and circumstance?

You are doing amazing at getting curious. Now get ready.... The next shift will allow you to move through this with even more ease to continue to create more and more of what you want.

13

Step #3:

What Do I Really Want? (In the Future and in This Moment)

I want... (to feel good right now, have an epic relationship, to be connected, to be experiencing love, etc.)

Other ways to get curious and gain insights in this step:

What do I want to be experiencing right now?

Is what I am believing, focusing on, or doing RIGHT NOW going to get me that?

Are the thoughts I'm believing really true, and what other perceptions and possibilities could exist?

What is the feedback I now get to use to get what I want in this circumstance?

Ask for what you want. In this circumstance, what do I want and how do I ask for that and create it?

Calling Yourself on Your Bullshit

Step 3 brings us to transitioning from what was unconscious to clearly looking at what is right in front of us and bridging the gap to now consciously choose something new. Ultimately, I see Step 3 as calling yourself on your own bullshit because you get to look at the result and reality you are experiencing right now and see if it matches what you want in your life and want to be experiencing. Identifying what you want can allow you to see all the things existing between getting that and what is very clearly happening now in front of you blocking it and therefore, what gets to shift.

You walk away angrily, slam the door, and leave the house. You get in your car, go to put the keys in the ignition, and you remember...*5 Steps. I can always do the 5 Steps.*

You begin to slow your breath and breathe more deeply, allowing yourself now to sway your torso just a bit from side to side. Breathing and moving the energy through you as much as possible.

It's all perfect.... Interesting that I'm experiencing this.

The tears rolling down your face begin to dry, your heartbeat slows a bit more, the burning sensation in your chest begins to soften, and the intense feeling to flee begins to release.

You put your hand on your heart to tune into your little girl or boy inside and apply love as you begin the dialogue with yourself and the 5 Steps to Freedom.

Ahh, sweetie, what are you feeling? What am I feeling?

The first thoughts that pop up are: *I'm pissed off* and *What an asshole!*

Then taking responsibility of it you say...

I notice I feel pissed off, angry...

Breathing... *Thank you for sharing that, love. It's OK to feel that. What else, love? Is there anything else you are feeling? Is there anything else underneath being pissed off and the anger?* You tune into your body and what you are really feeling even more deeply.

I notice I feel sad...

Why? Why am I sad? What happened that triggered you or when did you notice the feeling arise and something affecting you?

You replay and think about the situation and realize, *It was when he said* (that specific thing), *I felt hurt because I instantly felt rejected. I felt like he didn't really want to make time for me, I wasn't important, and he isn't really interested in being with me. I felt not good enough.*

Ahhhh, sweetie... Thank you, thank you, thank you, love... You hold your heart and allow the feelings of rejection, not good enough, and not important to come up and be felt fully, held in love.

Why? Because he said (that specific thing).

You breathe and soften even more into curiosity, noticing all the possibilities and simply taking ownership for what you are feeling and thinking as you now move into the next step of curiosity.

What do I want? This is the moment you can't get away with lying to yourself, hiding, or projecting because you get to look at what it is you really want and see if it matches what you are currently experiencing.

If you find your answer is, *I want him to do this, say that, etc.,* then that is never going to get you anywhere other than exactly where you are. You are still projecting onto somebody else what you want them to say to you, what you want them to do, or what you want them give you for you to have what you are seeking; you want them to fix it. This is the blame and projection game just keeping you stuck. Look at the boxed-in parameter of domestication you are operating out of by placing an expectation on them of how to operate for you to be happy. You're saying, "I will love you when you show up this way instead of you showing up for yourself in the way that is required for you to create the change and be the source of your own experience."

First, connect to what you want in the big picture of things or to experience long term.

If that is what I want, how do I now align to that?

If what you have wanted is an epic partnership and a relationship you love, is what you are doing right now, how you are behaving, and what you are perceiving or believing, going to get you that? Will getting defensive, leaving the situation, being angry and pissed off, and not communicating through it to solution or having these behaviors and patterns in your relationship give you an epic relationship?

This is where we clearly get to call ourselves on our own bullshit. No matter what happened, what was said, done, or went down, we obviously won't create a great relationship if our own patterns and behaviors don't align to it.

Now, bring it back to this moment. *What do I really want right now?* Tune into what your little boy or girl is really seeking. *What do you really want?*

I want to feel loved, accepted, appreciated, and important to my partner, and I want to have a great relationship. I want to be able to communicate through anything and feel safe to share.

Now, if that is what you want, let's evaluate the situation more so we can see what is in your way and get clear on how to align yourself to getting what you want.

Did you behave in a way to create an environment where it was safe to share? If that is what you want, then, of course, you would first get to be giving it to yourself and them by being the person that creates that type of environment and space to share. You can't ask of someone else what you aren't willing to do, give, and be yourself first. That would just be playing the victim role and waiting for someone else to someday give you what you want.

What else did you say you wanted?

To feel loved, accepted, important, and appreciated by your partner? In this situation, do you think your partner felt loved, accepted, important, and appreciated by you? Did you treat yourself with love, acceptance, importance, and appreciation? Did you allow them to be heard as though you appreciated what they had to say? Did you love yourself enough to allow yourself to be heard and share what you were feeling as though it was important?

Hmmm, Interesting. Were my actions in alignment with what I want to be experiencing?

You thought that what they said meant that you weren't important to them. What other thoughts were you having, and did you express them consciously?

Can you really know if what the person said meant that you weren't important to them? Did you allow the other person to share and get clear on what you thought they said or did, or were you operating out of assumptions and projections? Is it really true then, that what they said meant that?

What else can we get clear on from this to allow us to get what we want? When they said "that" specific thing, that is where you got triggered, and you felt sad because you felt like you weren't important, and so you felt rejected and not good enough. Is that what the person actually said? Did they say to you exactly and specifically that you are not important to them and not good enough?

Is what I'm believing really true? What else could be true or what other perceptions can I find?

You realize that you translated what they said into a meaning, you gave it an attachment, and it most likely wasn't what they intended; you don't really know what they intended because you are not inside them and didn't create that clarity. As you practice assuming the very best and getting curious, it flashes back through your mind now as you see what happened next. When that happened, you shut down, put up your guard, and got defensive. Feeling wounded and hurt, you were closed off and didn't listen because you had already decided what it meant, and to protect your heart and with your guard up, you became pissed off, lashed out, and then went into your survival pattern of leaving to get out of the overwhelming amount of feelings you were having.

What else did you think or project in the experience or have come up? What an asshole.

And now, taking responsibility, turning inward whatever you are seeing and projecting...

How am I being an asshole? How do I say things that are hurtful or act out? How am I rude, inconsiderate, or angry? What is the result? I am in the car right now because I stormed out. Who's being an asshole again?

Another question you could ask yourself is: *Why am I doing this, or why did I do that?* You can ask any curiosity question that leads you to evaluate what you usually don't pay attention to and allows you to see all the spaces you've been afraid, the things you've been hiding from and suppressing deep down that are creating your reality.

This shift is when we really get to look at all the thoughts you had and everything that came up because it reveals all of the gold. It is when you look within yourself for everything that you'll see what else you were putting outside of yourself and not taking ownership of and behaviors you were using that were not in alignment with what you say you wanted. Then you can change it. The more you are willing to look at, the quicker you arrive at clarity to create freedom.

This step doesn't have to take a long time either and it doesn't have to be a game of many questions. I want you to see how much gold is actually available depending on how much you want to see, how much you want to clear, and how deep you are willing to go. This step allows you to get right to what you're unconsciously operating from to consciously create a change. It really is up to you on how much you are willing to evaluate at the time, have space for, and what is required for you to move on effectively to get what you want.

It can be this easy: *I notice I'm angry because that was said. What do I want? I want to feel connected to my partner and have a fun night. I want a great relationship.*

Right there, even without all the other deeper evaluations, you can call yourself back to clarity of what is being created right now. You know you don't want to get in a fight and go through the drama, so you can catch it right now and get clear on what you want and how you can shift it to move forward into getting what you really do want.

It is so easy when you can connect the dots of what you are doing unconsciously to what you say you really want to be experiencing. *If I want an epic love relationship yet I just got triggered, closed off, shut down, and bolted, is any of that ever going to give me more connection or an epic love experience? No.*

Let's go back to this scenario you might've found yourself in or can imagine going through whilst sitting in the car. In just the first 3 Shifts, you can recognize and see what's really happening and decide how you choose to respond next instead of staying in an unconscious cycle and pattern.

Moving into the next step of the 5 Steps is to move you through it fully to create new experiences and results. You'll move into the new perceptions and the new actions. Now, the importance is to see clearly what you get to do to align with what you want. You get to see that what you have had so far in life has been what you've been committed to and you can now be committed to something else.

Maybe next time, you catch your feelings and thoughts before you go into a reaction and request a few minutes alone to get clear so you can have a conversation about it. You can utilize the survival pattern to serve you. Clarify that you are going to take a few minutes or some personal space, leave, breathe, and go through the 5 Steps to get clear on what you are feeling, why, and what you really want to create now. You can then return to the situation and move through the 5 Steps to create a completely different experience and align to the epic relationship you want.

The next time, you might catch it, breathe, and feel no need to take off or even leave the space or energy happening. You get present with it, breathe, and get soft and curious to start asking questions, see it for what it is, and make a clear request of what you want. Each time you create more and more alignment with all of your operating systems to create the results you are seeking.

You can use the 5 Steps for communicating through an issue with someone else, and always with yourself. It is always there as a constant tool and guide for you every single time you realize you aren't experiencing bliss, joy, peace, love, or what you want or you catch yourself going into a sabotaging pattern that also isn't going to support what you want.

Here's another example. What if you've been wanting to start speaking on stages and expressing yourself more, and suddenly the opportunity shows up when someone asks you to come speak. You notice you are filled with fear and suddenly you begin to find all these reasons why it just isn't the right timing or it wouldn't work out.

IF YOU SAY YOU WANT SOMETHING and you aren't moving TOWARDS it in some way (even a small inch), then you are in a bullshit STORY, EXCUSE or VALIDATION as to why you can't have it.

Obviously, the action or patterns you are going into of blocking what you say you want don't match and aren't in alignment. This is a clear red flag to go internal and do the 5 Steps. Nothing is going to change when you stay in the same behaviors.

What am I feeling? I notice I'm feeling scared and afraid.

Look at where you feel it in your body. Most likely, for fear of expressing, you will experience something in your throat. You might start to cough, or it may feel dry and scratchy. You could also be feeling pain or tightness in your stomach due to fear. Maybe your chest hurts because it connects to sadness that you feel not good enough.

Why am I feeling this way? I notice I'm scared because I am afraid if I get up on stage, I will freeze, I won't do a good job, and people won't like me. I don't feel like I look good enough to get up in front of people on stage. They are going to think, "Who is she/he to be talking about this? She/he isn't an expert. Why is he/she on stage?" The list could go on and on and on depending on your own personalized list of beliefs and experiences, which can create your own shit show that runs your life if you buy into it.

The moment you get to see, *Oh...I'm scared because I'm afraid to be seen and that I might not do a good job,* ask yourself, *What do I want? What do you really want? Do you want to speak on stage, share your message, talk about the things you love and the gifts you have to share? Do you want to be able to help more people, create an impact, allow yourself to experience things you are drawn to and get greater at them, and see what comes next from it?*

OR...

Do you really want to just stay doing exactly what you are doing and keep asking the Universe for opportunities you will turn down, which will stop showing up because you've also clearly responded to the Universe with what you really want? Do you want to hide, reaffirm your limiting beliefs, and stay in the comfort zone, receiving exactly what you have?

You can look clearly at what the energy and alignment is with your next action you're considering and determine if your response will really give you what you say you want. If not, begin to get curious about these thoughts and beliefs and evaluate them. You can, of course, just say, *I do want to speak on stage because I do want to share my message.* Then you can move into Step 4, and so on. The part to remember here in Step 3 is we want to get clear.

If you can't feel good about that and you are just forcing yourself and saying, *Yup, I'll do it,* and inside you are still thinking and believing all those reasons why these fears could show up, you are actually only planting the seed of fear into the very thing you are saying yes to and the energy hasn't changed.

That seed of fear will grow, and you will most likely find a way to experience exactly what you are afraid of, or you'll sabotage— maybe you'll pull out last minute and create some trauma drama that will be a good excuse as to why you now can't do it or make it.

I recommend you evaluate each one of the thoughts that came up and see if they are really true, in the words of the great Byron Katie, even ask, can you absolutely know that this is true? You can get more curious as to what other possibilities exist, what other things are true and could be true, and you can now find other possibilities.

Let's evaluate the reasons that came up in the last example and some possible responses.

I'm scared I'll freeze.

Ahh, sweetie, thank you, I can understand why you feel that way. It's OK that you feel that; that's from those old beliefs we used to think were true that we aren't good enough and everything had to show up perfectly. That's from that old program that said it wasn't OK to speak up and we had to sit quietly or that things had to look a certain way to be accepted.

What is really true? What else is possible?

I am afraid if I get up on stage, I will freeze.... OK, what if I freeze? Could I freeze on stage? What is the worst thing that can happen if I freeze? I can look at my notes. I can laugh it off with the crowd and share how this is a big new step for me. I could also create a PowerPoint or something to guide me and keep me on track. Ultimately, if I freeze, is that so bad? If I freeze, I will just be showing that I am human and doing the best I can, which means I'm just proving that I'm a real person who cares about my message.

What else? If that happens, I'm showing myself that I still can speak, and it doesn't have to look a certain way, and I love myself anyways, which is only going to create even more opportunities for me.

So, is it really that big of a deal that I could freeze, and is that more important to me than moving forward and getting to do what I've been saying I want?

It all becomes a lot more funny and lighter now as you say, *Silly human stories.... So, what is true for me? It's totally OK if I freeze; there are always options, and I can set myself up for support in many ways, and I'm excited to have the experience and see how it goes.*

Now, let's look at the next thought that came up.

I won't do a good job...

Talking to your inner child, *Mmm, yeah, babes, I can understand feeling fear around that. What is a good job anyways? What would classify doing a good job, and why would we think that we wouldn't do a good job? Do you know your information, and is this something you want to share? Yes...* Or even if it is a *No,* then you could ask yourself: *What would you get to do to support yourself in feeling more confident about what you share or finding ways to feel more prepared? If you share and make a difference for even one person, is that a good job? Is that worth it? Who can classify what a good job is? Can other people tell you what is good, or is that all based on perception? That's right.... I am the only one who can decide what is right for me, and if I share and get on stage, I've taken a step towards what I want and that in and of itself is a good job. I know that doing my best will be creating change, and I can never know what or how people will feel about it or how it will affect them.*

People won't like me. I don't feel like I look good enough to get up in front of people on stage.

Well, that's an interesting one.... I can totally understand how this would come up as a fear. We were taught to hide and not be seen because that was safer. Thank you, sweetie, for reminding me that we thought that was true, and what we now know is true is that hiding and staying in the dark is where we are the most unsafe. It is where we miss out on life; we stay feeling rejected because we are avoiding participating, and we only keep attracting the things that keep us hiding. When we step out and share, we find and attract the people that are like us, that will love us; we find even more amazing friends, associates, clients, and people to connect with. We can't enjoy others if we don't step out to interact with them.

What else? Who are "they" that we are trying to get approval from and trying to impress anyways? Is it any of our business what people think about us? You begin smiling and laughing now at the comedy show of it all and this fun game as you get even lighter. Remembering ... **"It's none of your business what people think about you; it's only your business for what you think about yourself."**

No, it's none of my business what people think. What's true is that I like me, and it doesn't matter what anyone else thinks. I am doing this for me and because I want to share it, and that is what matters. Where did this idea or story come from of what I'm supposed to look like and be like that requires others approval for me to be on a stage? Can I find examples of people choosing to be on stage that are in all skin colors, shapes, sizes, dress, and sharing all types of experiences, etc.? How many messages wouldn't be shared if sharing a message was based on what someone "should" look like or be like? I know I am the one who gets to love myself first to allow even more love into my life.

They are going to think, who is she/he to be talking about this? She/he isn't an expert. Why are they on stage?

Who am I comparing myself to? Again, getting lighter as you remember that **comparison is the thief of all joy,** and even though there are hundreds of other experts in the world, no one is me. I am the only one that can deliver this message the way I do, with the knowledge I have, and I don't have to be an expert because I am just going to be there to share. I'm sharing my experience, my knowledge, and what I've learned to be able to help others that are looking for the same. That is *why I am doing it, and I can drop the story of where I have to be in life, the amount of success or any labels, attachments, or expectations to be able to share my truth and service to the world.*

Can you see how through this step you simply evaluate all things and break down the stories that are going on in your head and showing up as emotion in your body that would have unconsciously shut you down? They are just thoughts and reflections of what is inside. You can de-story them and re-program what is true for you to move forward.

Each time you evaluate and move through the story, you can see it for what it is and feel differently about it. You've cleared the shit in the way to pave a path to move forward consciously and respond with what you want.

It doesn't mean that you won't, of course, be feeling and experiencing some fear as you move into it, yet each time you do, you get to break it down, bring it back to the truth, shift that fear into excitement, wonderment, and possibility, and reaffirm the new beliefs and perceptions that you do have, which is coming up in Step 4.

It, again, can be quick and easy as well.

I notice I am afraid of accepting the speaking opportunity because I am afraid I won't do a good job and I'm not ready.

Ahh, sweetie, what do you want?

I do want to start speaking and share my message more. I do want to get more comfortable with it and be able to attract more clients, share the message on a bigger platform, and step out of my comfort zone.

A quick evaluation can also call you on your bullshit to move forward. The main thing is that when you arrive at moving into the next step, you feel clean and clear with the energy to move forward, feeling good about it and it is something you can believe now inside. We don't want to surface sidestep it and just tell ourselves something that sounds good and is only going to be vibrating the opposite and work against us.

I even got to go through the 5 Steps around the process of writing this book. I suddenly would find myself getting distracted or doing something else when I wanted to focus on it. I stopped and asked myself a few questions. In the tiniest little voice, deep down, the little girl was saying, *Are you sure you want to put this out there? What if your friends and all the amazing people you know in the world read it and don't think it's that good? What if it doesn't make that much of a difference or impact for people? Can you really write a book?*

All of these reflected the deep old wounds, fears, limitations, and beliefs that I was stupid, I wasn't going to be good enough, that I could just be rejected for it, and it wasn't safe to be seen, heard, or take up space.

Ahh, sweetie, thank you for letting me know those fears were there. I got to fully feel and give presence to those fears. Then my inner child got to acknowledge that those were just those old, old, old stories we used to believe and this was something new so I could inner-stand how that could come up.

What is really true?

I know I'm being guided to share this information that has made a massive impact on my life and many others, and I trust that who-ever is called to it will be for whatever they get to take away from it. It doesn't matter what others think; it matters what I think, as does giving myself permission to fulfill my own purpose and express myself fully and unapologetically as me. I am excited to be able to share this piece of my journey and the freedom I've learned with others.

That was it.... One conversation to get clear, hear what was hiding deep down, and acknowledge it, love it, clarify what was really true, and set up the actions to support me in continuing to move forward.

Your old shit showing up isn't a sign of having a setback or going backwards. Your core wounds and past experiences are just that, your core wounds and past experiences. And so, as you move forward always in accepting and receiving more, these very same old patterns or beliefs can pop up to just ask you to get clear on what you really want. It is just a reflection of being able to receive what's next as well as showing you what else inside you still gets to be loved. You may continue to find layers, and layers, and layers to these deep core wounds, and it just is giving you access to more and more and more freedom each and every time you allow them to be there, accept them, embrace them, and choose how you want to respond.

Ask for what you want.

"You Never Get What You Don't Ask For"

This is something I chose to live by as I stepped into expressing myself fully, being worthy of getting what I wanted, and getting clear in my communication to get it. We get to stop trying to read minds and assuming or projecting. Just get clear and ask for what you want because you never get what you don't ask for. I use this concept of just asking for what I want as something I live by in many aspects of life. Here, we can also see how we can apply it in the 5 Steps to only get more support and what we do want more easily.

Step 3 isn't just to realize what you want; it is to actually move towards it by asking for it.

When we share our vulnerability, it is the greatest act of courage and the greatest gift we can give others and ourselves in creating our own freedom. I began supporting myself by being fully transparent with nothing to hide and nothing to prove as my way of living that would then give me the greatest freedom and allow me to be supported in asking for what I want.

I realized that by sharing what was going on internally and what my old patterns were, out loud if it involved anyone else, then there was nowhere to hide, and the old patterns were revealed.

Then I'd get to ask for the ultimate support I required to move forward and what I wanted in these moments that felt the scariest. This was just one of the greatest gifts I could give myself to support me in getting what I wanted, which was moving through my bullshit.

As I transitioned into this, it could look like this: "Hey, I just noticed my energy shifted, and my guard came up. My old pattern is to disconnect and leave right now. What I want is to continue to feel connected and create only an even greater relationship. Would you assist me, and could we go sit down that I can share with you what is coming up for me right now so we can stay connected and create an even greater relationship?"

The best thing I could do is call out my patterns and share. Instead of doing what felt comfortable, I leaned into the uncomfortable, which was just showing me I was on the verge of my comfort zone. The gift available was to step through parameters I had previously created as the comfort zone to now receive the love, connection, and epic relationships that were waiting when I aligned to different patterns and ways of being. It will always come down to you calling yourself on your own bullshit because you could find reasons and excuses to validate it all day every day and continue to stay exactly where you are at.

I also learned that if I was using touch, such as holding hands or facing the person I was communicating with and touching them as I would share what was coming up, I would more easily be able to soften, open up, and create connection. If I was standing across the room having the conversation, then it was easier for me to still put up a guard around my heart, want to stay in defense, and stay disconnected.

These insights into my own patterns only gave me more ability to ask for what I wanted to be supported in creating a different experience. I'd share what the old pattern was to bring that clearly out into the open, and then I'd ask for what I wanted that would support me in moving through it, even though it felt completely uncomfortable and was the opposite of what I wanted to do as my learned behaviors. Being aware of what would assist me in moving through the resistance in these moments, where I knew it would be the most confronting to my comfort zone, which was being stretched to an even greater capacity, I could request and ask for whatever would be the most supportive. In this case, to be held while I shared what was coming up so I could create a feeling of connectedness to move through the process. As I became aligned to my emotional wholeness, there wasn't anything outside of me required to allow me to be with all things for myself and others.

Only you can give yourself permission to experience what you want, and so you might as well be your greatest support system in creating what you want to receive.

Trust & Assume Only the Very Best to Be What's Really True

Begin to practice always assuming and looking for the very best in people. What would you want someone to think about you? Can you give the same to others? Before you choose to run with your projections or assumptions, what if you thought, *I'm sure that was not the person's intention.* When you practice looking for and assuming the very best to exist, you are also creating a belief system that, of course, you only attract the best people and situations and that wasn't what was intended. *I trust that, of course, the person loves me, cares, or didn't intend to hurt me, and so I'm going to now get curious about it, ask, and create clear communication.*

This is when we are called to RISE and create clarity to transmute any disconnect or chaos to unconditional love, acceptance, compassion, and to bring all things to a greater frequency and experience.

217

"Hey, I noticed a feeling of sadness came up when 'that' was said, and that I took on and interpreted that to mean.... I know that, of course, you would never intend to hurt me. Can you assist me in understanding what you meant by that so I can see a different perspective?"

The more you learn to clearly speak to the energy that is there and just get curious, the more you will find clarity and the ease of getting what you want.

When you are going through the steps with someone else, I suggest you go through Shifts 1 – 3 to share what is going on for you, then give the other person the same opportunity. When you are listening to them, remember to respond and reply with APPRECIATION: "Thank you for sharing"; "Thank you for letting me know that's how you feel"; "I appreciate that."

Listen generously and with genuine wonder and curiosity to be able to understand. Claim full responsibility of your own experience, appreciating the feedback no matter how it is delivered, and choose to see and hear it out of love. Practice assuming the very best is true and what's in front of you that scares or hurts you is a misperception, allowing the space of love, support, and acceptance over defending.

If you are willing to take it one step at a time, you can reprogram how you see it and the way you respond to it, from a complaint to a commitment of operating consciously in your relationships and with yourself. You can take radical responsibility to go from hiding, masking, and concealing to operating in full authenticity, vulnerability, and transparency with all of your feelings and expression of self, knowing freedom is having nothing to hide and nothing to prove. You can take any situation from chaos to clarity and unconditional love as you get creative to find and implement the new patterns and actions that are aligned with your True Divine Self that is a magnificent worthy BEING of Light.

Be Specific and Go Deeper
if You're Struggling

Specificity is an important part of this process. Describe what you want as vibrantly as possible, whether you're talking about your career, your dream home, your relationships, or anything in between.

It's easy to say what you want from a big-picture perspective. For example, you could say, "I want to be more successful," or "I'm tired of sabotaging my health goals and now I want to be thinner." However, if you try to move forward with those goals without changing the underlying perceptions and beliefs that have shaped your approach so far, you're going to keep operating from the same unconscious commitments.

If you say you want more success but feel in your body that success has always meant stress and hard work, you'll create more stress and hard work. If you say you want to be thinner but are used to fighting your body and seeing diet and exercise as a struggle, it will continue to look that way for you.

To begin to shift your core patterns and beliefs around what it is you truly want, you get to ask yourself some questions. Start by, again, examining what you're feeling in relationship to those goals, especially when you get stuck in negative energy. If you've clearly identified what you want but still aren't getting it, that's because it is vibrationally not in alignment at this time and your body doesn't believe you. It is an opportunity to get more clear with what's underneath and align it to something you can believe to move forward.

For example, say you're trying to shed weight but find yourself in the pantry looking for an unhealthy snack. What happened? This is the red flag to go internal with the 5 Steps because clearly your actions are not in alignment with what you say it is you want. You want to have an amazing healthy body, yet you are doing something to sabotage it. What's really going on? Why does this pattern come up, and when? Is it just the pattern you created for comfort every time you are stressed, and you are going to your associations for comfort, or does it show up when you get close to your goal? Why would you be afraid of actually reaching your goal? Is there a deeper fear? *If I look attractive, I'm unsafe; If I lose weight, I'll cheat; or I'm not worthy of feeling and looking amazing.* Struggle is the cue to look deeper, find what's there, and move inch by inch into new beliefs, patterns, and behaviors that support you to get what you want.

Ask curiosity questions and utilize the 5 Steps to dig deeper. If the sabotaging actions come up again, it is so you can continue to see what else there is for you to love and heal. You can say you want to be thinner on the surface, but if you don't change your beliefs and perceptions about what that means and creates, then the internal environment hasn't changed. How else can this be easy? What if you just focused on being 1% more aware, implementing just 1% greater micro alignment in your patterns, bringing in 1% more unconditional love, acceptance, and compassion with yourself and the world? You can always take the next step. We are just practicing and remembering.

If You're Not Defining What You Want, You're Also Making a Choice

Most people will get stuck on this shift. Why? Getting clear on what you want forces you to do two things: get specific about what's not working in your life and take responsibility for what you've created.

Maybe, quite simply, you don't know what you want at this point because you've never given yourself permission to ask that question. Maybe all you know is that you aren't feeling good and that something is off. Let's circle back to the relationship example because most of us can relate to arguing with a partner or some-one in our life at least once: if all you know is that your partner pissed you off but you can't put your finger on why, the more you practice giving yourself permission to feel and the space to ask questions, the more likely you are to discover a deeper fear or something you are avoiding. However, until that time, we don't want to stay in the shit cycle, creating our own suffering. If you are arguing and you don't want to be arguing, you can focus for now on wanting better communication. Identify something you know you want and move through the shifts—something, after all, is always better than nothing.

There's another side here, too: if you come this far and decide you're not going to get clear about what you want, you're actively choosing to stay in your shit rather than have the life you want. Inaction is a choice. You're saying you want more of what you already have, that the status quo is all you deserve.

To truly set yourself free, you get to keep moving to your free-dom. Be committed to moving through the entire 5 Steps, being careful not to get stuck here on Step 3. Remember, you don't have to be a psychologist to unearth your root beliefs and perceptions. And, when you do, you don't have to trace every one back to an event that occurred when you were younger than seven. All you get to do is know that happiness is a choice, and you can actively choose to pursue it, even if it's as little at a time.

Your Results Are Your Truths

By getting clear on what you want, you're owning your results as your truths. You're not projecting onto the world that everything you perceive as wrong in your life is someone else's fault, someone else's problem. When you can call yourself out on what you are doing, taking full radical responsibility of your life and all you are experiencing, you've mastered Step 3.

If you are still feeling struggle with aligning your life to peace and an experience you want, there is simply more you can receive as you look at your role in creating the struggle.

What patterns continue to keep you from having what you want? With every experience and interaction there are infinite ways to respond. Ask yourself why you're tolerating, allowing, or attracting this type of behavior; why you continue to act out of your own patterns that aren't serving you; why you keep putting up with the same repetitive patterns from yourself and others? Continue to breathe, open, and get curious as you look at each operating system and your responses, which hold the gold and greatest gifts you are just about to receive.

The next discovery opportunity will allow you to recognize some of the behaviors keeping you from what you want and what you can now do instead.

Discovery Opportunity #5:
Discover What You Really Want and What's in the Way

For this discovery opportunity, simply give yourself space to dive into more clarity and take radical responsibility of what you have been creating.

1. In your journal or on a piece of paper, write down and describe what it is you really want. Now, you are going to support that creation by evaluating your life and the patterns that are aren't supporting that.

2. Take out another piece of paper or choose another space in your journal and draw a line down the middle, dividing it into halves with two columns next to each other.

3. On left side, begin listing out all the patterns and behaviors you are currently doing in your life that keep you from having this. After you've made your list, go back through it, one by one, and decide on a different action, pattern, or behavior you are now going to practice doing instead whenever that old pattern shows up. Write this new pattern next to the old one in the right column. When you are finished, you'll have a clear reflection of all the things you could recognize you were doing to block having what you want and a number of things you are now going to be practicing instead as new behaviors to assist you in getting what you do want.

4. You could also now support yourself more by writing out just the new behaviors on a piece of paper, taking a picture of it with your phone to be able to pull up whenever it supports, or print them out. Put this reminder list where you can see it, and it can support you to remind yourself of the new behaviors you are practicing. Whenever those old patterns want to come up, now you have a resource to remember what you are going to practice and implement instead.

14

Step #4:

Align to New Beliefs and Perceptions

What is the NEW belief, perception, and focus I am choosing now to get what I want?

To have what I want, what would the new belief, perception, and focus get to be?

Choose Freedom

After you can clearly identify what you want, it's time to move on to Step 4—choosing new beliefs and perceptions that will align to what you really want.

Here you get to create new perceptions and possibilities when you look through the eyes of faith energy, which is excitement, wonderment, and curiosity.

This is where you begin to relearn, reprogram, realign, and integrate into the remembrance of who you really are—the being fully worthy and capable of having whatever you desire and who will always be fully supported in receiving it.

On the path to your healing, liberation, and peace within, many people stop at good or great. Why? They believe their current situation is "as good as it's going to get." They believe if one area of life is rockin', something else is going to have to suffer. Again, that's the belief system talking. If everything you are experiencing and every area of life isn't in peace, fulfillment, and joy, which you are fully worthy and capable of, then your results are showing you what internally and vibrationally gets to come into more alignment with your divinity. Your natural design and state is that of being light, bliss, and joy as a divine sovereign creator.

It is always as easy as you want it to be if you choose to see how easy it can be and what the next inch is. **It takes just as much EFFORT to suffer as it does to fly.**

Yup, it takes just as much effort for you to put your energy and focus on a thought, belief, perception, and feeling that doesn't give you what you want as it does to focus on what does give you what you want. STOP and breathe that into your body and cells and remembrance for a moment.

You've been effortlessly doing it for so long, so you clearly know how. It is just a choice, and now that you have this awareness, you can make a conscious choice to give something else your attention. You can allow each operating system to align its focus on what it is you do want, and it will actually become even easier than what you were doing before. I can understand that it might feel at first like it takes more effort, and that's just because it's been your norm and the pathway of least resistance. Really, a thought is a thought, a focus is a focus, a feeling is a feeling, and you've been and are doing these things all the time. You most likely just haven't paid close attention to how they've made you feel, behave, and therefore manifest.

Now you can reprogram to have the new program that you replace with the old and do it over, and over, and over again. As you match this with the new patterns, and practice these new ways of operating, soon they become effortless because they are how you've programmed yourself to operate, and they can work for you to manifest what you desire by just being. You won't have to think about it anymore because it will be the easiest way for you to be and receive aligned to your true nature. Change isn't hard; it is just different, and different is just what you haven't known.

Why Are We Afraid of the Unknown?

I'd say we actually aren't when we truly look at it. It isn't the unknown that we are actually afraid of; it is the known. It is living in the same known box because of the known fears, worries, constraints, and programs you've created and are all-too familiar with. The unknown contains all the infinite and exciting possibilities of what we can discover, how great it can be, what ways would work the best for us and give us our highest joys and freedom, and what would feel good. In the nothingness that exists, we find the infinite options of ALL that is available to dance with and play in. That is the unknown. If you realized that the unknown contains everything you want, you might stop running from it and start running to it.

That is how creation happens because it is only in each moment with the next inch and new discovery that we can allow ourselves to see what is there and where we want to go. It isn't from pre-planning or projecting into the future based on what you've had in the past. Let yourself learn to dance free in the unknown of possibilities of the greatest adventure that is your life. What if you saw and knew clearly now that this is actually the safest place for you to be because it is always you who is choosing each moment? There is a lot more freedom and security in this moment that you can *choose* than there is in what you've known in the past. You are an evolutionary being, and each moment is your creative expression of play and possibility.

Since this is a choice you are always worthy of, I would never tell you what to do because you are the only one who can choose your divine timing of freedom and what you want to continue to experience and learn. What I would suggest you consider is that if it is the same processes, time, and effort, why not just GIVE IN to your happiness.

My friend Michael Beckwith says, "You might as well give in and be happy, be great, be prosperous..."

It's inevitable that you are amazing, and as this divine and unique being, you can create whatever it is that you want and is perfect for you. You can obviously then continue to fight this greatness that is you from revealing itself and keep creating struggle, or you can let go, GIVE IN, and let yourself be happy and worthy of the ease, abundance, support, and infinite ways to experience joy and be loved. **Let yourself be the greatness that only you are.** Allow the Universe to support you and send you all there is that you desire. It is safe to shine, safe to be happy, safe to be fully supported, safe to be blissed out in peace, pleasure, passion, play, and prosperity. It is actually your divine birthright.

The Universe is just waiting for you to receive all it has for you when you clear what's in the way and vibrate, "Yes, that is what I want. I AM worthy." I'll remind you again, my friend, that only you are your greatest asset because only you are the creator of your reality. Only you can give yourself permission to receive all you are seeking and only you can choose which way you will learn. You can learn through suffering, and you can also learn through joy. You aren't a victim to the circumstances. You can choose now to end the feelings of confusion, anxiety, and overwhelm and free yourself of the unconscious commitments that sabotage your money, your business, your health, your relationships... EVERYTHING.

Are you game for making this your new reality? Are you committed to creating a new focus and aligning everything to that focus, allowing it to become how you operate?

Then let's begin the exciting adventure of new possibilities!

What is the NEW belief, perception, and focus I am choosing to get what I want?

To have what I want, what would the new belief, perception, and focus get to be?

This is really simple because you've already clarified what it is that you want, and you've seen the limiting beliefs and perceptions that were giving you the opposite.

If I discovered "WHY" is that I have a fear and belief that love won't last, I'm going to get hurt, and love is scary....

And I decided what I wanted was to embrace the love in front of me and feel safe and connected (instead of my old beliefs and patterns)...

I say, *What I want is to feel safe and stay connected.*

What would your new belief and perception get to be to create that now?

What would you get to focus on that reaffirms that to be true?

What are all the possibilities here? This is where you can use the energy of faith, wonderment, excitement, and creation to see all the things that actually can be true for you if you were creating safety, connection, and a love that lasts as your experience.

Love is where I am safe; when I run from love, push it away, close it off, try to domesticate it and make it conditional, or add a story, attachment, or expectation to it, I get hurt; that's when love doesn't last. I can see now that was because that wasn't me giving love; that was me closing off love. So, giving love is the safest place to be, and receiving love is the safest thing to do for me. Love is what is natural; all of the other stuff I add in makes it unnatural and hard. That is why I had ideas and stories that love didn't last and wasn't safe.

Now, from all you de-storied and evaluated in Step 3, you are just creating the new belief and perception in Step 4 that supports that.

Love is safe. Love is everlasting. Love is natural and easy.

What else did you declare you wanted? *To be connected...*

OK, what now do you get to believe and perceive about connection and choose to focus on?

I love having connection with others because it is so much easier in life to be supported and connected. I enjoy connection. I have the greatest experiences when I allow connection. Connecting feels fun and easy. I am worthy and deserving of being connected to the most amazing individuals that magnify my life and operate at high frequencies. Connection always brings so many fun gifts and surprises into my life. It is safe to be connected.

Can you see how there are infinite and limitless possibilities of new beliefs and perceptions you can find to reaffirm what is really true and what you are now choosing to focus on that becomes true for you to create that as your experience?

It doesn't require that you come up with a ton of new beliefs and perceptions; it just requires one that you can believe and feel to be true. The point is, if you let your mind run with all the possibilities and evidence you can find and now choose to focus on and believe, look at how much more you are re-affirming it. *Oh, that's right... Haha, silly human story that was making it so hard. We were believing all these other things... We can look at what is really true, and this can be my new experience.*

When you see all the new ideas, beliefs, and perceptions that you will now choose to focus on, you can simply say... *OK, my new belief and perception that I'm focusing on is that love is safe and that connection is fun and easy.* Before you move into the last step, you get evaluate whether this belief will really work for you.

Check in on Your New Belief

This is one of the most important steps apart of changing your beliefs and being able to actually imprint with new ones. If you skip this step, you'll just be blowing more smoke up your ass that reaffirms the limiting beliefs inside because your body doesn't believe the surface self-empowerment affirmations you are feeding it. If you just pick a statement and start declaring your new belief just like you would with stating an affirmation, it doesn't mean it is going to create any changes. You are shifting your focus, yes, but we know that the feeling you vibrate will always override what the thought is, and if you don't believe it, it will only reaffirm the old belief to be true because that is what you are feeling. So please pay attention here to this very important step of checking in with yourself to feel into your body if you can believe the new belief as true for you or not.

This is why it is important to tune in and ask yourself: *How does this new belief feel when I say it?*

Remember that lies feel heavy and truth feels light in your body. We are shifting things from heavy, low-vibrational density to be transmuted to light. This is how it is easy to see if you believe it by how it feels in your body. If you say, "love is safe," and your body feels heavy, that is a clear sign that your body does not yet believe that to be true yet. It is understandable; realize that you've had years and years of programming and looking for the old belief to be true.

There are two things to do here. Look more deeply at the belief. Why else doesn't it feel good to believe this? What else is there that needs to get broken down from your old stories and perceptions?

You also might just realize that the belief you are choosing is a bit too big of a bite for your system and body to believe right now, and that's perfect because we want it to be something small, simple, and the next inch that you actually can focus on and believe moment by moment. That is what will reprogram the pathway and create the new result, and it gets to be easy. It's about moving forward and aligning to it, even an inch at a time.

If "love is safe" feels heavy, then ask yourself...

What else could I believe right now that feels more true?

It could be as simple as adding "it's easier everyday" to your belief; that way it breaks it down into chunks of taking it one day at a time. For example, "Every day love feels safer," or "I feel more safely wrapped in love every day."

Tune in. Can your body accept that as a possibility to be true for you?

Can you feel it to be true in your body that every day, love feels more and more safe?

How about...

"I enjoy finding safe ways to love and be loved."

Can you feel that you can now find safe ways to love and experience love?

"I'm excited to experience all the ways love is always safe."

If you can believe that love being safe is a possibility and yet you haven't experienced it and so your body doesn't believe it's true, can you believe that you are excited to now get to experience it and find it?

It can completely change your feeling around it if you put it into a context of what you will be practicing and taking action on that allows you to get curious about it and allows it to evolve as you are practicing it. Can you feel good about it being your new exciting adventure? There are truly infinite possibilities to play with options to find something you can believe.

Can you feel that smaller step to be true in your body? Does it feel light and feel like you can believe that to be true? If the heaviness or resistance isn't there anymore, and it feels light, then you are golden. You might just feel nothing or neutral. That is a step in the right direction. Remember that neutral is great because in this state we have freedom of choice when it comes to what we want to believe. You can stay there and use what feels neutral, now knowing that you can continue to allow your body to believe it as you practice it. Or, you can get a bit more curious with the statement that is neutral and see if there is any other twist on it that feels like you can say, *Yes, I actually can believe that. It is possible for me to believe that now and to create that as my new belief.*

What If I don't believe it because my evidence doesn't show it?

There are two common ways I see people struggle with this step. The first is when they get stuck because they are looking at what is literally happening in front of them right now or just happened to them as their clear evidence that it doesn't match, and so, of course, it would feel like a lie to believe anything else. The second is when the mind has overwhelming proof and evidence that what you are now wanting to believe isn't true for you from your past experiences or beliefs about life and stops you in your tracks.

Let's start with the first.

You are going through the 5 Steps, and yes, you can see what you are feeling (Step 1), you can see why you are feeling it (Step 2), and you even are clear on what you really want to be experiencing (Step 3).

In the example above, maybe there is no way in hell you believe love is safe because what clearly just happened did not feel good and created a reaction of you feeling very unsafe. How then, can you believe that it's safe when this thing just happened that looks unsafe, feels unsafe, and reaffirms all of the evidence that it's unsafe?

And that is OK too. This could completely have been your experience, a clear representation of the past and, of course, a reminder and reflection of what you have believed and is ready to be healed. That is why it is happening, and it is also why you are here experiencing it. There is no thing and no one to fight and nothing to prove in this moment. No one is saying that you didn't experience what you did and trying to convince you otherwise.

If you were or felt attacked in some way or had an experience that says love is unsafe, with every bone in your body in agreement, trying to convince myself of something else only feels like a lie. The goal here is not to convince yourself otherwise but to **realign to something else becoming true for you.**

What it comes down to is choosing to see it from a deeper truth. We chose this experience, and so this person or experience was just holding up its contract to read our script and guide us to finding a solution and remembering who we really are.

Even if what is in front of you looks, feels, and smells like the very shit you've always experienced and have only known to be true, what do you want to be experiencing now in your life, and therefore what do you want to be true for you now?

If you do want love to be safe, even though you just had an experience where it didn't feel safe and you've got a world of evidence that shows and proves that love isn't safe, do you want to now change it and experience love being safe?

If we want love to create a different result in the future and align to love being safe as a part of our experience, what would we now get to believe?

What would you now get to choose to focus on instead of looking at the evidence and experience you just had?

Remember, your new belief and perception isn't based off of past experiences; it is a belief that will match up to what you want to experience moving forward and are now going to create as your reality.

So again, what would you GET to now believe to get what you want and create that as your reality?

What could you now practice looking for?

What perception could be truer and in alignment with your highest self and divinity?

Do you feel like your highest self really believes that experiencing love and having love is unsafe?

Do you feel like your highest evolved self would believe that love is scary and isn't safe?

Or, would your highest evolved self know something else to be true and see all the possibilities and options that you just haven't allowed yourself to experience yet? Does your highest evolved self know of the divinity you are and the worthiness you already hold to now experience in the divine frequency of unconditional love and the truth? Do you think it knows that what is beyond the fear is an infinitely eternal field that can hold all of you in love through everything you do and experience in every moment?

That might be more than your human mind can conceive at this time, yet your highest self can hold that vision of what is to come and what is possible for you.

What are you focused on? *It not being true...* So, now what do you get to focus on?

How it can be true.

Get curious. Can you see evidence that other people somewhere in the world are experiencing that love is safe?

Can you find examples of ways that love is safe?

Is it safe to love a pet? Have you felt safety in the love of a friend? Even if you haven't experienced it, can you see that it is a possibility?

So, again, what do you now get to focus on? You can then choose a belief that you can align to be true for you as we discussed above, and that might even be, *I am excited to find ways that love is safe.* Our mind is hearing "love is safe," our perceptions are looking for "love is safe," and we are focusing our new attention on "love is safe." That is moving the alignment dial towards love being safe instead of reaffirming and getting stuck in the same old shit. That gives us the possibility now of attracting and creating that as our experience. What we find is that we get a little taste or experience of how it's true, and then another, and another, and another... and soon you can easily say and believe love is safe because you've now got more and more evidence of how that is true when you are looking for it, focused on it, and creating it.

Easy, right? There are always solutions and infinite ways to move past what you once were stuck in to see all the possibilities available.

What about the classic ego mind fuck?

Let's get clear on the second way I mentioned this can feel blocked.

You say the new belief...and suddenly, ego mind speaks up: "Umm, excuse me. Nuh uh.... Remember when this happened to us, and then that happened..." and on, and on; it begins listing all the evidence that you've built up from the past that this new belief is not true.

The classic ego mind fuck jumps in to do its job... If we see this for what it really is; it is just doing everything it thinks you actually want by keeping you safe in the very comfort zone of what you have known to be true and have always focused and acted on, and it is just popping in to say hello and do what it thinks is saving your ass by getting you to stay put right here in that uncomfortable comfort zone. Our ego simply knows every trick and secret that will trigger the scared smaller self the most and bring up everything in you to want to stay in this comfort zone you've created together.

I see my ego mind as one of my besties and partners on this journey and a simple operating system doing its best to support my scared smaller self and the contracts my scared self made within myself out of my intention to do everything to keep me safe.

Shutting these voices up by trying to ignore them, throwing them in the dark closet where you think they belong, and slamming the door is what we've already been doing. It will only keep them there, growing louder, banging on the door, and crying out to be heard.

I simply appreciate what it wants to say and bring my awareness to knowing that it is doing it ultimately out of love for me and to keep me safe and for it to survive. There is never anything to fight; that, again, is a story to create struggle and pain. Instead, when I accept anything and everything that comes up, I honor that it is just there as an experience and reflection, and I can utilize the feedback to consciously respond. I can always be in the power of choice to create what I want from it.

I say to my ego mind, *Thank you, love, for those reflections; I can completely understand why we would think that from those perceptions and experiences. Thank you for bringing up what we used to believe. This is what we now realize, see, and know to be true, and we can have that conversation with all parts of us to shed light on the new evidence we see and are looking for and what we now believe to be true.*

After addressing the ego, inner child, and all parts that want a voice, we can focus on those things that we know to be true, even if it's a small step. These are the quick ways to just find a simpler or smaller belief that is working towards the bigger one that you are aligning to. Realize instead of playing along and going down the rabbit hole, looking for all the reasons why it's not been true for you, you get to choose to now appreciate it and acknowledge it as what you chose to experience and used to believe and turn your direction to what you now get to believe to create a new experience.

Your Inner Child Knows the Way

If you break down a more specific reason why love doesn't feel safe, you can zone in on a more clear and specific belief to replace it with.

To do this, ask deeper questions. Who has the answers? Well, all of you, yet your inner child is the one who created the decisions of your core programming and is steering your life. This can be as easy as playing a game of questions with your inner child.

If you say your statement as above where we began, "Love is safe and connection is fun and easy," and you notice heaviness in your body or some form of resistance, tune in to your body and see where the heaviness showed up.

Ahh, sweetie, when I say, "Love is safe," what are you feeling?

Maybe the feeling is in your stomach. *Why are we still afraid to be loved?*

Stay soft; remember you are just playing a game and ask more curiosity questions.

You can only come up with even more clarity and unlock even deeper hidden stories, ideas, or fears that the little boy or girl still has. Obviously, these want to be seen, and they hold more truth and power for your inner child than the new belief does when it comes to the safety of love. It won't matter how many times you say the new belief if there is something that feels truer to your inner child that hasn't been acknowledged.

When you allow these to be fully witnessed, embracing them with love and acceptance, you can feel and heal them to move through your system and dissolve the heaviness into light.

Ahh, thank you, love. I can understand why we would still be afraid of love being safe with those past experiences and those old beliefs, thoughts, and worries.

Imagine you really are having a conversation with a child because you are. What else does he or she require to know from you to feel safe and to trust that the old stories are just lies? Listen to this sweet little wounded child and make him or her feel comfortable by applying love and listening to what the fears are. You get to build a relationship with your inner child because you might have completely neglected him or her and shut down that part of you because you thought quieting this aspect of yourself would help you cope or survive. It might be that you haven't listened to him or her for a long time, and he or she doesn't really feel heard, or like you care, or like you can be trusted you to keep you both safe. You are now building a relationship with all of you.

Ahh, my sweet little one, thank you. I want you to know that no matter what happens, I've got you. I'm not leaving you. My Sweet one, we can get through any situation. I'll take care of you. I'm always here for you, and we are safe. I will hold the space for you. I have always got you, and God (or whatever language resonates for you) has always got us.

Thank you for letting me know and reminding me that is what we have known in the past to be true based on our experience. I know you are just trying to protect us and keep us safe.

What we know now is that we used to think and believe that love is unsafe, and that is also why we have experienced what we have. This is how we made love not safe; by believing that, and putting up our guard, and pushing love away. That is how we can get hurt.

What we now want is to have more love and connection and for it to be safe.

Now we can see how we can be safe in experiencing love. Continue to gently talk to your inner child as you get to again look at all the new truths and what new perceptions you can find and reaffirm.

You get to learn to actually parent yourself and nurture yourself to build this relationship. Instead of continuing to live your life from these outdated and old stories continuing to unconsciously operate as the five year old, you can begin to share with and teach your little inner child the new evidence. You get to give them the love they require and provide them with the new truths and healing statements they and you both require for your healing and to upgrade the conversation to the conscious, aligned version of you to be able to create something different.

You can also ask the question: *Whose voice is that? Who does that thought, belief, or story really belong to? Is it really yours, or was it one of your parents', grandparents', caretakers', or teachers'? Does it come from religion? Is it someone else's idea and story that you took on?* You can always breathe into it, thank it for showing up, and recognize this was never yours in the first place, and as you breathe, consciously choose to now release it and see the energy of it being released from your body, returned to source where it is transmuted back into light. Witness it becoming light, as you now love seeing it for what it is and only honor it for what it taught you and the person you received it from for being a part of those sacred contracts. You can now reclaim those fractals and parts of you that got lost from this and giving your power away to someone else's story and beliefs. See these pieces of light fractals come floating back into you, restoring even more of who you are, knowing you can return to the remembrance of who you are and what you now choose. You always have the choice to choose what is best for you and be the source of your experience based on what you now choose to believe and how you choose to respond.

Are you seeing the string of evidence and how we break it down to each thought process that connects us to the next step of understanding and acceptance?

Wherever there is any type of resistance is where we get to go because it is being revealed to be healed, and on the other side of the resistance is what is even greater waiting for you to receive.

Changing the mindset by just looking at a new perception isn't the answer to creating the solution. The mind is, however, the tool we use to fill in the gaps and connect all of the operating systems for it to become true. It is clarifying what is happening in the body, what the thoughts, patterns, and behaviors are, and with each piece of information, we get to decide if that will give us what we want. As we realign all the systems, it does become what feels true, looks true, and is true because we are also choosing all the patterns to align to it and receive it.

State your new belief and perception, and again tune into the body to see how it feels.

Did that clear it up now that your mind has connected the dots with your body and for your little boy or girl to see clearly and understand? If not, you can continue to get curious or bring it to a smaller step, belief, perception and focus that you can now believe to be true.

Break Down Will Always Lead to a Break Through

The more you are willing to get curious and break it down, the faster and the easier it becomes and what follows will always be more space for you to expand and receive.

If you continue to ask curiosity questions for anything you are in resistance to such as in our example above, *Why else isn't love safe?* or *Why else are we afraid to feel more love?*, then you'll be able to go deeper. Maybe the initial response was: *We always get hurt,* but if you continue to probe, you might find that your inner child believes that love is unsafe because he or she associates love to a loss of control. Suddenly, you might see a whole grander string of why you operate the way you do and what you are really fighting. You see how Mom lost control of her life because she was giving up her life for the man in it, or she was emotionally controlled by someone else, or she didn't have her own voice or stand up for herself because she was afraid of losing love. Again, there are infinite possibilities for you to uncover when you ask yourself these questions out of softness and love.

Maybe it is that you feel like you have no control over what happens in love because you can't control the other person; you feel then extremely vulnerable to being rejected. All of this shows you that there is a deeply held belief that you have to control things to be safe and that you will never be free until you realize that anything you are fighting to control is in fact the thing that *is* controlling you.

When you break down the idea of losing control, or having to be in control, and you remind yourself of the truth, you realize you actually are always in control because you can listen to yourself and do what feels good. You can feel your feelings and tune into what boundaries support you, what environments you want to be in, and the type of people you choose to be around and share your energy with.

You also might feel out of control and that you get hurt because you believe people are mean, bad, and abusive because that is what you were programmed in and have experienced.

The moment you see this, you can now allow that belief to surface, be recognized, and take radical responsibility to accept your position as the creator of your life. You choose who you let in your life and to be around, and you now focus on how you only attract the very best and most amazing people of integrity that magnify your life. You align yourself first with your own behaviors to be that person, and therefore you can only attract the same. If the behaviors and results someone is living in don't align to the type of people you choose to let into your space, then you are the source of your experience that gets to set new behaviors and boundaries to support the life and relationship experiences you are now choosing into.

By digging deeper and asking your inner child these questions, you discover and clean up a whole other area of your life, freeing yourself from a program you didn't recognize was keeping you away from people and away from receiving more love.

Anytime you feel resistance, it is easy to quickly get curious and see what idea or story you are holding onto that is creating it. It just takes a quick internal look to get clear and tune into what you want and how to focus on and align that to the new truth that will serve and support you. Then you are free to move forward in creating and receiving it. The same thing is applied in money, your passion and purpose, sex and pleasure, and every aspect of life you are leaning into that you can only receive more.

My Association to It Is SHIT

There is one more area that can keep you trapped on the hamster wheel of creating the same struggles—keeping the same internal representation to the very thing you are looking to change.

Let's say you are now focusing on believing you are worthy of success. If you say, "I am successful, and success comes easy," it makes sense to look at what success really means to you. I had a client who always sabotaged his business when it was expanding, and as we looked deeper, we found it was because he believed successful people were assholes and he didn't want to be an asshole. "Successful" to him meant that you start treating people poorly, lose your relationships, and care only about money. If the association doesn't change, then the internal system still doesn't want to create success no matter how many times you reaffirm that is what you are focusing on.

So, if you say, "I am successful," and feel heavy or like you can't own that, this is the cue to look at your associations to success, or whatever you are feeling resistance around and what that means. Where do some adjustments get to happen internally so your whole self is clear on what success really means for you and gives you? Can you see that truly only you can give it to yourself, and then can you feel as though you are worthy of creating and receiving it?

Oh, that's right…. That's just from my past association. Haha…silly human story. This is what we know to be true and what is true for me now. Successful people are kindhearted and have the resources to serve and support many others. Success is easy because I love helping people, and when I serve and give value, I receive value back in the exchange of money. I use this money as a tool of creation to do even more good on the planet. I am always supported by the Universe and will receive the people who are seeking what I have to give.

Let's go back to our core example, "love is safe," because we all can identify with having love or a lack of love show up in many ways.

Now that you understand that, you get to connect all the pieces of the puzzle by having all of your operating systems (aka your mental programming, beliefs, perceptions, language, and feeling) on the same page and aligned. It's easy.

Yet, maybe you notice a little fear because you think you've tried this before. You tried to believe that you could have a great relationship. You want to believe that love can be safe, supportive, and awesome, and you think that you did really try to focus on love being that in the past. What happened?

Obviously, you continued to have the experiences you had because there is something else that you get to reveal, embrace, love, and heal.

Let's say that after the last relationship you had, you did all the self-empowerment techniques. You started declaring that you are worthy of love and you began to focus on receiving love, how you love, and how love shows up in your life.

Pause for a moment and ask yourself: What is your RELATIONSHIP to love? You'd do the same thing for money, sex, health, and any other area.

To continue going deeper with this example: what comes with love? What happens when you are in love? What are your general associations and your internal references to love? Your relationship to different kinds of love can be very different. Love with your friends might be supportive, fun, uplifting, and amazing and yet love with family might be scary and painful. It was when I questioned what my relationship to any relationship, such as money, my body, sex, expression, and relationships with others, that I found my deeper connections to where any

243

resistance was still remaining and what unconscious associations I had to it.

If your internal representation to an intimate love relationship is that of struggle, difficulty, sacrifice, or pain, then that is the kind of love you are calling in as you focus on receiving more love.

You will therefore continue to create love that reflects that exact kind of love you have experienced and what you associate love to be. As we reviewed earlier, we also create the exact programs that call us to heal these patterns, beliefs, and behaviors so that they can change. They are only reading our scripts and bringing up exactly what you can discover to heal so you can create a love that is fully honoring and loving of yourself and the other.

If you see that your relationship to love was hard and you had a pattern of sacrificing yourself or getting out of balance, you can get a lot of clarity as to why exactly your relationship to love becomes hard. If you step into playing a hero role or a mother, father, or rescuer archetype in your relationships, then it's no wonder love can be difficult. That isn't sustainable unless that is the kind of relationship you want.

Taking radical responsibility that these are the types of patterns you are operating out of allows you to see that staying in them isn't going to give you the fulfilling love you want. You'll also see why you have attracted the types of people and relationships that you have if this is the pattern that shows up. It will give you feedback to the relationship you have to relationships and what your beliefs about them and associations you have to them are.

So, if you are calling in love and haven't yet recognized these associations, so you continue to have these types of love experiences, the gift is right in front of you now to see. You get to take full responsibility here about why you used to see it that way and behaved that way in the past so you can heal it. Everything, and I mean everything, is always working for you. This applies to your relationship with all things, and as you question your relationship to anything, you can create the clarity that you aren't calling in the same experiences because the reference point hasn't changed.

The process is still working for you each and every time you go through the 5 Steps because each step is reaffirming a new belief, pattern, and behavior that is creating a different story and experience for you. You are now looking for what you are reaffirming and aligning to new behaviors, and all of it is creating a better experience with love, money, sex, pleasure, health, expression, worthiness, and all you continue to expand into.

It's time to create a new representation, which starts by getting more descriptive when it comes to love, success, health, abundance, or whatever you are choosing to focus on.

Let's continue to look at how you can create a new internal representation and association of what LOVE now is to you as our core example here. If you think about the relationships you've had and you can see the patterns you went into or the things that didn't work, then what would be the opposite of that? What would give you what you really want?

I encourage you to visualize and get really specific as to what it would be like to feel the type of love you want to experience. Rather than simply saying, "I deserve an epic love, and it will be beautiful" or "I am receiving love," which are fairly basic sentiments and can carry associations from the past, we want to now get all of our systems clear as to what we now refer to and mean by "love" and what we experience with it now. Apply this clarity with each thing you are recreating and get specific.

Close your eyes, or do an open-eye visualization if that is what you are mastering, and give yourself permission to begin to see what love, success, abundance, bliss, worthiness, peace or whatever you are creating now looks like and what your new experience with it is. In this example, see how you interact with this love partner in all the facets of life experiences, from the day to day, to the depths of unconditional love, pleasure, adventures, growth, and the infinite possibilities of the most aligned sovereign divine experience of love. See how this relationship magnifies your life, is fun and easy, and is a container of love, support, and acceptance to continually grow and expand in. What do all of your experiences look and feel like?

What does it look like when you're just driving down the road together? Are you holding hands, belting out songs, laughing and grooving and having a blast with each other? Can you allow love to be that fun and enjoyable all the time? What does it look like to go get groceries with this person and be in the day to day experiences? Expand from day to day and into all the areas of relationship you want to experience. Are you a great team and support for each other in all of your passions, purpose, and growth?

How much expression, authenticity, and vulnerability can you experience together as growth partners? Can you feel held in love to be completely transparent with who you are? Do you feel worthy of being fully seen, heard, expressed, loved, adored, honored, cherished, and appreciated? How does that feel? Can you see yourself being that for yourself and reflecting that field for your partner or partners, depending on the type of love relationship/s you seek and choose?

What does your sex life look like? How does it feel to be so completely held in safety of your relationship to fully express, be seen, ask for what you want, and allow full pleasure? How does it feel to be committed with someone to grow increasingly in receiving more pleasure, joy, passion, fun, and play? What does that journey look like, feel like, and sound like? Can you see the laughter, the play, and feel the safety and joy that is available and what that feels like now?

If now you are describing or seeing love as: "I love being with my beloved and how much fun we have in all we do and experience in life. As we drive down the road, we sing songs and laugh.

We love being connected and love holding hands, even as we push the grocery cart together down the aisles, planning what we want to cook and create together. We have deep and beautiful authentic conversations and hold a field of divine unconditional love and acceptance for all our hurt, scared parts that are healing into love and light. We share in complete vulnerability and transparency and hold the space for each other to be unconditionally supported in all we are experiencing. We laugh. We play. He/ she is my amazing co-creator of divine sacred union and mirror reflecting all the bliss, abundance, and joy available on this adventure together as we continually grow together and find ways to have even more fun, pleasure, and play." Can you see the difference in vibration as opposed to the simpler description? Can you begin right now to imagine what that feels like? Can you feel all of your desires met now by yourself as the source creator of this experience and by being it, receiving it? Can you begin to feel completely supported now?

Just imagine that you have all of this now, without looking outside for evidence.

If that type of love is too outside of your vision and grasp right now, if you can't relate and connect to that, then that's OK; get more curious. In what way can you describe the love you want that you can imagine to be true for you? Where can you see examples of it that prove it does really exist? Look at where you have good associations to love and support in your life. You can take those, such as the love you've experienced from a friendship, and now associate them to love being supportive. You can imagine feeling the same support with an intimate love partner if that is the area of greater love you are aligning to.

What is the new belief and perception I can believe? What can I focus on that is moving me towards that new pathway of freedom and what I want in this area of my life? What can I claim and believe to be true?

Once you break your shit stories down, they'll begin to lose hold on you or any power in your life and you will truly find the gift in the shit. Those limiting beliefs and perceptions will fall, and you'll become the creator of a new story that gets you where you want to go—to the life you really dream of and actually are now aligned to receive. You are worthy of it, and it is already done. It's already on its way. It's already available. Open your arms and receive.

You Can Completely DESIGN a Brand-New Story

I want to share another way that you can completely design the story from one my personal client's own experiences of this from his words. I mentioned earlier in the book that I would share a timeline-hopping process that can completely change where you are existing so you can create a new reality.

This client was and still is an amazing and powerful coach. He spent countless years processing this one traumatic event that happened to him as a child, from which he had anchored in some deep wounds and beliefs around abandonment and not being enough, which was therefore capping his growth and ability to expand and receive. No matter how many times he worked on it through self-empowerment processes over the years, and no matter how many different perspectives he looked at it from, it still remained.

This is because it still always felt like the truest perception in his system. Along with 37 years of continuing to reaffirm this through his life and experiences, it is understandable. I want you to hear why that is so important to understand and that you will always continue to receive based on what you really believe in your body.

Here is his experience:

I want to share a story about the work that I did with Marci and how it completely transformed my relationship to myself, my relationship to my parents, and many, many other things.

I've been doing personal development work for about 15 to 16 years. I've spent a tremendous number of hours and probably close to a million dollars on my education, including books, videos, seminars, and coaching programs.

There was, however, this one instance when I was three and a half years old that created many, many situations in my life and belief systems that I struggled with. So, by the time that I had started working with Marci as a personal client, I had looked at this one instance to try and shift it a good thousand times. Basically, to sum up what I took from this experience was that my parents left me, I'm abandoned, I'm a loser, I'm bad, I'm not enough, and I have to prove that I'm enough. These beliefs shaped the course of my life.

This particular day I was speaking to Marci for a coaching call, a situation was happening in my life that I was having a really, really tough time with, and I basically got on the call with Marci bawling, as all of this stuff was being triggered back from this moment I experienced when I was little.

Marci took me through a really powerful exercise, which took me back into that situation, looking and experiencing it from my soul and higher self. I was able to capture so many more things from the experience that had created hidden disconnects for me. We were able to catch what had created my ability to be independent, do things on my own, and take care of myself, which obviously are amazing strengths that I have.

I was able to connect to why my soul had chosen and created this to bring a lot of these gifts and abilities into my life. I was also able to then connect to the shadow frequencies and aspects I had taken on that were never true and only created through what I perceived at the time. I had tried to just pick a new perception many, many times before over the years, but these just didn't land or work for me because I could not believe them as more true then what I had experienced.

What was absolutely amazing about what Marci took me through was that I actually got to reprogram the moment to be a completely different experience and completely shift the timeline then see how it affected the rest of my life.

Now I have two young kids of my own, who are seven and five and a half years old. I was able to visualize and imprint into this experience what I've learned from Marci in how to be fully with my kids, love and comfort them, listen to them, and hear and accept them in what they are experiencing. I was able to recreate and recode the experience to be that which my little boy was seeking, give him the healing he was requiring, and completely change how it felt in my body and played out into my life. It wasn't just a perception shift or reframe; it was a completely reprogramming of the experience.

As this was all happening, I could feel a tremendous release in my body from the weight being lifted. The next piece that happened was really crazy and fascinating. As we were reprogramming, and I was seeing all these connections in my timeline that happened from this, I was able to witness all these other related experiences also completely shift because the experience and timeline had changed. What got reprogrammed were the feelings and fear I had of losing and of being abandoned; these were replaced by this beautiful, loving, feeling of completely supported and taken care of. I saw and experienced a completely different experience that supported me.

It was a really beautiful experience. I realized that my inner child wasn't necessarily looking for support from my parents; he was looking for me to love and support him. It was like he told me: "I've been waiting for you for 37 years. Thank you so much for finding me." Ever since that moment, we've just built this incredibly loving beautiful relationship, almost like I have with my kids, of just supporting him and letting him know that no matter what happens, I will always be there for him.

That whole exercise just opened up my entire world so beautifully, and then watching how it then has played out with my wife, my kids, my parents, and others has been absolutely monumental. Thank you, Marci. I love you and am forever grateful.

I hope what you can get from this is that you can completely choose new beliefs and programs to operate from and experience a completely different timeline and reality now. In a non-dualistic reality, it was a timeline experience you chose and reality that you manifested into your hologram, but you can shift the timeline and time hop into a different experience by changing the experience you had internally. Everything can then shift from that internal shift you chose to reprogram. You are the source of your experience.

15

Step #5:

What Is the Action I Get to Take to Give Me What I Want?

What is the ACTION I get to take NOW to give me what I want?

AND... How does it get to be fun and easy?

In this circumstance, what would I get to do to get what I want?

What is the next step?

Ask for what you want to create the solution.

CHANGE YOUR VIBE and STATE to feel good and take the ACTION to create what you want.

Create Your Solution

After you've figured out what you're feeling and why, discovered what you truly want and deserve, and adopted new beliefs and perceptions, you're ready take action.

It's time to up-level, my friends. It's time to ask for what you want and start creating the solution. It's time to feel the freedom of ultimate clarity. It's time to change your vibe and move into the light of peace, prosperity, bliss, and awesomeness that is your new reality.

You just decided on what your new belief and perception is, and so in this moment, Step 5 is to now act on it. *In this experience I am in right now, what is the action I get to take now to give me what I want? What would be the step I could take right now to move towards that new belief and perception as my experience? To be experiencing that new belief right now, what would I get to do and be doing? How can I now create that? What is the most powerful action I can take right now?* Any one of these is a way you can communicate with yourself to spark how you can take the next inch and action step to align it into reality.

In Step 5, if you continue to practice operating out of faith and creation energy, which again is curiosity, wonderment, and excitement, you can find infinite possibilities to step forward. Get excited and change your perception to excitement and wonderment if you feel any resistance come up with taking the action. *I'm excited to see how I can feel better right now and to see what else I can be experiencing. I'm excited about the possibilities.* You are finally here at the turning point of creating a new experience and operating out of your new belief system; it just takes choosing an action that matches the new belief and creating new patterns that will give you this freedom.

Bring It to This Moment

First, we want to bring it to this moment because HOW we respond to our trigger, and the old shit showing up, and the patterns is what will determine what we get next. *What in this moment can I do to align to that and be a clear declaration to myself, my core beliefs, the Universe, and all the energy involved of who I am now and what I now get to experience?*

This can be super simple and easy.

Let's walk through a scenario: You were working on a project for your business and found yourself getting distracted; you kept putting it off or felt resistance in sticking with it or doing it at all. Perfect! Time to see what's really happening and go into the 5 Steps.

You discovered you were feeling afraid. You felt this way because the thoughts coming up were that the project might not be good enough, you aren't sure people will like it or respond to it, and that it might fail.

You give yourself some love and see where it was all coming from; it is just from your past and old beliefs and programs. Then you get clear on what you want—to complete this project because you are passionate about it; it is a piece of you. You reaffirm and see that you are doing it for you.

Your new belief and perception you choose could be any of these: *It is safe to be me. I am safe to express myself and to be seen and heard. I am worthy of creating masterpieces for me and I also love sharing them. I love the freedom I feel when I express myself and I'm excited to share it with the world.*

What would the action now be in this moment to align to that? And, the second part of Step 5, how does it get to be fun and easy?

The action is simple, right? Get back to working on your project. It is just doing the action that takes you back into alignment of getting the result you want.

What if it doesn't feel that simple though?

The key: make it fun and easy!

You can also try on: *How do I get to experience more joy right now?* or *How do I get to feel good right now?* or *How would I make doing this super fun?*

How would you get to now view doing this project as something you are excited about? What would change your entire vibration from the heaviness or resistance you were experiencing to energy aligned with getting back into your project?

The reason this is important is because the energy you project now is what will create exactly what you get.

If in this scenario, again, we walk through the 5 Steps and go *OK, so here's my new belief "I'm convincing" myself of. What do I now get to do? Get back to work and get in it.* Just notice that energy of "convincing yourself" if you still feel an energy of fear like you aren't completely on board with that new belief and perception.

If you implement the action out of forcing yourself, pushing past your resistance, just to get to that end goal, it is planting the seed of fear into that very project and message and creating exactly what you were afraid of because it's now carrying that vibration and those thoughts and those worries. Doing the project or thing itself and adding the energy of force, fight, try, struggle, lack, or scarcity will only create more resistance.

Now, you might have found a belief and perception that really does feel good to you, and you really can believe it to be true and yet, you are still feeling or holding some energy in your body that feels scared about moving forward and taking the action.

This is why we get to consciously ask, "How does this get to be fun and easy?"

In doing this, our minds find all these solutions for how we can create with ease, receive with ease, have more joy, and allow this to be our experience. We get to consciously add in the energy and perceptions of fun and ease to what we are doing because remember, it is always as easy or as hard as you want to make it based on your perception. If you consciously choose the perception and energy of fun and ease, that is what you will find and will create as the feeling in your body and your new belief around doing what you want.

That might look like turning on your favorite jam and rockin' out some dance grooves so you feel light and joyful. It might mean that you meditate and give yourself a few minutes to visualize yourself completing the project and how good it feels to share it, how much impact it will make in the world, and how you are discovering more ways for your gifts to come through. Maybe you go take a walk or do an energy shake out to release any of that stuck energy and give yourself permission to feel good. Now you feel really aligned to this feeling and are excited to jump back in.

You can process a bit deeper to see if there is anything else to be heard, expressed, or addressed. There might be another thought your inner child has that is holding onto a bit of fear, so you hear it, acknowledge it, present what is really true, and get back into it, allowing it to feel good and in flow.

That might be that you realize overwhelm at the idea of completing the whole project, and that is why fear is still there. Instead, what serves you in this moment is just to focus on the next inch and the next step you are working on and drop any attachments, stories, or ideas of the time frame that are creating the stress. You can decide that you are going to take action by focusing on it for the next hour, and whatever you get done in that hour, you get done.

It might also mean that you notice you get to have some play and self-love because your energy really isn't in alignment for this project right now, and if you focused on it, you would only be forcing yourself. So, maybe you can do other productive things that feel in alignment right now before you focus on the project. That might mean you also let everything go and choose to go hit the beach and lay in the sun, go for a swim in the ocean, take a drive, or do anything that feels like it is you giving yourself the love you are worthy of. How do you get to allow yourself to be back in that vibration of love, light, joy, bliss and your worthiness that is bringing it back to the alignment of who you really are, remembering that your vibration is always the highest priority?

It isn't about creating a distraction; it is about leaning into why you were distracted or resistance came up and coming full circle to feeling good and awesome to reaffirm it is your new norm that you get to always live in awesome, things do get to be fun and easy, and you are worthy of always feeling good.

If you ran to do one of these things out of avoiding the project because you were afraid of it not being good enough, you'd run into the same issue the next time, the next day, and the next, and it would continue to reaffirm the fear and become a life pattern of procrastination.

Sometimes the very thing you get to let go of is the story that you should be doing that thing right now or it has to look a certain way. You being in the highest vibrational frequency is the highest priority because that is what creates everything else. If you aren't feeling good, you are in some kind of a story.

There have been many times I got to honor that what I had planned for the day or to do just didn't feel good, and so I got to ask, *What would feel good right now? What would be the most nourishing for my soul? What am I really seeking?* I got to realign my day because it wouldn't be authentic to do the things out of force anyways, and I know that my alignment is the greatest priority for creating the highest and greatest good. It is so easy to produce, create, and manifest when I feel good because that is creation energy. It would only create more shit if I tried to force something or fight it. When you get clear, you operate from a place of alignment in all that you do and so, of course, it becomes easy and your norm is flow, fun, and ease.

You might find that it just doesn't feel good because you are requiring some clarity on the project or thing in front of you. *Well, how would you get that clarity? What research would you do? Who would you talk to?* Those are the actions you step into when you realize, *Oh, I do want to do this. I am just feeling resistance because of this, which has me afraid it won't be good, so now how can I receive that support to get that clarity and to move forward?*

If your new belief is, *Relationships are a joy,* how do you get to make that true for you right now? What can you do right now to experience joy in relationships? What can you do to allow yourself to create more connection, fun, and joy?

If an ankle injury has set you back on your workout plan, for example, ask yourself what you're feeling (likely frustrated) and why (because you're afraid you won't get results). Then, remind yourself again why you want the results you do. Do you want to have more energy to play with your kids? To feel more confident in your love life? Focus on that while applying more curiosity.

Understand that yes, you've created an ankle injury for yourself. You can't change that now, but you can examine it closely, use the feedback, and create what you want to be experiencing out of this situation. Issues with the ankles signal inflexibility or the inability to receive pleasure. Consider whether that rings true for you.

With such a high level of clarity, you can then lean into your belief that although you had something show up that you might've seen as a setback, which we know showed up for a reason. It doesn't mean you can't still be creating and receiving what you want. You're still worthy of a healthy, rockin' body. You decide, *I am worthy of being in tune with my body, living in health, having energy, and feeling good every day.* That means, of course, you get to take care of yourself every day and you love how that feels.

Then, ask yourself, *What else could I do to move forward with my new belief and perception? What else is possible? What action would align to that? What would be the most powerful thing I could do to support myself and create that?*

And your action? Instead of doing cardio, you might focus on exercising your upper body and fully supporting your body with the best nutrition as your new behavior you are aligning to while your ankle heals. It might be that you look at what you can do to move and exercise that doesn't involve using this area that is healing and showed up to share with you what was going on inside. You get curious to see how else you can make your new lifestyle of exercising fun and easy for you. Maybe you'll involve a friend or even just do a few minutes of movement because doing something is reaffirming that new belief versus an old one that says now you can't.

The point is that you move forward to leave your comfort zone in the dust.

Let's say you just had a fight with your partner. In this circumstance, how would you get what you want, which might be returning to love and connection? The action right now to align to that could be that you get to drop your guard, get soft, and choose to communicate through it. How could you make that easy? Ask for support, tell them you are aware of how deeply you are triggered and hurt and that what you want to create instead is a soft, peaceful conversation to return back to love and understanding. Ask for what you want, and if they are open and willing to have a conversation to support you in moving through it. Then you set yourself up for support by breathing, moving, and reminding yourself that you can't possibly know what is true for them, you only assume the very best, and you are excited to find more clarity about what is really true, and you settle into softness and curiosity to go into the conversation.

How could it be more fun? I have some dear friends who are relationship coaches, and they have a practice of putting on silly masks when their tension is high, and they get to go through communication with each other. They can't help but begin to laugh at it all when they make the whole thing silly and realize the cosmic joke they are in and how they each were just reading each other's scripts and really, they both are just seeking to feel loved. They found a way to make communication fun and easy. It allows them to do something that sets the mood to see the things they used to make painful as silly and easy to move through to return to love, solution, and the relationship they want to be experiencing.

You get to take radical responsibility to create the energy of the action matching the energy of what you are claiming as your new belief and perception if you want to actually create that as your result and new reality.

Now you have made a CLEAR response to the Universe and yourself and aligned the energy by taking the action in this moment. Celebrate that success!

If you want to truly implement this as a new belief system and create the pathways of this becoming how you operate as your new norm, it is important to look at how you are going to now integrate this into your life. Just doing it this moment isn't going to continue to imprint the new pathway and create the result. It is choosing to bring all your patterns and behaviors as well as operating systems into alignment with what you say you want over and over again as it becomes how you operate.

Whatever you are seeking, GIVE it to yourself.

By using the 5 Steps, you are taking radical responsibility of your world, and this final step is where you create it. What you really want to look for is whatever the little girl or boy inside is seeking and give this to yourself.

Alignment Comes from Inside

Let's say you realize you only wanted to reach for the sabotaging food because you are wanting to celebrate your success for the day, something you accomplished, and to have fun. How, then, can you do that without the sabotaging pattern? How do you celebrate you and your success and fill yourself up with love rather than seek something to be the source of your acknowledgement? How do you give it to yourself? It isn't going to come from the food; it is going to come from you. If you are reaching out in a particular pattern or behavior and you realize what's behind it is that you are wanting connection and love, how do you give yourself the connection and love? Yes, you can always create behaviors that support and create what you want, such as building up friend-ships for connection, yet if you are looking to be fulfilled from an outside source, you will always be seeking and always be looking for someone else to provide it for you.

To become whole, you get to be whole, and that means you are the source of your experience and the creator of your world. It will always come from within you and not from outside of you. The more whole you become, the less you will require and expect others to fulfill you, validate you, or show up a certain way. The more whole you become, the less you will dance the dance of manipulation you once weaved unknowingly in the silly human patterns that kept you striving to control your world. The more whole you become, the less you will expect others to carry your responsibilities, do your inner work, create your solutions, or give you permission to experience joy and pleasure and live in your purpose and highest calling. You'll find your own energy, vitality, and life force within as you withdraw from depending on others' energy for your own ability to operate. You shed the identity that you once believed was required to protect you and you now understand was enslaving you. You are free to dance your own dance in the movement and flow of life that feels good for you and allow others to do the same.

And so, I'll say it again: whatever you discover you are seeking, give it to yourself.

Set yourself up for successful implementation and think long term. Ask yourself, *How will I Implement this in my life moving forward?* If you want to have great communication in your relationship, what are the patterns and behaviors you can take ownership of that keep you from that, and what are the ones you will now implement and practice to create that?

Step back to look at the big view of what you are really wanting and all the possible ways you can begin to live as that person, be that person, and think and behave as that person. How do you set yourself up for support to continue to practice this belief and BEING this person? You BE the person first by doing the things that person does, and you will receive it as a result.

This reminds me of watching the fly who just couldn't get through. As I'm traveling the world right now, location free, I'm currently enjoying Croatia and have had a month at a gorgeous place right on the ocean front and on a private area of an island. My place has a huge stretch of windows and doors—all leading right outside to the ocean—and I have them open most of the time to hear the waves, enjoy the sounds of the ocean right out front, and to feel the wind.

I sat and watched this fly in front of the one window that was closed. It continually kept banging itself repeatedly into the window, trying to get outside. Then it would pace and walk all over the window, only to return to flying itself again and again into the window, as if to have a different experience. We all know this as the definition of insanity: doing the same thing over and over and expecting a different result. If it simply paused and considered the options that could be different, backed up to really look at the obstacle and opportunity in front of it, flew around, and got curious about all of the options, it would see several doors and windows open, giving it access to the outdoors, the very place it wanted to go.

You can stop the cycle by applying curiosity to your situation. Say, for example, you're sick of friendships that aren't honoring to you. Maybe you examine your friendship experiences and ask yourself why you experienced what you did and what you judge about the other people involved. Then, ask yourself what you were doing to play into that scenario? How have you ever portrayed those traits in some form at any time in your life that you aren't claiming or recognizing? As you work through both of these questions, remember not to place blame. Instead, focus only on the feedback you're getting.

Keep moving the focus forward on what you really want to do—have epic and fulfilling friendships—and breathe and sway. Breathe and sway. Move that energy through your body and understand that just because a scenario you are going through may look like your old life, that doesn't mean that it is true, or that you have to accept it. Instead, you get the opportunity to take a different action; you can now change how you see it and how you respond.

I highly suggest you pause and sit with curiosity as to how this idea, story, belief, or scenario that you were doing the 5 Steps for really happens. What are all the ways you stop yourself from having what you really want. One of the greatest things you can do for yourself to really SEE exactly what things you have unconsciously or consciously done is to make a list like we did in Discovery Opportunity #5. I highly, highly recommend taking the time to do this and looking at what you have been doing or now "used to do" that has kept you from doing the things you really want and that has in any way sabotaged what you want.

Then, make a list of what you will practice instead. When those patterns come up, now you will see it because you spent time to get really clear and acknowledge it. Now you will be prepared for when the triggers show up. You also have already set yourself up for support, have new replacement patterns in place, and will be ready to practice them.

Be Proactive About Your Action

What are the ways you can create those changes to more quickly get to what you want? If you want more friendships and connection, that might mean that you commit to going out to meet new people two times a week and lock that into your schedule to be repeated every week. If you are practicing loving yourself more, it might mean that you have a date night with yourself once a week and that is always in your schedule and set.

When I first intended to create date nights with my boys, I noticed we still struggled to get it to happen because there would be extra homework one night or other circumstances. As I evaluated how else we could create this to be fun and easy, I realized if we planned on it and set it in our schedule, we weren't just waiting for it to happen.

Now my boys and I always have set date nights that we plan on. Monday was date night with my beloved, Tuesday was my night with Gavin The Great, Wednesday was my own date night while the boys had a night to themselves, Thursday was date night with Super Sky Guy, Friday was date night with my beloved, and the weekend we left open to shift to whatever we wanted to create, whether that was family time, friend time, personal time, etc. These were set and locked into our schedule that everyone planned on. Of course, if things showed up that we wanted to attend or do, we would just communicate and shift our plans for the week, yet we always had these set and would rearrange accordingly to still meet our committed family, personal, and date times every week. If one of my boys had extra homework or school stuff, we'd adjust, moving our time together to another night, trade their night with someone else's, have a quicker date version to flow with the homework or even doing homework together as a part of our date.

That set pattern in our life completely up-leveled our relationships in more ways than I could ever explain and was one of the greatest gifts for creating the awakened, amazing relationships that I had set as my intention.

Look at what you've done in the past or what is getting in the way of what you want. If your focus is to align to your new creation with health, look at what has been sabotaging you living in health and what are you now practicing in place of those behaviors? You'll be practicing new beliefs, and you also get to practice new behaviors that match what you want. How will you support yourself in the lifestyle of health and implement that every day?

I'm Just Practicing

Sometimes you might stumble around as you are getting familiar with and practicing these new beliefs and patterns. Sometimes you'll get pissed because old patterns start to creep back into your life just as you're trying to get away from them. If something doesn't feel good, resist the urge to shame it back into submission. Let it be there. Learn from it.

Your ego mind is simply doing what it knows has always worked in the past to stop you in your tracks, and it will do the same thing to keep you from moving forward. It's actually a sign that it's working. Your oldest patterns will usually reappear just as you're about to up-level to your next level of receiving, even when they've been patterns that you thought were long gone. These core patterns and behaviors can show up because your ego mind is trying to do all it can to keep you from moving beyond that comfort zone that seems safe and because there are even deeper layers that are ready to be healed. You can begin to see these as easy red flags to spot when they show up—giving you feedback to go inward—and a celebration of what is ready to heal.

We invest a lot in our illusions, so de-storying and transmuting them so that we can create something new takes intentional focus. Choosing something different and consciously acting on that choice is how you confront the comfort zone and step through what I call "The Lock Law of Ascension and the receiving effect." This is how you step through and into receiving more awesomeness, love, and light.

I want to remind you that you are just practicing. It gets to be fun and easy by just practicing. We are always perfect, whole, and complete in whatever we are experiencing, and with each thing that shows up, you are just seeing it and realigning by practicing something new that will give you even more of what you want to be experiencing.

As you are practicing, keep this in mind: The more often I FEEL this state of BEING, the more FAMILIAR I become with it. Therefore, the more familiar I become with it, the more it is my new NORM and natural state of BEING. The more often I choose the patterns, behaviors, thoughts, ideas, stories and feelings that MATCH this STATE and the more I FEEL it, The more I ATTRACT everything and everyone that aligns to this frequency of joy, bliss, pleasure, prosperity, play, unconditional love, acceptance, and light.

See, my loves, each moment you have a choice that will feed the next moment and what you will then receive because how you choose to respond will always create the vibration you give out and what you will manifest next. So, all that is required is the focus on this simple moment and the energy, attention, and focus you choose to give it.

It can be super simple and super easy to just take the next step in alignment to your highest divinity. If anything doesn't match the energy of what you want to be experiencing, it is your opportunity to shift it and align it to that which does. This then effortlessly compounds to the next moment, and the next, and the next and the next. The more this become your new norm and natural state of being and what you expect from life, the more easily it becomes your experience. I expect magic and miracles every day because that is what I choose to look for, experience, and find in each moment.

It is my belief system and the program I operate from as my natural state of being and what I believe I am worthy to experience and receive. Because you have choice and because all things have a right to exist, you can also choose this or the opposite. You can choose to react unconsciously in each moment and feed it with the energy of blame, shame, and judgment and focus on what you don't like and isn't working. It will then effortlessly compound in each moment and bring you even more of it because you are being very clear on what ways you want to continue to grow, evolve, and learn in.

You can also learn through bliss, peace, joy, ease, and the discovery of how much love is available just as you can learn through hardship, suffering, sacrifice, struggle, separation as you discover how much of that is available if you choose. It is always a choice, and you are a divine being of infinite possibilities and therefore, have always been worthy of whatever you want. Focus on practicing the thoughts, beliefs, behaviors, and feelings and frequencies of what you want to be, and this will become what you are familiar with as your natural state of being.

We can discover how extraordinary life was actually meant to be and is when we are willing to look for it and receive it. We can choose to keep it simple and let go of all the complications that can create illusions in each moment instead of what is actually available in the here and now, which is having the time of your life. It doesn't actually take much to allow the deepest parts of ourselves to be incredibly happy. It only takes being here now and appreciate it. We came here for awe, wonder, and the experience of it all. Choose to feel the joy of being alive, feel into your heart, and be grateful for this breath and this moment. You can expand it even more by choosing to share that joy of being alive by who you choose to be and how you interact with people, the world and all of life. That is how simple it really can be.

If you want to have a life you truly love, then you can only receive that by loving yourself. Practice loving yourself unconditionally by dropping the struggle you create by dropping the judgments on yourself and the expectations or attachments of what you think it should be or that anything in this moment is wrong. It is always perfectly playing out for your greatest and highest good, and you can now receive it.

Practice remembering you are the example of how the world gets to love you; only you can create the conditions to receive more love by giving it first to yourself and others. Always remind yourself and repeat, *I love myself unconditionally, even when I witness old behaviors. Every single day and moment, I am practicing new patterns, beliefs, and ways of being in peace, bliss, flow, joy, and ease as my new experience.*

A beautiful dear friend and spiritual teacher of mine who leads our retreats in India in my Ascension Adventures program says, "I think anything worth doing is worth doing badly first. It's not going to be perfect because I've never done it before. That would be unrealistic, and I get to be patient, kind, and loving with myself when I try new behaviors." You know that whatever is showing up is perfect because you are perfectly doing it in whatever way it is coming through you. Your mind might want to judge something as bad, wrong, a mistake or not good enough, but the truth is that it's just the silly human conditioning of old ideas or stories. Every single time you do it, it is perfect and good enough, and it can only give you greater and greater wisdom, experience and access to discovering yourself to now accept a greater and greater life experience. Knowing this, how could we ever downplay or speak into anything being wrong or not in divine order? To do that, we only keep ourselves in the lie and cycle of being a victim unconsciously operating. You have the power to now see and experience everything out of the truth, love and light that it is to serve you fully in all your expansion, magnificence and glory.

Remember that whatever is showing up for you today is a simply a byproduct of what you were believing and thinking yesterday, an hour ago, or even a moment ago. The next moment you enter and what is on its way now—bringing what you receive tomorrow—is created based on what you choose in this new moment of today. It's time to choose a fantastical life that reflects all you truly are.

Discovery Opportunity #6:

Act Accordingly & Create the Support to Achieve

Accountability is simply taking responsibility for reaching the results you desire.

Part 1: Daily Integration

In the last Discovery Opportunity, you were able to get clear on what you want and specifically clarify what patterns and behaviors were blocking what you want, as well as new patterns and behaviors you could now replace them with and practice.

Take this opportunity to look at what you are now committed to practicing in your life as these new behaviors.

Now, get curious about what other actions would create the most change for you and how you can incorporate actions to support those changes for you to practice every single day.

How can you support yourself with implementing these new behaviors into your daily life?

Write out a list of the specific daily practices you are committed to incorporating into your schedule.

Maybe it's waking up an hour earlier to get in some exercise, breathwork, or meditation. Maybe it's writing out and putting up little sticky notes with affirmations on them to remind you of how amazing you truly are and to continue to look for the good. There are so many ways you can support yourself in practicing new behaviors. If you are committed to doing a date night each week with yourself, your spouse, or your kids, then that is something you can have conversations about, you can set up babysitters, or you can just put these dates into your calendar so that it supports you in this new routine.

Write out a list of specific daily practices you are now committed to incorporating into your schedule.

In addition to a calendar and sticky notes, you can set alarms to practice new behaviors and have these reminders on your phone to do your check-ins, which is one of the greatest tools to support that I'll share next. Put the 5 Steps up everywhere to remind yourself to go through them when you're feeling less than awesome. There are countless ways to support yourself every day in making these practices a part of your daily norm. In the Lock Last Formula teachings, we have a check-off sheet to support every area of upgrading your life every day, and every day I have my list of the things I do to embody the way I live life to simply remind me and check off daily. These are everything from my breathwork, meditation, listening to my own frequency recordings, taking time to dance and sing, and anything I am incorporating.

Part 2: Set Up Accountability

Who can you share with, learn and grow with, and check in with on what you are specifically practicing this week and implementing into your life?

The greatest way we can reach our results is to receive support and support each other. Most people want to stop themselves on the path because those triggers want to come up and they want to hide, back down, or buy into old programming. When you are connected and committed to something greater than your own willpower and strength, it is that support of each other and giving each other the tools to continue to move beyond these points that allow us to reach the results we want.

Be the example of the change that is possible and get others involved. Together we can all create a greater life experience. If you don't feel like you have anyone to create accountability with, then I encourage you to check out the Best Life Tribe, an entire community here to support you and much more. I am here to support you, and you are worthy of that support. Please allow yourself to accept support and declare to the Universe also that you are worthy of receiving all you desire. You can find out more at https://members.marcilock.com/best-life-tribe or visit marcilock.com.

16

The Power of Checking In

How fast things can shift for you depends on how much energy, focus, and intentional integration you apply in your life.

What I realized on my journey and with utilizing this 5-step shifting tool that came through me was this: *Why would I just wait for shit to show up so that I can apply the tool? How could I experience the life that I desire more quickly?* I got really curious about how to become PROACTIVE with my internal journey instead of REACTIVE.

We are trained to be reactionary beings; take, for example, how you often react unconsciously when you get triggered instead of consciously responding. We can train ourselves to operate differently. When your shit shows up, it is definitely powerful to be able to shift through it and create something different, continually moving forward. I found that we can also completely bypass the shit showing up at all when we get proactive about it.

You can wait, or you can choose to create.

From that curiosity, the ultimate tool that I give my peeps, clients, and tribe to use to catapult their life as quickly as they want into an even greater timeline of awesomeness was born. This tool will allow your world to evolve and change more quickly than you can imagine and will massively up-level your life into what you want to be experiencing.

How do we get PROACTIVE? With just a simple internal check in.

When you begin to allow life to be your guide, accept what is happening in front of you and what your body is telling you, and acknowledge what's really going on, then moving through the 5 Steps will become easy. It won't be work. It won't take conscious effort. For me today, the 5 Steps are as natural as breathing. One of the fastest ways to get to that point is to implement the check in.

By consistently using this check in, you can quickly reprogram and integrate this way of operating into your life and what comes with it is the new life experience you get to create and receive.

Tying It All Together: The 60-Second Shift to Awesome and Check-In Tool

With this check-in tool, which can be even a quick 60 seconds, you'll see how fast situations can turn around if you take a proactive role in choosing to live in the life you want and deserve.

As you work through the method of the 60-second shift and check-in tool, remember to relax. Life gets to look whatever way we want it to, and this will allow you to proactively create that and quickly shift into experiencing it. Shifting into liberation, abundance, bliss, peace and overall awesomeness in every area of your life is your greatest adventure. The new game we are playing is to have it be fun and easy.

The 60-Second Shift: The Steps

It is this simple: set your alarm.

Easy right? Well, the alarm is the first part; it will be a reminder for you that it is time to do a quick check in. I recommend setting an alarm on your phone or something that will be near you to go off every single hour. If that feels like too much to you, aim for three times a day—maybe morning, afternoon, and evening. If that still feels like too much, you can choose to set it for once or twice a day. Whatever you decide, remember, it's perfect as long as you start implementing this tool to support you and move towards what you want.

When you start, It might seem like you are taking more time by stopping to do the check in, yet you'll recognize the amount of time, effort, and energy you actually save by catching what's happening with this proactive tool and avoiding the shit that was on its way from what was operating unconsciously to show up. You'll avoid the resistance altogether and set yourself up for success to create a phenomenal day and life, and you'll probably be inspired to do it more frequently.

So, the first step is to set your alarm and make a commitment to check-in with yourself every time it goes off. During this fun and easy check-in, just ask yourself one simple question: *What am I creating right now?*

How will you know what you are creating right now? It's easy. You can always know what you are creating right now by tuning into two things. What are you feeling in your body, and what are you focused on or perceiving?

If what you're feeling or focused on is going to give you anything less than amazing results, then aren't you so glad you caught it and saw what was happening unconsciously under the surface? Now, all that's required is that you give yourself permission to quickly go through the 5 Steps to shift yourself into alignment to receive what you want—to be living in the feelings of joy, bliss, play, prosperity and the awesomeness you want.

If you are having limiting thoughts or feelings in your body that are not serving you in what you want to be creating and experiencing, then some form of resistance is on its way as a byproduct of those underlying frequencies, even though you aren't consciously aware of them. By catching it and shifting it, you avoid the potential drama shit show and what would eventually show up as a result from those thoughts, feelings, and energy.

Now, you also might be slightly aware of what is happening, yet not enough to do anything about it. Again, the power of getting present and checking in. How can you create your everyday norm to be a life of liberation if you are unaware of what is creating a prison unconsciously and you are just OK with feeling alright or not bad?

Most of the time, because we have been operating unconsciously for so long as well as not being aware of the subtle things going on, we can't catch it until the shit gets bigger, is going down, and is ready to fly. Now you can begin to practice letting your body know what it feels like when it is even slightly off; you can practice being truly aware of how you are choosing to operate and see what is happening unconsciously in your thoughts and energy body, and now proactively reprogram and realign to that new pathway.

The 60-Second Shift: Example Application

If you were prepping for a business proposal or meeting, your alarm goes off, and the thought you were having or feeling in your body was, *I'm nervous it won't go well...*, then you could respond, *Wow... Thank you. I'm so glad I caught that...* You know that if you let that continue, you would only plant the seed of fear into the meeting and would be vibrating a low frequency that could sabotage what you really want as the experience.

What Am I Feeling? Nervous... Why? I want this to go well. I'm afraid it won't.

Awesome (the other word I tend to say no matter what I find because it truly is awesome to see what is keeping you in the comfort zone so that you can move beyond it).

What do I want to experience?

I want to rock this meeting and interaction and let them see the value that I have and the vision of what I believe is possible.

Cool... Then, if that is what I want, what would I get to think and believe right now?

I'm so fuckin' stoked for this meeting today. I'm so excited that I get to meet cool people and share my genius with them of what is possible, and I'm excited to see if it aligns and is a fit for them to work with me. I know that what I have prepared will offer value, and it'll just be a fun connection and time to share these ideas.

Let go of attachments and expectations and get clear on your intentions of who you are and what you are worthy of. Trust in the process of life that you only deserve the best, and if they are the best to work with, then it will align. If not, you just learned even more about how to find and align to the frequency of those you truly want to work with.

How much more effectively could you continue to prepare and go into that meeting feeling this way about it, rather than what you caught that was operating before? What you caught were the seeds that you were planting to soon receive. We know that if you choose to continue to operate out of anxiousness, the laws of energy will apply, and out of anxiousness everything will lead to complexity.

What is the most powerful ACTION I can now take to have that as my experience, and how does it get to be Fun and Easy?

I can choose to be excited about it and all the possibilities available. I am going to stop and acknowledge myself and reaffirm all the things that are awesome about me and how much value I bring to others so that I am remembering all of my gifts. I'm going to envision this meeting interaction playing out in a way where all of us are having a great time and the business part being fun and easy. I know that I'll be guided with the perfect flow and direction of communicating all the possibilities and options we can find together.

You take your powerful action—just a few minutes of giving yourself appreciation and love and visualizing what you are creating and intending as the experience for the meeting.

WOW. I feel good. Yes, I am excited. Let's do this!

And you dive back into preparation with the energy of excitement.

Now you might discover more clarity as you get curious. Maybe you are nervous because there are details you want to understand to the best of your ability. Dive into any type of resistance until you get to clarity and a solution for you to feel good.

See? Sixty seconds of going internal can do a lot. It can propel you into receiving what you are intending to manifest, help you move beyond the stories you've created for yourself, and get the beautiful, badass life of bliss you deserve.

Remember, you aren't pushing past what comes up; you are doing whatever is required to realign to feeling good and experiencing awesome as your birthright and as your natural state.

The 60-Second Shift: What If I Check-In and I Find Awesome?

What if you check in with yourself and discover you're already feeling amazing and awesome right now? Nothing is weighing you down at all. You're feeling fantastic about your life and everything feels in alignment.

First of all, it's beautiful, isn't it? Letting the Universe love you, knowing you're worthy of that love, and everything being flow and ease is an indescribable feeling to be living and vibrating at.

This is one of my favorite places to be and has become where I am operating at most of the time, and would you believe that this is also one of your greatest opportunities to up-level and receive even more in this moment?

WHAT?? Yup, you heard me. How much greater can it get? Well, it always can because there are infinite possibilities for more joy.

There is always more love, peace, pleasure, prosperity, play, joy, and even greater to receive. So, let me fill you in on exactly how to now up your vibration even more and clearly declare to the Universe you are ready for more and open to receive it.

There are a few ways I consciously do this by asking the curiosity question to then receive.

First, I ask myself, *What else would bring me more joy right now?* Or, *How else can I experience more joy right now?* You can ask for really anything to be up-leveled; allow yourself to get curious and creative. It could be: *How else can I experience more pleasure right now, more play, more passion, more presence, more abundance, more connection, more fun?* If you are focusing on creating a life of more play, then as you ask, you find ways to incorporate more play.

My "go to" in getting curious is: *How can I experience more joy? What would feel good right now?* or *How can it get even greater?*

Notice what is really happening. You just requested more greatness from the Universe and tuned into your core being and reaffirmed your worthiness to receive as well as the opportunity to really be heard in what you would really love and what would create even a greater experience for you. Please recognize the power of this pause in your life; to declare and receive more is a huge step that will only catapult your life into greater and greater.

This can be as simple as realizing you would love a cup of tea to sip on as you are working on your laptop. It might mean you realize you can turn on some tunes or you can stop and appreciate and hug and love on yourself to experience even more love and joy. You can take a dance break, sing a made-up song about your amazingness, or go put your feet in the grass for a few minutes to recalibrate your system. It might be a much bigger thing that you can do that allows you to realize what is there waiting for you to accept, create, and receive.

As I consciously checked in with myself, I became consistently aware of how else I could live a life I love, love the life I'm living in and experiencing now, and move beyond the comfort zone to receive more and more and more and more. You can access a training we made available for free "Living in 100% Joy Now" at marcilock.com/joy-now to also support you in embodiment tools and shifts to integrate more joy.

Giving yourself the simple little things is how you increasingly upgrade your frequency and vibe to be able to receive more, and that includes the big things that are on their way based on how you are vibrating moment by moment. You being in the highest frequency and vibration is the highest priority for creating abundance in your life and business, having the greatest sex life and love relationship, feeling awesome in your body and your body aligning to health, and being fulfilled in all of life, no matter what you are experiencing because you are always in choice to love what is and create more joy. It all depends on your vibration, and so, of course, we want to PROACTIVELY elevate that frequency and what is our norm.

I live a magical, fantastical life, and even I am still finding ways to create more abundance, pleasure, bliss and play for myself. I was in Costa Rica for one of my Ascension Adventure retreats with a group of my clients and those in my masterminds and programs. We had just spent the entire day in paradise trucking through the jungle, having magical adventures through deep transformational healing and inner alignment experiences and play. Driving back from the excursion to the villa, we rolled all the windows down. The cool air was surrounding me. The landscape was lush and green. The music was perfect in my ears. I was in a dream location with glorious beings and leaders of light, choosing to fully live and doing kickass things in life, sharing with them these gifts to greater freedom, which is exactly what I love.

Someone's phone went off for their check in, so, of course, we all checked in as well. I asked myself how the moment could get even greater and more joyful—then I found a very simple way because it always can be fun, easy, and simple.

I put my arm out the window, making a wave motion with my hand as the breeze rolled off my skin. I began to feel the music more deeply as my arm moved with the flow of the music and wind, and I danced with it out the window. I smiled even bigger as I felt the vibration of enjoyment rise even more in this very beautiful experience of just sitting in bliss, driving in a car with really amazing people, healing and freeing themselves and the planet, and celebrating that as I danced with life. It was just a little gesture that made my experience even more beautiful, fun, and passion filled, and that tiny little action to upgrade my experience and frequency signaled even more to come into my life. You get to begin to know you are always worthy of even more and begin to look for even more ways to create and receive it. These micro actions, upgrades, and alignments create the macro shifts in your life to be received.

I know I'm always worthy of more. You are, too.

Consciously Choose to Feel Even MORE

Can you accept any more greatness in your life? Of course, you can.

One of my other favorite ways to up-level is to ask, *If this level of bliss, awesome, peace, joy (or whatever I am focusing on) I'm experiencing right now was just 50 percent of what I'm capable of, what would another 50 percent feel like? What would it look like? What would that experience be like? How deeply could I allow myself to feel all that is available in this right now?*

Can you embrace fully feeling it and receive it at an even greater level?

Looking back at my Costa Rica experience I shared, I was already feeling awesome and I got to look for how else I could embrace those feelings and let them vibrate in my being even more. In that moment, it didn't require anything else outside of me. Just me, just choosing, opening, and expanding my heart even more to allow more love, fun, play, and bliss in. You have the power and ability to create that feeling without anything outside of you; you could literally just choose to allow your body to open up to, create, and feel even more right now.

It could be as simple as relaxing into it and being present with it to enjoy all that you are feeling. It can be consciously upping the game by envisioning channels of light, the energy of love, and fully being supported by all of the Universe and Angelic realms around you giving you this energy that is always available and right here when you open yourself up to it. You can open yourself up to receive even more vibrational upgrades, life force, and love to flow to you now. You can ask the angels to bring you the opportunities of your greatest joys and see the Universe taking care of all those details as you float in bliss, right now feeling yourself open to even more receiving and bliss.

If you were having an orgasm, how could you allow that orgasm to be felt even more deeply, to last even longer, to lean into the expression of it, the appreciation of it, and in it, request even more as you continually allow even more? Each time you did this, you'd find a new wave of bliss and pleasure to receive and experiences to have that were available beyond the comfort zone of where you would've stopped in the past. As you shower, can you fully appreciate every inch of your body, be so grateful for the water, the soap, your amazing body of health, and every part of the experience? You are training yourself to open up and expand in this beautiful dance of an upward spiral into greater and greater, receiving more and more. If you tune into your body and open your heart, there are infinite ways to how much light, love, joy, acceptance and bliss you can generate for yourself.

The game of receiving is a reflection of how much you are willing to love yourself and allow yourself to be supported as the divine being fully worthy of support and receiving all you desire.

Lack is not a reality. We only experience lack when we aren't operating out of our highest self and are buying into the illusions and lies. It is really a reflection that there is more we get to allow ourselves to receive.

Many times, as I up-leveled my experience, I found myself noticing that my heart would literally feel like it couldn't take any more and I was on the verge of all it could handle. I would breathe into it, physically even tap my chest and massage or pull the energy outward as if opening the space in my heart and chest even more to expand, and ask myself, *How much more can I receive?* I lift my chest to the sky to open even more, I open my arms outward to receive, and say "Thank you, yes, I accept, I receive... How much more can I receive?" Repeating this several times, allowing tears of joy and gratitude to stream down my face. I might then move down towards my womb and tap and open up my womb, connecting to my womb consciousness, my creation center, and the ability to feel my creation center even more fully. You can ask your heart what it knows, ask your womb what it knows to be true, ask your highest self what is available as you connect to and see yourself through your highest self consciousness.

I have a set of mudras I'll place over each area of my body as I say, "Yes, thank you. I accept. I receive. I see," as I end with a mudra over my third eye and vision center and I envision my life and the life I am choosing to live and create. I can hug myself and begin appreciating every part of my glorious physical body as the vehicle and vessel that allows me to experience this holy human journey. I can communicate with my cells to receive being filled with unconditional love, acceptance, compassion, and light and give love to all of my body.

I share in my "Marci on Medicine" podcast show on the *Awakened Being: Conversations to Create Change* how this simply beautiful song came through me in one of my Ascension Adventure experiences and retreats in Colombia, which is now one of my "go to's" I sing to myself all the time. I sing... "I love you so much, so much, so much.... I love you so much, so much, so much.... Repeated two more times, and I effortlessly sing into existence the love for myself. In this show and experience I also share how I was directed to sing this to my knee that I'd been healing to greater degrees through my journey. I hadn't realized how I could just take the opportunity to constantly sing to, love on, and give my knee that healing. It has since completely healed.

Even after experiencing this, I can ask again, "What would 50% more feel like?" and I can repeat that as many times as I can open myself up to. So much joy is available by being fully WITH yourself. This might lead to a full-on dance party with myself, getting naked outside with the earth, receiving the sun on my skin and in my eyes as I receive the healing of the codes of the sun and sun gazing, which is another powerful tool to receive. I might go into some breathwork that accesses more life force energy and flow in my system. You also can just sit still and choose to open yourself to access all the love and peace that is available all around us right here and now without actually "doing" anything.

This simple question allowed me to consciously allow my body and all comfort zones to expand. Each time my ego mind and body wanted to say, *No, it's too much,* I would ask a question of curiosity, reminding my system of the truth that I can always allow and receive more. As I go into the game of wonderment and curiosity, I can allow myself to continually receive even greater, inch by inch. You are always RICH when you Realize I Create Happiness, which is what I see RICH really stands for. It can be easy when you remember that every moment you are experiencing un-happiness, you are looking for what's wrong instead of what's right.

How? Breathe and sway to allow the energy to flow, creating even more room to lean into. As I simply breathe and lean in, the next opportunity to access more appears. I feel my heart suddenly open into a whole new level of love, joy, abundance, pleasure, and feeling that expands my capacity to receive.

I used to contract, shrink, settle, sacrifice, compromise, hide, and survive because I expected fear, pain, rejection, and struggle. Now, I consciously choose to expand, as I expect the most fantastical, magical, miraculous, blissed-out life of flow, ease, prosperity, peace, passion, pleasure, joy, blessings, and play. You can begin to expect the miraculous and open your mind and heart to the expanded possibilities.

Now imagine getting the opportunity to up-level your frequency, make a clear declaration to the Universe of what you want, and reaffirm to your inner self how valuable and worthy you are EVERY SINGLE HOUR. You can see how we can massively shift our worlds when we choose to become proactive and intentionally look at what is going on now and what we want in the here and now.

Each time you do this, whether it's every hour or once a day, you give yourself the gift of catching the countless golden nuggets and hidden gems that would've just passed by. The more you allow yourself to look at, the more you are able to clear, heal, and transmute it into a different frequency and way of being. These suggestions I shared are all things that have now become a part of my daily embodiment tools to live in a high frequency and they started with my own checklists to remind me to do these things daily to open up more and with my own check ins.

The more often you are reaffirming and practicing these new pathways, the faster they will become your norm and the way you live. This is when it becomes effortless because it becomes the pathway of least resistance for you and the one you now easily follow. You will always manifest what you are vibrating, and now you can clearly catch and see exactly what that is.

Another favorite show that can give you support and ideas to this is "Luscious Love affair WITH Myself." That show, the ones I've mentioned above, and many more are all available at marcilock.com/show and on any major platform to tune into and receive more tools to support you in creating and receiving.

Specific Check-Ins

You can utilize checking in for any area of your life you are looking to up-level on. I specifically have the couples I coach do a nightly check in together, which we call the Break Down to Break Through tool. This gives them a clear time and opportunity to be able to voice anything, clear any negative energy, misperceptions, or assumptions from the day and break it down to then find the truth and the solution. They go to bed more connected and in love every day and wake up more in love every day, which is a choice. As they practice this, it becomes their norm to feel your feelings, authentically express, and get clear so life is easy. It also integrates new patterns, views, understanding, and clear way to practice and upgrade their relationships every day.

Operating at your highest frequency is the highest priority. To do that, I highly suggest that you continue to get curious, ask, and create a habit of checking in and remaining conscious of what you're creating because you don't have to stop at good, great, or even amazing and awesome. You can always continue to find greater and greater levels of joy, abundance, bliss, and love as you allow and access greater remembrance of your divinity.

Your check ins will most likely become less frequent, organized, and structured because you will constantly be operating from a place of feeling good and choosing to shift. It will just become what you do and how you are all the time.

Check in with Your Inner Child:

The fastest way to change your reality is to spend time within, not without

Are you ready to receive even more? We can go even deeper and receive even more by also practicing a check in with your inner child. Remember that you get to build a relationship with your inner child and learn to support and parent yourself while creating the life you want. Think of it this way: whatever we don't heal shapes all of our reality; it is continually shaping all of our relationships and all of our world. The distance we keep ourselves from our pain is the same distance keeping us from our divine partnerships, prosperity, pleasure, play, passion, freedom, fulfillment, and liberation.

Anything you continue to emotionally suppress is what you embody; it becomes a magnet of attraction projected out into the Universe.

There is a reason why truth feels light and sets you free while lies always feel heavy and limit you.

How do we access that and shorten that distance to receive more and more? We uproot and emerge what is stuck, hiding, and afraid to be seen, allowing us to play in the playground of our inner life that will only give us access to more joy, play, and freedom.

Intentionally checking in with your inner child allows whatever is deep within to emerge and allows you to guide it to freedom. It doesn't have to be scary or locked away anymore for fear it will unleash on you because of suppression. It is like opening the door to the closet where everything has been in the dark, and you just turn on the light switch and say hello. Giving access to what is there, giving it a voice, and allowing it to be heard and seen is what allows you to become closer to your freedom and accepting a fulfilled life because all parts of you are complete and whole when all parts of you are allowed to exist. These shadows waiting to be found are only gifts to remember the light we forgot that existed. It only gives us more capacity, power, understanding, and gifts to utilize. It is when we explore the past that we no longer have to repeat it, and what is no longer hiding can be free.

As you check in, listen, allow, and begin to build a relationship of trust with your inner child, you are breaking down any resistance that would come up in your path as well as reaffirming all that is true for you and your inner child to imprint with and integrate into your being. Again, this only speeds up the process of how much you can allow yourself to receive.

This can also be very simple, and I suggest starting off in the morning and evening, and eventually, you'll be in connection and communicating all the time to always be aware of what you are actually creating. I like to put my hand on my heart to signify connecting with my little girl inside, and so if there is a way that brings you more present to this, then do so.

Simply ask, *Hey, sweetie, how are you feeling?* See what comes up and have an actual conversation. Is there a part of you that feels unheard? Unseen? Unrecognized?

Yes, you might decide it feels weird at first, yet if that is the case, then it is exactly why you get to reconnect with the little inner voice and being inside that is running everything. The question really is: Can you be that brave enough and compassionate enough to get to know these parts of yourself? Can you let the deepest areas of your being come out to be seen, heard, expressed and valued? Can you feel it, get to know it, and give it the right to exist? Claiming it and feeling it is how we heal it. We get to feel our way to freedom accessing all that we are to ascend and rise.

This evolution of our being is always awakening a greater and bigger understanding of who we are. It is through being fully transparent with yourself that you become fully intimate with yourself. Intimacy is "into me I see," and you can only be intimate with another to the degree you are willing to be intimate also with yourself. When you see into your soul, you also see into the souls of others because we are all source, sharing one collective heart, one collective mind, and arriving at the allness and oneness that exists; within reflects without. Fulfillment comes from fulfillment within, and what that gives you is the gift of being fully accepting of all things, in harmony with life, and the ability to receive even more.

Having a real conversation with your inner child might take some time; he or she might be pissed off and not trust you. Your inner child may have a little bit to say or a lot to say. Just start checking in. In the evening, I have very clear attunement processes because I know that whatever I go to bed with is soaking in my subconscious and system all night long. I'm only going to wake up to it already well on its way to being manifested the next day if it is left unheard, unseen, and suppressed. So, at nighttime, I always clear any and all energy and check in to make sure I'm not going to bed with anyone else's ideas, experiences, attachments, expectations, ideas, stories, or any energy that doesn't serve me. Think of this as an etheric shower, which doing even once a day or, if you can, several times a day to continually move energy, cleanse, and keep your vibration in alignment, I believe is much more important than even a daily physical shower.

As a part of my clearing, I always ask, *Is there anything else that gets to be heard, felt, or seen?* It is just giving space to become present with anything that exists and wants to emerge. This could be something from the day or it could just be the time to reveal something in the unconscious and give it access to healing.

As you do this, you can go deeper and deeper with your capacity by asking yourself if you are really allowing yourself to feel it. We have run from feeling for so long that many of us can say "I feel sad" yet hold back from actually fully feeling sadness, which then accesses it at a greater intensity and creates a much deeper relationship with the self of feeling safe, feeling fully expressed, fully seen and heard by upping the dial of how much you are actually willing to embrace the feeling and fully be with it. This is also the process of emotional alchemy, which is what causes manifestation to happen. The deeper you are willing to fully be with it emotionally is what allows the greater capacity to receive

Lean in, let go, and fully be all of who you are. Access the depths inside you that have been waiting for freedom for far too long and give yourself permission to play in your internal playground of possibilities and the pearls of pleasure that comes from it. If you want more support on connecting with your inner child, I do have an inner child connection and timeline hopping activation that will take you through a deep healing, clearing, and activation to a new timeline from childhood healing. This can assist you in building this relationship with your inner child to move forward into working together to create and receive. You can always tune into infinite resources to bring you back to your remembrance. If you are struggling with feeling abundant, you can turn on the Abundance Activation to bring you back into the re-calibration of the abundance available everywhere and in everything. You can find these activations under the activations section on marcilock.com or in the book resources section at book.marcilock.com/resources, and they are also all available in the Best Life Tribe Community.

Remember that the ACTION is to discover whatever the inner child or any part of you is seeking and give it to yourself. You are and will always be the source of your experience. We are held and healed by the container and we are also the container. The entire Universe exists in every cell of our bodies, and we are and have never been separate. We are always connected to all that is available; the question is: how much are you willing to allow?

Discovery Opportunity #7:
Create Joy

Make a list of all the ways you can practice experiencing more joy.

Having a "go-to" list of ideas as you check in and continue to implement more and more actions of joy in your life can support you.

This could be singing every day, dancing, giving love to yourself every time you look in the mirror, breathwork, chanting, meditation, going for a walk, turning on music and jamming out, or sending out a message of love and appreciation to someone daily. If you want support in this, you can also access the free training "Living in 100% Joy Now" in the book resources guide Book.marcilock.com/resources to support you in discovering all the ways to create joy.

The list can continue to grow. You can utilize this list of ways you experience more joy, so you have a go-to, then get curious in each moment and let yourself discover even more.

Conclusion

At the time of this book's completion, I was experiencing a whole new level of freedom as I was called to enter into a new journey as a Global Citizen, to serve humanity around the world to an even greater degree. The new adventure of growth was to follow wherever I was guided, learning to embody even more, fully living from divine feminine flow, giving myself permission to even more freedom to serve and experience whatever I was called to in the moment and serve in whatever way I was guided, bringing these codes to wherever I was directed to go and be.

I kept hearing the words, "This is your 'Journey of Aloneness,' and you get to go alone."

I didn't know why; it didn't feel like I had anything to heal in my "aloneness," as I loved my alone time. I did remind myself that you can't "intellectualize" your healing, and something deep down felt a bit scary about it, even though I couldn't comprehend at the time what was awaiting me. The only thing I knew was that it was what I was being called to do. This was the calling to embody the next level of freedom. It was a deep shedding to completely let go of all attachments, possessions, identities of self, or anything that could validate my life and what I'd built or created, all ways of "doing" that I knew in business and ways I had previously been called to share my gifts, creations, and messages.

I got to create space and step into the next realm of creating and receiving. Everything was cleared off my schedule, all commitments shifted, so I was completely free to do what I was called to and step into the allowance of being solely with ME. Could I be with ALL of me and create solely from that place that was my divine essence?

I saw there was a new layer of freedom awaiting I had to be willing to give myself. How could I ever share complete liberation if I wasn't willing to give it to myself first? Leaders go first by leading themselves, and I was again always being asked to trust the process of life. This was really putting it to the test of living moment by moment, following the energy of life guiding me, receiving through the embodiment of feminine flow, and creating what wanted to come through me with each step.

It was earlier in the year that the Universe began pre-paving and preparing the way for this to take place. I began getting the direction for us to not schedule anymore retreats on the calendar, stop filling future masterminds, and to not take on any more personal clients that when their contracts were complete, there was literally nothing I had made commitments to for my time, effort, or energy. This meant we'd be letting go of all ways I had known the business to serve as well as provide the income to support my team, family, and the countless philanthropy projects we were supporting monthly.

I didn't know the pathway was being created for all of this at the time. It began to unfold as one day I had surprised Super Sky Guy by showing up at lunchtime at his school to take him out for some quality time. I had felt his energy carrying and holding onto something and felt pulled to create some time and space for whatever was there to be revealed. I asked if there was anything he was thinking or feeling he wanted to share. He opened up and shared that he had been noticing he was afraid to fully express himself on his YouTube channel, in fear that our family would see it and judge him. When we were in the jungles of Colombia doing deep transformational work, he had experienced a complete release to fully be himself fully expressed. He had committed to himself since then that he would fully be and express himself.

All of our family, including my sons' father, live in accordance to the ways and doctrine of a specific religion. Sky had a deep desire to face this and felt called to go live with his father so that he could decide who he truly was, what he really believed, and what resonated for him.

Sitting across from me, I didn't see a 14-year-old teenager; I saw a divine light being called to his own path. Of course, all I could do was support exactly what he felt called to and be a field of divine unconditional love and support. This was a reflection for me as to how much I had grown and evolved as the past me would've done anything and everything to keep them out of that environment and belief systems because I had believed that was the best way to be able to support them in every way I could.

Now, I had no desire to control anyone or anything, as I knew any form of trying to control was only controlling myself, and my only desire was for him to know I unconditionally loved, supported, and accepted him and whatever his journey called him to.

I had already received the awareness that his younger brother and he had such deep sacred contracts; that they had been partners on their journeys in some way in every lifetime experience. I felt that at some point they would really desire to be together again, even though the thought of not having either of them with me completely felt like the scariest thing I could ever be asked to embrace. Again, I got to trust the process of life and live in accordance to what I believed to only honor my divine growth partners in whatever their journey was. We moved Skyler out to Utah to begin the school year, and Gavin and I began to look for all the ways we could adventure, grow, and stay connected and supportive to Sky.

Feeling the sacredness of this time with Gavin the Great, I began to do all I could to prepare him in every way I felt would support him and wherever his journey would call him. We usually processed the day every day after school to support him in releasing and seeing things out of light, as he is gifted as an empath to sense and be aware of energy. My desire was that he could be fully empowered to move through things without me there, knowing intuitively that he would feel a desire to continue to learn and grow with his brother.

Gavin and I had the most magical, amazing quality time traveling and growing together for six months. I began to feel his pain inside; he was missing his brother and counterpart on the journey. Even though he told me he wanted to stay with me, I offered him the option of joining Sky. Gavin began to open up to the possibilities of joining Sky and experiencing a new way of life, building an even greater bond with his Dad by living with him full time for the first time since he was just one year old.

Six months later, at the beginning of the year, we moved Gavin the Great out to be with his brother on this new journey for the growth that their souls were obviously seeking. With my boys now completely supported in a new environment, everything began aligning and telling me it was time to let go and step into flow, trust, and allowance on this journey globally. I was directed to complete the teachings with some of my spiritual teachers and was initiated as a Swami and received my activations as a Priestess to support my next level of awareness. I was in India with my beloved and one of our spiritual teachers when I received the clear direction that this was my "Journey of Aloneness" and it was time. We returned home from India, and I had three weeks to release my entire life and identity.

I got to come to divine sacred completion with my Beloved, say goodbye to my Divine Soul family and community, and release the Magical Manifestation Mansion in California that I had just manifested the year before as my ultimate temple and home space to support community, have retreats at, and even spend time with personal clients and VIPs that would come stay for personal time with me.

My team and I began giving away beautiful furniture, clothes, and items that could support others and boxed up just our keepsakes and a few sacred family items to store. I got onto a plane to the first destination I was guided to and began my Global Citizen Journey.

This divine journey brought everything up for me that was ready to be revealed, loved, and healed. I discovered that this journey was what was required to reveal the greater levels of healing; to trigger deep fears and imprints within me. The journey of aloneness through my healing became the journey WITH me. Traveling the world WITH myself was what I was called to DO in order to RECEIVE a mentorship with my soul, to truly SEE myself even MORE fully then I ever had, HEAR myself more fully, ACKNOWLEDGE myself even more fully, and unconditionally love and accept myself completely. **The only wound we ever have to heal is the separation we've created with our sovereign divinity.**

With this journey came the healing of deep multigenerational imprinting in my DNA and, as you can imagine, intense healing work through the paradigms of relationships, letting go of all the fears of separation from my boys, continuing to de-story the paradigms of what parenting looks like. We got to continue to build our connection and relationship from across the world, honoring our own perfect journeys of growth from wherever in the world we all were currently.

I was guided and invited to participate in the most sacred ceremonies, portal activations, immersions, and experiences with enlightened masters, reincarnated avatars, gurus, and teachers all over the world. I was called to support philanthropy projects wherever I was and serve in many different ways, from teaching in ashrams and villages, to supporting in places with extreme catastrophes, to bringing activations and codes to specific areas and portals, and much more beyond the description of words could entail.

We have forgotten who we are and are here to unveil, de-story, un-program, and unlearn to come back to full remembrance of the divine, sovereign being of light that we are. There are continuous levels and layers to reveal and receive to continually access greater levels of freedom. We are not designed or meant to be stagnant. It was on the first stage of my journey that I began channeling and writing about 8 to 12 hours a day until this book came to completion. An intense force of creation was waiting to be poured out.

Along with this, I kept getting the direction to track my deep healing work, immersion experience, and all that I had been learning and growing in on this journey. I kept hearing "The Awakened Being," so, I began tracking each location and experience the best I could, with no attachment as to why or what it was for. About a year into this journey, fully immersed in service and expansion, I got a clear vision and assignment to create the podcast show I've referred to called "The Awakened Being: Conversations to Create Change." I was being called to share my journey with full transparency, through even greater depths of my soul. This assignment was not to be a typical podcast; it was created to be a change agent for the world—a platform with divine purpose, where you are invited to participate in conversations that transform the world, and it was created to be in service to all beings to be able to receive.

These conversations are completely free of boundaries or limits, with nothing to hide or prove and all things exposed. It was designed to create a standard of authentic and deeply impactful conversations, which, in turn, create a calling from within to follow the call to create the change in the life of anyone listening to utilize the truths, teachings, and tools revealed.

Starting this podcast was a whole new level of expression, which felt scary and, of course, led me to receiving even greater. This show is meant to open up, activate, and shine light for all of us to live life as the grandest adventure in our remembrance and divinity. This journey definitely led me to living fully FREE and authentically in all of who I am and revealed the desire to share how we all get to fully accept and honor all that we are.

I began recording these shows of the deepest healings, immersions, and experiences from my journey, along with channeled truths and teachings I'd been blessed to receive. I could only teach and share these next level codes of living, alignment, and freedom after I first lived it. Again and again, I was reminded that leaders don't ask people to follow; they go first by leading themselves. It has been an honor to receive the messages daily of how it has changed lives. A beautiful individual who came to one of my live speaking events shared with me that her entire women's group's curriculum was just to listen to each show I released and then they discussed it along with the ways they were implementing the tools shared.

On the journey of letting it all go, I felt the calling to shift the focus simply to how many more could I serve, and trusting that as I served, I would always be taken care of and we would always be provided for. I was directed to teach all over the corners of the earth and host events charging only a small fee to cover costs. It was completely opposite of the standard high-level experiences I had held in the past other than the many times I had been asked to speak on stages at other events. I learned so much through the process of letting all attachments, identities, and ways of being go that gave me such greater depths of love for all of humanity.

I also began to access whole new levels of multidimensional capabilities, channeling and working with many high-vibrational light beings, accessing light language, and I became more and more known as a spiritual teacher.

It was also on my Global Citizen Journey as I was called back to India and invited to spend time with an Enlightened Master in the Himalayas that I received my spiritual name, SunDari. It means Divine Beauty and Universal Beauty. When I received it, I instantly began to bawl, recognizing that it signified my soul's journey perfectly, as I had grown up completely fighting beauty, being seen, heard, expressed, taking up space, and that it also matched my soul's desire to teach the Universal Beauty of all things. My journey had been to learn unconditional acceptance of self and all things which gave me the gift of discovering the beauty in all parts of me, all parts of us, all things, all experiences, and the Universal Beauty that is everywhere and in everything.

I began to re-code and activate true abundance through all aspects of life and being supported by the infinite intelligence and abundance that is everywhere. I began to feel some high-level leaders of light creating big shifts for the world coming into the energetic field, opening me to begin consulting and mentoring again. I didn't "decide" or "put out any offers to do so"; I felt them and the knowing this was coming, and they effortlessly showed up, requesting I personally coach them. Following the divine alignment, it continues to be at this time one of my greatest joys to go to the depths with the individuals I'm called to personally support through the depths of soul remembrance with. The guidance and desire came in to again host my Ascension Adventure retreats all over the world, doing the sacred experiential transformative healing work. This truly lights up my soul, as I love diving into the messy parts of being human and accessing our multidimensional gifts and bridging the gap to all we are. I host retreats wherever

I am called in sacred portal sites all over the globe as well as some of the most sacred spaces, working with plant medicines and deep healing modalities.

Letting go of it all accessed so many parts of myself to be discovered, and then, as these were called back into my life, it has expanded beyond what I ever could've imagined along with my capability and capacity to serve and facilitate more healing into even greater depths of freedom. I continue to live in flow, committed to peace as my highest priority, living by "BEING" and what is always the most nourishing for my soul, creating from my essence and where I'm divinely guided and inspired to go, surrendered to and always trusting the process and flow of life. What a glorious adventure it has been, and it can only get greater.

As our world has been confronted with massive change, I was given another direct assignment from our higher light beings of support to create "Peace for the Planet" and share live channeled activations to recode and recalibrate our systems, along with the integration and embodiment tools to the laws of New Earth consciousness, allowing us to operate from a highly evolved New Human frequency to allow us to bring in and receive a New Earth experience. We also, together in these activations, receive our own healing and peace within to become the frequency of peace for the planet and together send out these frequencies in a much greater capacity to bring healing to the world. You can find details in the book's resources section to access the free tools in "Peace for the Planet."

This new calling forth became my next greatest adventure to step into, which again felt very scary. Can I hold this container of support worldwide and bring this much healing to the planet? It felt easier to just run away to meditate on the mountain top and hang out with the Ascended Masters and vibrate peace from there. I remind myself that it is actually scarier to stay in the comfort zone that would deny myself of my greatest light, liberation, love, and joys. I, too, continually get to lean into what feels uncomfortable and step into my next level of expression, gifts, capacity, and ability to serve in even greater degrees to allow myself to also receive even more.

I was clearly shown that this is why I've had my perfect journey of EMBODIMENT to these new codes and frequencies of the future human, the New Human of the New Earth, and teaching how to awaken to be the alchemists of light we naturally are as sovereign creators. We share these guided teachings through the Aligned to Manifest Program and Masterminds.

We all chose to be here at this time to transmute our deepest wounds into the greatest strengths, shedding separation, lack, scarcity, disease, suffering, and anything that was not in alignment to who we truly are. We came here to free ourselves. It is like putting on your own oxygen mask first to then be able to fully breathe, fully function, and fully give to all beings as we hold a high-vibrational field of unconditional love, as we together can only rise in love. Take a moment to remember how excited you were to be here right now and to take part in this transition into the New Earth that is available. You too were born for this, and we came to anchor in the light at this time. Will you become a New Human to bring in the New Earth and be the change for the planet by first creating peace within yourself?

Wherever you are at in life and whatever you are experiencing is perfectly here for you. My desire and intention is that through this transmission you remember....

You are here for your greatest fulfillment and joys...
You are your grandest adventure....
You are your purpose,
You are Source.

I honor you and thank you for choosing to be here to light up the world by just being here and being you, and I'm honored to journey with you as we expand into even more of the discovery of all we are through remembering our Divinity. Thank you. I love you infinitely, completely, always and in all ways.

SunDari
The Alchemist of Light
Marci Lock Mentor

Parting Thoughts as You Continue Your Journey into MORE

The opportunity in these pages is simple: to love everything you are, everything you've ever experienced, everything you have yet to experience, everything you know, and everything you don't. If you exist peacefully within that vibration—accepting all things, loving all things—you're in the energy of alignment to be at peace and receive the abundance that is available in all aspects of life. It can look whatever way you want as you operate from your sovereignty.

Yes, my loves, you are already perfect, whole, and complete. There only question is: how much more wholeness do you want to experience and receive?

So, where do you go from here if you want to journey with us into even more?

Of course, we would love to receive you in the containers, programs, and experiences we have for even greater expansion, and yes, that is all available if it calls to you. Above that, I desire everyone to receive access to even more of the tools for greater healing and alignment and I am so happy and honored to have shared this space with you. May you receive all the blessings your heart desires on your continued journey.

As I've shared throughout the book, there are several other free resources available to you. Please check the book resources guide for additional gifts, access to Peace for the Planet Activations and all things mentioned and shared in this book transmission: the discovery assignments, 5 Steps quick reference guide, and how to access all the other resources I'll share below.

Where to Start:

Free Resources – All links in the book resources guide at: Book. marcilock.com/resources

- "The Ultimate Life of Having It All" activation that you can begin to utilize every day.

- *The Awakened Being: Conversations to Create Change* podcast show is one of my greatest contributions to the planet. I'd encourage you to check it out, and we'd love you to subscribe and continue to receive access to each show that can shift and activate a new reality.

- "Living in 100% Joy Now" – Access open now for free. This is one of our favorite trainings.

- Peace for the Planet – Activations, trainings, and tools.

My Top Contribution for the Most Value

If you are truly seeking and ready for the path that supports all aspects of the journey, then I wholeheartedly recommend The Best Life Tribe community. This was created to provide step-by-step support on the journey to living your best life. Inside, you'll discover access to activations and meditations, programs and coachings, embodiment tools, breathwork, and even access to all 24 of Marci's Body Break Through workout videos from her days as TV's Body-Mind Mentor. BLT also offers a massive deep dive library of additional trainings to support your health, wealth, relationships, and spirituality, for you to grow and expand in every area of life with the supportive environment to guide you to living an absolutely amazing life. Plus, The Best Life Tribe Facebook community will surround you in an environment of support and accountability as you grow.

This is the BEST place to connect directly with me also, as I do live Break Down to Break Through open mic calls every quarter with the tribe, answering questions and doing personal Break Through sessions with Tribe members so that everyone is supported through their deepest resistance.

Most Popular Coachings & Programs

Aligned to Manifest
Releasing Your Unconscious Commitments & Liberation Codes
Money Medicine
Awakened Relationships

Meditation & Activation Bundles

There are many mediation bundles and activations for greater expansion to recode your neural pathways and entire system to step into a new reality now. If these call to you, check out the different options to select what supports you best at this time.

Worldwide Retreats / Experiential Events / Mentorship

If you are interested in the Ascension Adventure Events and VIP and Group VIP experiences coming up, then check out the section of our website, and the book resources guide will also link you directly there. Any interest in personal mentorship simply requires an application submitted.

My team and I are here to support you in each step of your liberation, and for any additional support, you can email info@marcilock.com You can find the details to everything mentioned above in the book resource guide at Book.marcilock.com/resources and you can also get daily messages and inspiration on Facebook on the Marci Lock page, MarciLockMentor@instagram for our Instagram followers, as well as on YouTube at http://www.youtube.com/c/MarciLockSunDari.

Thank you so much for being a part of the Beautiful Journey. Again, I'm honored to be on it with you and for your willingness to lean in and heal your life—healing the planet—and for the example you are that gives others the ability to access and choose their best lives as well.

CPSIA information can be obtained
at www.ICGtesting.com
Printed in the USA
JSHW012219110820
7239JS00004B/36

9 781950 367177